Stories, Stats and Stuff About Michigan Football

By John Borton and Paul Dodd
Foreword by Lloyd Carr

Printed in the United States of America by
Mennonite Press, Inc.

ISBN 1-880652-60-9

PHOTO CREDITS Photographs were supplied by
The Bentley Historical Library, the University
of Michigan Athletic Public Relations Office,
Bob Kalmbach, and Scott Eccker.

ACKNOWLEDGMENTS

Taking on a book project is a little like taking on a Big Ten football season. You need more than a few good people in the right places, with the right capabilities, to push you through to the end.

When push comes to shove, Bob Rosiek is The Man regarding Michigan football history. A not-so-mild-mannered advertising executive by day, Rosiek is Michigan football's chief historian by heart attachment. He loves the Wolverines with the intensity of a Yost or a Schembechler. Beyond that, he has the head to back the heart.

He spent many hours on this project, in addition to providing voluminous research materials. His input, direction, advice and good humor — not to mention his unbridled passion for U-M football — helped make this a labor of love. Thanks Bob.

Thanks also to those in the Michigan Athletic Public Relations Office, whose pillaged files provided much of the artwork presented here. U-M Sports Information Director Bruce Madej offered advice and encouragement, while assistants B.J. Sohn and Jim Schneider came up big regarding a number of technical and logistical matters. They are at the heart of handling the massive Michigan football information flow, and they're always appreciated.

Photographers Bob Kalmbach and Scott Eccker came through with several more recent photos, and their efforts help bring the book to life. Greg Kinney of the Bentley Historical Library in Ann Arbor led the way through the maze of early photos and writings.

A tip of the winged helmet also goes to all those at Coman Publishing Company involved in the editing and production of the book. Publisher Stu Coman, managing editor Mark Panus, and contributing editor Joey Mustian earned the eyedrops award for this one.

Finally, a sincere thanks to U-M football coach Lloyd Carr and the entire Michigan football program. Carr's own passion for Meeshegan is reflected in the forward to this book. His team, and all those that have gone before, are the inspiration and ongoing legacy. Go Blue.

— *John Borton and Paul Dodd*

To Darlene, Benjamin and Courtney, who make every day a national championship.
— *J.B.*

To my family — Mom, Dad and Elizabeth — who have always carried the banner for me and Michigan, and all of my Maize and Blue friends.
— *P.D.*

FOREWORD

Lloyd Carr

The rich football heritage at the University of Michigan began on May 30, 1879, with a game against Racine College. In the ensuing 115 years, many of the greatest names in the history of college football have helped to build what is arguably the finest football tradition in the country. It is a tradition filled with championships and Rose Bowls, All-Americans and Heisman Trophy winners, legendary coaches, incredible performances, and unforgettable games.

The showcase for this great tradition is the crown jewel, Michigan Stadium. The colors are the Maize and Blue. The symbol is the winged-helmet. The incomparable sound is "THE VICTORS." The expectation is always victory! The standard is forever excellence!

The leadership came from Yost and Crisler and Schembechler, three of the greatest coaches who ever coached THE GAME! But it also came from outstanding administration and loyal, talented assistant coaches. Their common cause has been to provide a positive and memorable experience for the young men who wore the Block M and won in the true spirit of the game.

The heart and soul of the Michigan tradition, however, is the men who traveled to Ann Arbor to go to school and to "Win for Michigan!" Their spirit, their determination, and their effort have inspired Michigan teams to win more games than any school west of the Allegheny Mountains. The camaraderie and the esprit de corps of these Michigan men have established Michigan as a place where the game is played as it was meant to be played: A TEAM GAME!

All of us who coach and play at Michigan are proud to be part of this great legacy. We are equally determined to shoulder the responsibility for carrying it forward in such a manner that all who love Michigan will be proud. To this we pledge our very best efforts.

HAIL TO THE VICTORS ... GO BLUE!

Lloyd H. Carr, June 11, 1996

TABLE OF CONTENTS

Beginnings 1879-1900

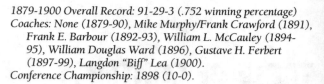

1879-1900 Overall Record: 91-29-3 (.752 winning percentage)
Coaches: None (1879-90), Mike Murphy/Frank Crawford (1891),
  Frank E. Barbour (1892-93), William L. McCauley (1894-
  95), William Douglas Ward (1896), Gustave H. Ferbert
  (1897-99), Langdon "Biff" Lea (1900).
Conference Championship: 1898 (10-0).

WOLVERINE QUIZ

1. What team provided the first opponent in Michigan football history?

The embryo of Michigan football saw no majestic spirals silhouetted against a western sky. It heard no proud throng of bandsmen blaring "The Victors" to the delight of 106,000. It put on no winged helmet — or any helmet, for that matter.

What ultimately would lead to a grand spectacle looked then much like a wild tug-of-war in the Civil War era. One reference in the Michigan student newspaper, *The Chronicle*, noted that "42 sophomores were beaten by 82 freshmen."

Michigan students began referring to themselves as "Wolverines" in 1861, and those of an athletic bent were intrigued by the football contests, which themselves were constantly evolving. The Michigan graduating class of 1867 had selected maize and blue as the school colors. The immediate successors to that class had no idea how prominent those colors would one day become, but they were anxious to have at this new sport.

The widespread interest culminated in the first intercollegiate football game in 1869, played between Princeton and Rutgers.

By 1870, football was getting more organized at Michigan, with teams from the classes of 1872 and 1873 locking up in a campus struggle. In 1873, a football association was established at Michigan, and an all-campus team was formed.

Michigan appeared ready to play an outside opponent that year. Representatives from the school negotiated with their counterparts from Cornell, arranging to play what would have been Michigan's first intercollegiate football game at a field in Cleveland, Ohio.

WOLVERINE QUIZ

2. Who scored Michigan's first touchdown?

It never happened. In a letter to Michigan President James Angell, Cornell President Andrew White wrote, "I will not permit thirty men to travel 400 miles to merely agitate a bag of wind."

It would be six more years before Michigan men would agitate that bag in earnest.

In the meantime, football itself didn't stand still, at Michigan or elsewhere. Rules were decades away from uniformity, and for years — even after Michigan entered the fray — schools hammered out rules compromises for weeks prior to engaging in battle.

The Ann Arbor contingent discovered a guiding influence in the person of Charles Gayley, who arrived in 1876 from Shanghai, China, where his father was an American missionary. The younger Gayley, educated in England and Ireland, persuaded his classmates to adopt English rugby rules for their campus-bound football games.

The Michigan students kept at it, honing their skills and adapting to the changes in the game, including the paring down of players to 11 per side. Classes came and went in Ann Arbor, but the Wolverines had yet to take the field against an opponent from another institution.

Once they did, there would be no turning back.

FOR OPENERS Michigan's first football game occurred precisely a decade after that Princeton-Rutgers clash, and involved Racine College of Wisconsin. The schools agreed upon the neutral site of White Stocking Park in Chicago and set the game for May 30, 1879.

The Chronicle recalled it this way: "May 30, opened warm and continued so the whole day. The heat was oppressive, but despite the heat, about 500 students of Racine and citizens of Chicago witnessed, what we may call, the finest game of Rugby foot-ball ever played this side of the Alleghenies. The White Stocking grounds were not in the best condition, half of the space being very soft."

Those grounds were chewed up by masses of men (scrummages, as they were called), clutching, shoving, scrambling, and stumbling to push the pile and a pig's bladder toward the opposing goal. It wasn't long before Michigan recorded the first touchdown in its history, a bolt by engineering student Irving Pond. Pond would go on to become the architect for the Michigan Union and Michigan League, but it was his effort that day that inspired onlookers to yelp, "Pond forever!"

Dave DeTarr missed the point-after try for a goal — officially. *The Chronicle*, reporting the first U-M officiating beef in history, saw it otherwise.

Irving K. Pond scored Michigan's first touchdown, against Racine College in 1879.

The account noted "… a kick was made by Captain DeTarr for the goal, which, according to the referee's decision, missed; but our umpire and the whole team and the spectators declared the goal was safely made; however, we did not wish to dispute with the referee, yet, we must suggest, he is as liable to be mistaken as anyone else."

The Michigan men had waited too long to allow mistakes of any sort to stop them on their inaugural foray into football. They fought "like dogs of war," playing Racine to a standoff the remainder of the 45-minute first "inning."

Michigan's first football team, of 1879. The Wolverines went 1-0-1 that year, beating Racine College in May and tying Toronto in November.

After that, *The Chronicle* stated: "A rest of ten minutes was given the teams, during which time Mr. Keeler and the other graduates amused themselves with a few kicks, but they only succeeded in covering themselves, not with glory, but with dirt."

The glory followed shortly.

Michigan's first shutout continued unblemished, and with two minutes remaining in the contest, DeTarr successfully placekicked a goal. The game officially went in the books as a Michigan victory, 1-0. The result delighted the students back in Ann Arbor, who received telegraph reports posted on a board near the medical building.

Back in Chicago, *The Chronicle* observed: "Our team was used in a very courteous manner by Racine, and the best of feeling was displayed through the whole game. The University alumni (will) banquet the team this evening at the Palmer House. The boys are feeling splendidly and only regret that more of their University friends are not here."

FORAGING FOR FOES The triumphant Wolverines wanted to test their skills again and again. Unfortunately, rugby football hadn't caught on in the "West" as it had in the East, where football powers were agreeing on a line of scrimmage, a system of downs, new scoring values, etc.

Michigan had difficulty finding foes.

As a result, the Wolverines went international, taking on the Varsity Blues of the University of Toronto on November 1, 1879. That contest ended in a scoreless tie. But the following year, the Wolverines won a rematch, 13-6. The victory was Michigan's only game in 1880.

Bolstered by its early success, Michigan managed to schedule the first college intersectional games. The Wolverines already considered themselves the best in the West and knew the real challenge would be in playing established Eastern teams.

In 1881, the Wolverines took on Harvard, Yale, and Princeton, all within the span of one week. The three sovereigns of rugby football royalty swept Michigan, saddling the Wolverines with the school's only season without a win.

Michigan hardly embarrassed itself, though. The visitors lost by one goal to Harvard, and two goals and two touchdowns to Yale. The Wolverines scored three safeties to Princeton's one goal and two touchdowns. Their efforts earned them an invitation to join the Eastern College League.

U-M's faculty declined that offer, citing the distances involved. Still, games with Harvard and Yale were negotiated for 1883, following a one-year football hiatus for the Wolverines.

That 1883 campaign began with Michigan's first home game, in which the Wolverines pummeled the Detroit Independents, 40-5. The Wolverines then lost three straight games, two of them on an Eastern excursion during which U-M was humbled by Yale at New Haven, Conn., 46-0, and was edged, 3-0, by Harvard at Cambridge, Mass.

The next several seasons saw the Wolverines focus on developing regional opponents, of which by then there were many. Michigan didn't lose a game for four straight years, going 2-0 in 1884, 3-0 in 1885, 2-0 in 1886, and 3-0 in 1887.

When the Wolverines encountered an opponent ill-acquainted with the increasingly popular game, they were ready and apt to instruct.

Thus it was on November 23, 1887, that the Wolverines taught the game of football to a gang of students from a small Catholic college in South Bend, Ind.

GUIDING THE IRISH Former Notre Dame students George DeHaven and Billy Harless (members of the 1887 Michigan varsity squad), along with Patrick Connors from Notre Dame, facilitated that first meeting. Michigan was heading for Chicago that Thanksgiving to face Northwestern and agreed to stop by South Bend the day

WOLVERINE QUIZ

3. Who first coached the Wolverines?

WOLVERINE QUIZ

4. When was the first homecoming, or Alumni Game, played?

before the contest.

The trip was almost scrubbed when Northwestern backed out of the Thanksgiving Day game. A Michigan advance man had taught the rough, new game to the Chicago-area scholars, and their reaction was to wire in a cancellation.

Money for the train trip had already been raised, though, so the Wolverines made their way to South Bend. The players were greeted warmly and given a tour of the campus, then led out to a field of muck, caused by melting snow.

In his book, *Bitter Enemies — The Notre Dame-Michigan Football Feud*, author John Kryk details that first encounter:

"At about 11 o'clock the elevens trotted onto the slop, which we can only assume was somehow marked to proper proportions. Before the players were set to have at it, (Notre Dame's) Brother Paul informed DeHaven that the Notre Dame boys — several of them former classmates of DeHaven and Harless' — had trouble playing by the book. Brother Paul then suggested the teams at first be mixed for a brief period of hands-on instruction. The Wolverines agreed.

" 'So we played gently with them that day,' DeHaven recalled, '… and carefully taught Notre Dame how to play modern football.'

"When the Notre Dame players learned just how physical this game was, they took to it with reckless abandon. Too reckless, actually. One student in attendance recalled DeHaven and company having to caution their eager pupils against playing too violently.

"After this brief tutorial, the players segregated into their proper squads and played a 30-minute game. When both sides finished slipping, rolling, and tumbling in the mud, Michigan had tallied two touchdowns to win, 8-0. (Touchdowns were worth four points.)

"Both Michigan scores were unconverted because, of course, there were no goalposts."

It was said the Notre Dame players, as well as the students in attendance, appreciated the fact the Wolverines did not try to run it up on their disadvantaged hosts.

The Wolverines then made it a clean sweep for the holiday, beating The Harvard Club of Chicago (the substitute for Northwestern) the following day, 26-0. Michigan finished 3-0 that year, and 8-0 over a three-year period, during which it had outscored opponents 222-0.

The Notre Dame tutorial managed to whet the football appetite of the Irish. The eager South Benders agreed to back-to-back games with Michigan the following year.

Those two clashes opened Michigan's five-game 1888

WOLVERINE QUIZ

5. Who was Michigan's first athletic director?

season, and the Wolverines swept the Irish at South Bend, 26-6 and 10-4. The second game, played one day after the first, proved an immense tussle for the injury-depleted Wolverines.

The Irish led 4-0 when Michigan struck back for a controversial touchdown. The Notre Dame student newspaper, *The Scholastic*, saw it this way: "(Ernest) Sprague took the ball, while the other players were settling some dispute, and made a touchdown for his side, and a goal kick by (John) Duffy gave them two more points. Notre Dame claimed the touchdown was illegal, asserting that Sprague neglected to put the ball in play, and furthermore went out of bounds on his way to the goal. The referee, however, could not see it in this light."

A later Notre Dame touchdown *was* nullified, intensifying the Irish ire. The Michigan-Notre Dame bitterness had not come close to the boiling point — as it would reach early in the next century — but it was simmering.

A full decade passed before the schools would meet again.

STREAK SNAPPED Michigan continued to win, moving from the final game of the 1883 season (a 17-5 victory over Stevens Institute of New Jersey) to the final game of 1888 without a loss — a 15-game win streak. But in that 1888 season-ender, the University Club of Chicago rose up to stop the streak with a 26-4 win.

The following two seasons produced records of 1-2 and 4-1 by the Michigan eleven, including lopsided losses each year to Cornell (56-0 and 20-5). The first meeting, in Buffalo, N.Y., occurred 16 years after the original, ill-fated matchup was scheduled.

That year, 1889, Gayley added to his University contributions by composing Michigan's alma mater, "The Yellow and Blue." Soon after, the Michigan football team had something new as well: a coach.

COACHING ERA BEGINS By the end of the 1880s, football had become the most popular sport on the nation's largest campus (2,153 students). The 1890s saw the enchanting Wolverines break more new ground.

Michigan played its first game against a team that would become a member of the Western Conference (the forerunner of the Big Ten) in 1890, knocking off Purdue, 34-6.

The following year, Michigan's first coach — in this case, coaches — took the reins. Mike Murphy, a trainer at the Detroit Athletic Club, and Frank Crawford, a graduate student from Yale, teamed up to guide the Wolverines through the 1891 season.

WOLVERINE QUIZ

6. In what year did Michigan win its first conference championship?

Coaches in that era were brought in for a short time, sometimes for only a few weeks, to teach specific skills or different approaches to the game. After the Wolverines went 4-5 under Murphy and Crawford's tutelage, Frank Barbour from Yale was hired as coach in 1892.

The Wolverines went 7-5 that year, beating future Western Conference opponents Wisconsin (10-6) and Chicago (18-10) but dropping games to Minnesota (14-6), Purdue (24-0), and Northwestern (10-8). U-M was 7-3 in Barbour's last season, winning its last five games by a combined score of 202-14.

WOLVERINE QUIZ

7. Whose dramatic touchdown run made the difference in U-M's 12-11 win over Chicago in 1898?

FORMING A FIELD In the decade from 1883-1892, Michigan posted an 18-1 record in games played in Ann Arbor. Those games took place on the old fairgrounds — later called Burns Park— in the southeastern part of the city and at a site where Waterman Gymnasium was eventually constructed.

In 1891, the U-M Board of Regents purchased 10 acres in what is now the southern part of Ferry Field and made the required improvements in drainage and grading so the land could be used for student athletic activities. In 1893 the real estate, complete with newly constructed wooden bleachers, became the football team's home.

First called The Athletic Field, the site would become known as Regents Field. Barbour guided the Wolverines to their first victory on the field — 6-0 over the Detroit Athletic Club — and then stepped down as head coach at the end of the season.

U-M hired William McCauley out of Princeton, and in 1894 Michigan began to pick up momentum. The Wolverines rolled to a 9-1-1 record, including a 12-4 win over Cornell at Detroit — the first time a western team had defeated an established Eastern power.

McCauley's second, and last, Michigan team was no less successful. It went 8-1, a mark blemished only by a 4-0 loss to Harvard at Cambridge. Michigan outscored its opponents 266-14. The season was capped by a 12-0 Thanksgiving Day win over the University of Chicago at Chicago's Marshall Field.

How popular was football becoming? On that day, a crowd of more than 10,000 braved biting temperatures to look on. Three inches of snow and slush had to be cleared from the field, and officials spread a layer of sawdust to protect the players from the frozen ground.

CHARTER MEMBERS The popularity of the game did not come without concern. The loose and sometimes vague rules governing games and teams were stretched to the limit. Coaches inserted themselves into games at times, players participated for six or seven seasons, and some team members were paid.

To answer the challenge on campus, the U-M Board of Regents instituted a Board in Control of Athletics, composed of five professors and four students. The board was charged with supervising Michigan's athletic programs.

On a larger scale, Michigan was represented at the Palmer House in Chicago on February 8, 1896, in a historic meeting. Seven Midwestern universities — Chicago, Illinois, Michigan, Minnesota, Northwestern, Purdue, and Wisconsin — banded together to form an association that would establish common standards and means of control. In years to come, it would be known as the Western Conference.

The Big Ten was born.

LEAGUE OF THEIR OWN McCauley turned over the coaching reins to another Princeton product, Doug Ward, who saw the Wolverines through their first conference season. Because of scheduling difficulties, Michigan played just three teams from the new association in 1896, but the schools that had been unable to meet the Wolverines were not heard to complain.

In Ward's one year in Ann Arbor, the Wolverines reeled off nine straight wins to start the campaign, outscoring opponents 256-4 (touchdowns counted four points, field goals five) heading into the final contest at Chicago. Michigan knocked off conference foes Purdue (16-0) and Minnesota (6-4) but couldn't fend off the Maroons, falling, 7-6, before a crowd of 8,000. U-M wound up 2-1 in its first year in the new association, good for a second-place tie.

Far from the crowds, relatively unnoticed, another of Michigan's greatest traditions was beginning. The University of Michigan Band conducted its first rehearsal in Harris Hall and gave its first performance the following year at a Michigan Law School event. As time marched on, so would the band, ever more entwined in glory with the football team.

The Wolverines hired one of their own to coach the next three seasons. Gustave "Dutch" Ferbert had played at U-M from 1893-96. As a coach, his teams would compile a record of 24-3-1 and be involved in a number of firsts. During his first year (1897), the Wolverines played their initial game against Ohio State (winning at home, 34-0); their first homecoming or Alumni Game (Michigan's varsity lost to an alumni team, 15-0); and their first game indoors (losing to Chicago, 21-12, on Thanksgiving Day at the Chicago Coliseum before a crowd of 9,000).

WOLVERINE QUIZ

8. Who wrote "The Victors?"

HAILING THE VICTORS For two straight seasons, Michigan's efforts in its new conference had been foiled by Chicago and its legendary coach, Amos Alonzo Stagg. The Maroons were a powerhouse in the Midwest, but the Wolverines of 1898 were not of a mind to bow to anyone.

Notre Dame fell, 23-0. Michigan Agricultural College (later Michigan State) made its first appearance on a Michigan schedule, losing, 39-0. Nine in a row went down, leading up to the season finale in Chicago.

The Maroons proved tough as ever, leading the Wolverines as time slipped away and darkness drew near. Then in a magical moment sealed forever in Michigan lore, halfback Charles Widman raced 65 yards for the winning touchdown.

The Wolverines had done it — the 12-11 win gave them a perfect 10-0 record, their first conference championship, and the right to call themselves the "Champions of the West." The feat so inspired U-M music student Louis Elbel that on the way back to Ann Arbor he penned these immortal words:

> *"Hail! to the victors valiant*
> *Hail! to the conqu'ring heroes*
> *Hail! Hail! to Michigan the leaders and best*
> *Hail! to the victors valiant*
> *Hail! to the conqu'ring heroes*
> *Hail! Hail! to Michigan, the champions of the west!"*

Elbel later recalled: "There was never a more enthusiastic Michigan student than I, but that team and that Chicago game pushed me way up in the clouds,

The U-M football team of 1898, Michigan's first conference champion. Its 12-11 win over a mighty Chicago team on the final day of the season gave the Wolverines a perfect 10-0 record and inspired young music student Louis Elbel to pen "The Victors."

Center William Cunningham, Michigan's first All-American, played on the conference championship team of 1898.

and all I had to do was fill in the notes, and there was 'The Victors.' "

The following year, John Phillip Sousa's band became the first to play "The Victors" in public, performing the piece in Ann Arbor. Sousa would later deem it the finest college march ever written.

Michigan's 1898 season carried with it more unique events. The Michigan Band made its first appearance at a varsity football game, Charles Baird became U-M's first athletic director and center William Cunningham became the Wolverines' first All-America selection.

Meanwhile, Indiana University and the University of Iowa were admitted to the Western Conference, bringing its membership to nine schools.

Ferbert's 1899 team couldn't match the previous season's glory, going 8-2 and dropping the season finale to Wisconsin, 17-5, to go 1-1 in the conference. He stepped down after that season and yet another Princeton man, Langdon "Biff" Lea, took over the team.

In his only season as head coach, Lea guided the Wolverines to a 7-2-1 record, including two losses and the tie (0-0, with Ohio State) in the final four games. Still, the Michigan Band of 30 men played "The Victors" at every home game, and school spirit was high.

They hadn't seen anything yet.

A Legend Comes Calling

Fielding H. Yost led Michigan to 10 conference titles in 25 years.

1901-1926 Overall Record: 171-31-10 (.830 winning percentage)
Coaches: Fielding H. Yost (1901-1923, 1925-26), George Little (1924)
Conference Championships: 1901 (11-0), 1902 (11-0), 1903 (11-0-1), 1904 (10-0), 1906 (4-1), 1918 (5-0), 1922 (6-0-1), 1923 (8-0), 1925 (7-1), 1926 (7-1).
National Championships: 1901, 1902, 1903, 1904.

"Hurry up! Hurry up! Hurry up!"

That beseeching soon became as much a part of football practice at Michigan as the grunting of sweaty men. The speaker, Fielding H. Yost, was always in a hurry. Born in the hilly environs of Fairview, W.Va., this bundle of brilliance and bombast already owned one-year coaching stops at Ohio Wesleyan, Nebraska, Kansas, and Stanford when he arrived in Ann Arbor.

Now, he was looking for a place to settle and build a football powerhouse. It was a match made in heaven.

Michigan legend has it that Charles Baird, who served a decade as U-M's first athletic director, observed that

UNPARALLELED EXCELLENCE

Fielding H. Yost is perhaps the most storied Michigan man of all time. The architect of Michigan's "Point-A-Minute" teams of 1901 through 1905, Yost ushered in a level of Michigan football never before experienced. His winning percentage of .833 (165-29-10) over 25 seasons is unparalleled among U-M coaches. Yost won four national championships (1901-1904), captured 10 conference championships in 15 conference seasons, ruled over Michigan football for a quarter century and went on to serve as Michigan athletic director through the 1940 season. He oversaw the construction of some of U-M's finest facilities, including Michigan Stadium, and built a legacy second to none.

COACH YOST.

Yost orchestrated the "Point-A-Minute" dynasty. His teams won four national champion-ships and posted 50 shutouts during his first five seasons at the helm.

Yost looked mighty young to have made so many coaching stops and had so much success.

Yost is said to have replied: "Mr. Baird, there are three things that make a winning football team: spirit, manpower, and coaching. If your boys love Meeshegan, they've got the spirit, you see. If they'll turn out, that takes care of the manpower. I'll take care of the coaching."

Did he ever. In the first 56 games — spanning five seasons — he ran the show in Ann Arbor, he never tasted defeat. It was dubbed the "Point-A-Minute" era, and it was marked by four straight national championships, 50 shutouts, and the beginning of the Yost legend.

WOLVERINE QUIZ

9. Who led Michigan with a still-standing team record of 26 touchdowns in the 1902 season?

THE DYNASTY BEGINS Fielding H. "Hurry Up" Yost invigorated Michigan's football machine in a way never seen before. He introduced one of the most successful trick plays in football history, (Old 83, a type of reverse used by Michigan teams for nearly 60 years). His fire and determination gripped the Wolverines, as did Yost's unabated sense of urgency.

In one of Michigan's famous "This I Remember" segments (a series of reflections by former U-M football players that ran in game programs for nearly 30 years), Judge Paul Jones, a player on the 1901 team, recalled: "(Yost) quickly instilled into Boss Weeks (165 pounds), as quarterback, the urgency of lightning fast offense. Boss would call signals for
the next play while he was still under the pile of the previous scrimmage. If you did not get into the play fast enough, Yost would shout at you from the sidelines, 'Are you just a spectator? Hurry up, Hurry Up!' That is how his name originated."

Yost also rushed Michigan toward unprecedented success by bringing with him one of the game's greatest running backs. Willie Heston would score an incredible 72 touchdowns in 36 games, rush for more than 5,000 yards, and average more than eight yards a carry from 1901 to 1904.

Michigan wasted no time rushing into this new era of greatness in 1901. The Wolverines buried Albion, 50-0, to open the season. Victories over Case (57-0), Indiana (33-0), and Northwestern (29-0) were just a prelude to a 128-0 humiliation of Buffalo. (Touchdowns, it ought to be remembered, only counted five points.)

In those days, the team that had been scored upon could choose to kick off again. Defensive mindset often dictated a team would take its chances and boot the ball away. But even after Michigan's Al Herrnstein rambled back 90 yards with the opening kickoff, Buffalo kept kicking — and getting kicked.

Judge Jones recalled: "After that game, Dad Gregory,

Al Herrnstein scored 38 touchdowns in two seasons for the 1901 and 1902 teams which went 22-0. His nephew, Bill, starred on the 1923-25 squads and great-nephew John played for Michigan from 1956-58.

George "Dad" Gregory, left, and Willie Heston, two of Michigan's standout players from the "Point-A-Minute" era.

who played center, said there was one thing we couldn't stop Buffalo from doing and everybody wanted to know what it was; Dad replied, 'We couldn't stop them from kicking off.' "

Nothing could stop Yost's band of sudden stars, including Weeks, Herrnstein, Gregory, Heston, Neil Snow, Dan McGugin, Herb Graver, Bruce Shorts, Everett Sweeley, Curtis Redden, Art Redner, and captain Hugh White. They mowed down Carlisle (22-0) and Ohio State (21-0) before encountering the team Baird warned Yost he would have to contend with to achieve ultimate success: Chicago.

For Yost's first homecoming game in Ann Arbor, his crew sent a message, treating the Maroons like everyone else and shutting them out, 22-0.

Herrnstein then scored six touchdowns in an 89-0 mauling of Beloit, and the Wolverines ended the regular season by blanking Iowa, 50-0. They were 10-0, having outscored the opposition 501-0. Snow, who earned

MICHIGAN'S BEST BACK EVER?

Willie Heston was the most famous player on Yost's "Point-A-Minute" teams and is considered by some the greatest running back in Michigan history. Born in Grants Pass, Ore., Heston came with Yost to Michigan in 1901. He never lost a game in a Michigan uniform, starring at halfback on the 1901-04 teams that went 43-0-1. He gained more than 5,000 yards in his career and racked up an astounding 72 touchdowns in 36 games. Heston earned All-America honors in 1903 and 1904 and is a member of the College Football Hall of Fame.

Willie Heston never lost a game in a Michigan uniform.

All-America distinction, and Heston led the team with 19 touchdowns each.

This miraculous season wasn't over, though, by any means.

COMING UP ROSES Yost's powerhouse earned an invitation from the Pasadena Tournament of Roses Association to play in its first New Year's Day football game (which eventually became known as the Rose Bowl). Michigan traveled to California to take on Stanford. The cross-country trip took eight days for the Wolverines, who left behind sub-freezing temperatures for 80-degree bliss.

There would be nothing blissful, though, should Yost's first perfect season be spoiled in the warm California sun. The coach was concerned enough that he tried to persuade Stanford Coach Ralph Fisher to shorten the scheduled 35-minute halves.

Heston recalled the meeting: "On Saturday morning preceding the game, Coach Fisher drove up in front of our hotel with a two-seated buggy, drawn by two horses, and told Yost he had come to take him for a buggy ride. Coach Yost got into the front seat with Fisher, and I climbed in the back seat with two of the Michigan players. We had not driven far before Yost began talking about the hot weather. Then he said to Fisher he thought it would be wise to cut the two halves down to twenty-five minute halves because of the heat. Fisher replied, 'We can't do that, Mr. Yost. We have sold a great many tickets for the game and they are entitled to see two full thirty-five minute halves.' So the subject was dropped."

Eventually, it was revisited.

Michigan manhandled Stanford from beginning to early end. The Wolverines blasted their way to a 17-0

WOLVERINE QUIZ

10. What was the highest-scoring game in Michigan football history?

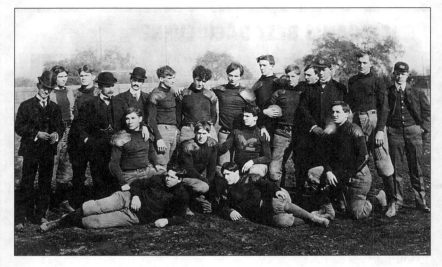

Michigan's 1901 team in California for the football contest that would eventually become known as the Rose Bowl. Standing (l to r) are unidentified individual, Everett Sweeley, Bruce Shorts, Fitzpatrick (a trainer), athletic director Charles Baird, Al Herrnstein, Dan McGugin, another unidentified man, captain Hugh White, Curtis Redden, coach Fielding H. Yost, Neil Snow, and Carfts (manager). Kneeling are Ebin Wilson, Herb Graver, Boss Weeks, and an unidentified individual. On the ground are Willie Heston and Art Redner.

lead on touchdowns by Snow and Redden, along with a Sweeley field goal. In the second half, U-M pounded in six more touchdowns, including four by Snow, another by Redden, and one by Herrnstein.

With the score 49-0 and eight minutes remaining in the game, Fisher approached the Michigan bench. After a brief conversation with Yost, the game was called.

On the train ride back to Michigan, Yost moved up and down the aisles, jovially slapping players on the back. He paused by Heston and whispered: "You know, Willie, I do not believe the Stanford boys were in good physical shape, or they would not have bruised so easily. You know what was in Fisher's mind when he crossed the field to talk with me? He came running up to me and said, 'Mr. Yost, we will have to call off the game. We haven't eleven boys able to take the field.' Do you know, Willie, what I told him? I said, 'Fisher, we can't do that. All of these people who have bought seats to see this game are entitled to see two full thirty-five minute halves,' and what do you think he replied? 'Well, 95 percent of this crowd are Stanford fans and I think they feel they have seen enough and would like to go home.'"

Home they went, putting this Rose Bowl football idea on the shelf for 16 years. The association replaced it with chariot races. Meanwhile, Snow was named Most Valuable Player for his five touchdowns — still a Rose Bowl record — and wound up in the College Football Hall of Fame.

Heston burst onto the scene with a flourish, igniting a Hall of Fame career that would see him score 19 touchdowns on plays covering more than 50 yards. Meanwhile, Yost became an instant icon.

SNOW STORMS PASADENA

Neil Snow played on the Michigan teams of 1898-1901 that went 36-4-2 and won two conference championships. An end his first three seasons and a fullback his senior year, Snow won All-America honors in 1901. His finest moment came in his final game, the first Rose Bowl on January 1, 1902. Snow scored five touchdowns in Michigan's 49-0 rout of Stanford (to this day a Rose Bowl record), was chosen the game's Most Valuable Player, and ultimately earned inclusion in the College Football Hall of Fame.

BIGGER AND BETTER   The following season saw Dexter M. Ferry, a generous U-M benefactor, purchase and donate 20 acres north of Regents Field to the university. The entire complex was named Ferry Field, which included Regents Field, where the football team continued to play through the 1905 season.

And did they play! Michigan roared through the 1902 campaign 11-0, outscoring opponents by an astounding margin of 644-12, extending its winning streak to 22 games. The Wolverines humbled several formidable opponents that year, including Notre Dame (23-0), Ohio State (86-0), Wisconsin (6-0), Iowa (107-0), Chicago (21-0), and Minnesota (23-6).

Judge Jones took particular pleasure in the Buckeye-bashing: "Late in October, Ohio State came to Ann Arbor, with a large band, and a special train of about 1,500 rooters. Perry Hale, their coach fresh from success as a player at Yale, had made a public statement that

Action at Michigan's Regents Field, where the Wolverines played through 1905.

Michigan's 1902 football team. In the front row (l to r) are Everett Sweeley, Bob Carter, Dad Gregory, Dan McGugin, Bill Cole, and Curtis Redden. In the backfield are Boss Weeks, Al Herrnstein, Paul Jones, Joe Maddock, and Willie Heston.

'Michigan had never played a hard team.' This proved to be a very unfortunate statement as Michigan beat Ohio State 86 to 0, and it was said that Perry Hale did not appear on the Ohio State campus for a week thereafter."

Minnesota provided the real challenge, though, and the Gophers came to Regents Field on November 27, Thanksgiving Day. A crowd of 9,000 was on hand to see the conference championship decided. Heston's TD runs of 30 and 35 yards spurred the Wolverines to a 23-6 victory, capping a second consecutive conference and national championship.

Herrnstein led the team during the season with 26 touchdowns, still a school record. He posted seven TDs (another lasting record) in one game, the 119-0 milking of Michigan Agricultural (Michigan State). In his two seasons in a Michigan uniform, he tallied 38 touchdowns on teams that compiled a 22-0 record.

JILTED FOR THE JUG By now, anything but a "Meeshegan" win under Yost's wizardry appeared unthinkable; in his first two seasons, Michigan had not lost. The Wolverines were to play the 1903 season without a loss as well, going 11-0-1, outscoring opponents by a whopping 565-6 and posting conference and national championships.

The only opponent that managed to score on Yost's squad was Minnesota, one of the region's biggest, toughest teams.

A crowd of 30,000, in full cry, had gathered to inspire the Gophers to victory, if not violence. When the Wolverines trotted onto the field, the fans chanted, "Poor old mushy, mushy, Michigan." And their team quickly tried to prove it true.

Fred Norcross, a slight, inexperienced quarterback on that Michigan team, recalled vividly this moment: "Herb

Graver used to come back and handle kicks with me. Minnesota's first one went to him, and I ran over to block. He had been tackled and was falling forward. Just as I got close, Webster, left tackle, rushed into Herb head-on and straightened him up and over backward (he was not slugged). Herb got up wiping blood off his face and said: 'Norky, this is going to be a round afternoon.'

"I'll never forget the words and the casual, deliberate way he said them. From then on it was every man for himself, and apparently everyone was in agreement. Sig Harris, their quarterback, and I were the only polite men left on the field. We had to be, because of our weight."

Norcross also recalled another bit of the game's brutality.

"... they began jumping on Heston after he was down. Willie (Heston) always used to twist and crawl and roll after being tackled and often picked up extra yards," Norcross noted. "Captain Redden protested the piling-up. Willie stood there with legs spread apart while they were arguing and finally said, 'I don't know any easier way to make yardage on those birds, so let 'em jump.' Well, they sure did and with such success that Heston nearly lost an ear."

When the blood and the seconds were wiped away, the teams had fashioned a 6-6 tie. Minnesota scored late in the game to grab a share of the conference championship and put the first nick in Yost's faultless Michigan record.

The Gophers secured something, too. Michigan student manager Tommy Roberts had purchased a brown water jug for 35 cents, and it accompanied the Wolverines to Minnesota. In the postgame bedlam, though, the jug was left behind. One of Minnesota's field caretakers found it and turned it in to his athletic department.

When Michigan officials later inquired about it, they were told, "Come and get it." It was a challenge to win it back, and the rivalry for The Little Brown Jug had begun.

That was the only disappointment for the club, led by Heston, Redden, Graver, Weeks, Norcross, Joe Maddock, Tom Hammond, Frank Longman, John Curtis, George Gregory, and Henry Schulte. Heston earned All-America accolades, and the Wolverines finished off the season in dominating fashion, blanking Ohio State (36-0),Wisconsin (16-0), Oberlin (42-0), and arch-rival Chicago 28-0.

Michigan had to beat the Maroons in terrible weather to secure the championship, but did so, as this report in *The Daily Maroon* lamented: "Historians have already recorded that on the twenty-sixth day of November 1903, it snowed in Chicago. And not only that it snowed snowflakes until the ground was covered to a depth of four inches, but that it also snowed touchdowns and

WOLVERINE QUIZ

11. Who was regarded as the greatest player in the "Point-A-Minute" era, with 72 touchdowns in 36 games, more than 5,000 yards rushing and an average of more than eight yards per carry?

Curtis Redden, captain of the 1903 Michigan football team.

Michigan's "Point-A-Minute" teams were 55-0-1, outscoring opponents by a margin of 2,821-42. The Wolverines of 1901-05 recorded 50 shutouts in 57 games and won four national championships.

goals from the field. Beneath a drift of these touchdowns and field goals, twenty-eight inches deep, were buried Chicago's hopes of a Western championship."

YOSTMEN DELIVER Michigan continued its death grip on college football in 1904. The men of Yost reeled off 10 more wins, capturing both a fourth consecutive conference title and a fourth straight national crown. Outscoring opponents by an amazing 567-22 margin, the Wolverines stretched their unbeaten streak to 44 games.

The rampage included a 130-0 bombardment of West Virginia, the highest-scoring game in Michigan history. Curtis and Norcross accounted for six and five touchdowns, respectively, in that one. The Wolverines also hammered Kalamazoo, 95-0; American Medical (of Chicago), 72-0; and Ohio State, 31-6. But the championship still hinged on the season finale with Chicago, which brought a crowd of 13,500 together for homecoming in Ann Arbor.

Hammond scored two TDs and Heston one to push the Wolverines to a 17-6 advantage. Chicago standout Walter Eckersall returned a fumble 45 yards for a touchdown to close the margin to 17-12. The Wolverines put the game away by driving the length of the field, with Hammond punching across a final TD on an 8-yard run to secure a 22-12 win.

Heston's 23 touchdowns earned him All-America honors for the second year in a row. His 72 career touchdowns still have not been eclipsed in Michigan history. Adolph "Germany" Schulz was another of the standout Wolverines that year, but it was his stand-up act that became fixed in football lore.

Germany Schulz, football's first linebacker.

An article in the 1950 *Football Digest* burnished his reputation:

> "Walter Camp named him the greatest center (a defensive noseguard, in today's parlance) in the history of football and since his time no snapperback has been able to displace him. There never was another center the equal of Adolph George Schulz and there probably never will be another.

> "He stood six feet plus in height and he weighed 250 plus. He had the strength of a Samson and the speed and agility of a halfback. He revolutionized center play early in his college career of 1904 to 1908, being the first pivot man to drop back behind the line on defense. The first time he did this, without consulting anyone beforehand, Fielding H. Yost was startled and horrified. At the first time-out he called Schulz to the sideline.

> " 'Dutchman,' said Yost, 'what are you trying to do?'

> " 'Stop 'em,' said Schulz.

> " 'You're supposed to play in the line.'

> " 'I think it better to play behind the line.'

> " 'They'll run over us.'

> " 'Listen, Yost, if any of 'em gets by me, I'll move back into the line and stay there.'

> "Yost had to agree.

> "From that day on, Schulz played behind the line and since then nearly all centers back up the line on defense."

MAROONS HALT ANOTHER STREAK The first middle linebacker in football history may have shocked Yost but not as much as the stunning denouement of 1905. The Wolverines appeared capable of steamrolling through yet

The 1904 Wolverines. In the front row (l to r) are Harry Hammond, Walter Graham, Charles Carter, Germany Schulz, Henry Schulte, John Curtis, and William Clark. In the back row are Thomas Hammond, Fred Norcross, Frank "Shorty" Longman, and Willie Heston.

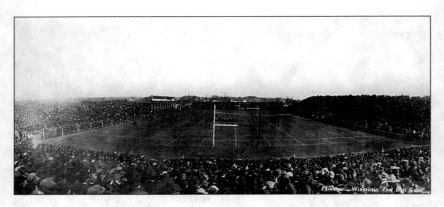

Regents Field, site of a matchup between Michigan and Wisconsin in 1905.

another season without a defeat and shut out 11 straight opponents with a combined score of 495-0.

Their only scare of the season was a 12-0 homecoming win over Wisconsin — that is, until the season finale with Chicago. To that point, Baird's warning to Yost had been unnecessary. Yost had pocketed four straight wins over the Windy City warriors, three by shutout.

Coming off a 75-0 win over Oberlin — the final game at Regents Field — the Wolverines had to travel to Chicago. The Maroons put just two points on the board that day, but two proved enough. A 60-yard punt by Eckersall in the final minute, and a subsequent safety, made all the difference in the 2-0 Chicago victory — Michigan's first loss in 57 games.

Graduation, along with sweeping national and conference football reforms, put an end to the Point-A-Minute era. During those golden years of four consecutive conference and national championships, Michigan posted an unparalleled 55-1-1 record, outscoring opponents by a margin of 2,821-42. The Wolverines won 50 of their 57 games by shutouts and set a standard to be forever recalled by Michigan teams that followed.

WINDS OF CHANGE At the end of the 1905 season, President Theodore Roosevelt ordered colleges to clean up football, marking a new era in intercollegiate athletics. Delegates from 29 schools gathered to form the National Intercollegiate Football Conference, which eventually grew into the National Collegiate Athletic Association. The organization produced a series of changes, including establishment of a rules committee, specific eligibility requirements, shortened schedules, and the legalization of the forward pass.

The Western Conference had reform ideas, too. During a two-day meeting in Chicago, the conference adopted regulations calling for the abolishment of training tables, a five-game maximum schedule, and a three-year retroactive limit on participation. Michigan opposed several of the rules, especially the schedule limitations.

Cutting the schedules, U-M argued, would jeopardize its strong ties with Eastern schools. Michigan reluctantly adhered to the change but requested modifications.

The Wolverines regained a share of the Western Conference championship wrested from them a year earlier, but a 4-1 season record could hardly be compared with earlier campaigns. Michigan's only loss that year was to Penn, 17-0.

In 1907, Penn won the return engagement in Ann Arbor, ending Michigan's 50-game home winning streak, which dated to 1901. The Wolverines finished the year 5-1 and Schulz was voted an All-American, giving fans plenty to cheer about. But it wasn't the same.

After the season, Michigan's Board in Control of Intercollegiate Athletics contacted the Western Conference, asking for a seven-game schedule, a training table, and repeal of the retroactive three-year eligibility rule.

On January 4, 1908, Michigan's requests were rejected by the Western Conference. The Board voted 5-3 to pull out of the league, and on February 1, 1908, Michigan officially withdrew from the Western Conference.

Michigan football found a new home in 1906. A new stadium with seating for 18,000 was constructed on the donated land north of Regents Field. It was named Ferry Field.

ALONE AGAIN, NATURALLY Michigan's first season apart from the conference was up-and-down, a 5-2-1 campaign highlighted by a 12-6 win over Notre Dame (making the series 8-0, Michigan) and a 10-6 downing of Ohio State. The year came to a disheartening close, though, in 29-0 and 28-4 losses to Penn and Syracuse, respectively.

The Irish came as close to the Wolverines as they ever had, scoring the only touchdown and not allowing U-M inside their 20. Michigan's Dave Allerdice made all the difference, booting three field goals (then worth four points each) to give U-M the win. Allerdice kicked 10 field goals in eight games that year, an unheard-of feat.

The loss was the only one Notre Dame suffered during a 27-game stretch from 1906 to 1910, and one the Irish would recall vividly the following year.

That 1909 season was the first for U-M Athletic Director Phillip Bartelme. Another, unthinkable first also occurred — a loss to Notre Dame.

Frank "Shorty" Longman, a fullback on Yost's indomitable Point-A-Minute teams of 1903-05, had taken over as coach of the Irish. He guided the Irish to an 11-3 victory over his old coach — to that point, the greatest athletic achievement in the history of Notre Dame.

E.A. Batchelor of the *Detroit Free Press* wrote: "Eleven

WOLVERINE QUIZ

12. Where did Michigan play its home football games from 1893-1905?

fighting Irishmen wrecked the Yost machine this afternoon. These sons of Erin, individually and collectively representing the University of Notre Dame, not only beat the Michigan team, but they dashed some of Michigan's fondest hopes and shattered Michigan's fairest dreams."

The loss to Notre Dame not only came against one of Yost's better teams (U-M went 6-1 in 1909), it finally shattered the aura of invincibility that had surrounded the Wolverines through the first eight games of the series. (That wasn't the last fight of 1909 with the Irish. The teams didn't meet on the field again but battled it out in the press over who was No. 1 in the West.)

After the loss to Notre Dame, Michigan went on to stun a powerful Penn team, 12-6. The Wolverines finished the season with a convincing 15-6 victory over the ever-solid Gophers, while Notre Dame could do no better than a 0-0 tie with Marquette — a team Michigan had edged earlier, 6-5.

After the Minnesota conquest, Yost didn't hold back his feelings.

"Of course, we are champions," he said. "What else did we come up here for but to carry away a title? It is well enough to put Notre Dame in as a claimant, but that doesn't get the Hoosiers anything. They don't approach (Michigan or Minnesota) in eligibility rules. We took on the Indiana team because we needed work, and we got it all right. But as for any championship claim of Notre Dame, that doesn't go at all. There are men on the Notre Dame team who have played years beyond the recognized limit in the West, so that bars them. They have a good team down there, but you must recognize the fact that we went into that game caring little whether we won or lost. Practice was what we wanted."

The Irish were indignant, screaming a charge of sour grapes. Yost continued to cast aspersions on Notre Dame's adherence to regionally accepted standards, and the feud intensified. The next Michigan-Notre Dame matchup wouldn't come for 33 years.

GOOD SHIP MICHIGAN While the Notre Dame clash marked the nadir of the 1909 season, the 12-6 upset of Penn represented an emotional zenith. Prior to that game at Franklin Field in Philadelphia, a delegation from the USS Michigan, led by the Marine Band, marched onto the field and presented the Michigan team with the ship's colors.

The Evening Telegraph described the spectacle:

"Reminiscent of Army and Navy games of yore was the entrance of the delegation from the United

WOLVERINE QUIZ

13. What was Michigan's record from 1901-1905?

WOLVERINE QUIZ

14. In the 57 games U-M played from 1901-1905, how many shutouts did the Wolverines post?

States battleship Michigan, 400 strong, headed by the Marine Band and silk banner of the vessel. They marched in through the northeast entrance and paraded up the field. Each blue jacket carried a Blue and Maize flag, and as they lined up before the north stand, they broke into a cheer for Michigan.

" 'Wow! Wow! Wow!'
" 'We're here now.'
" 'Two stack, twin screw, battleship queen,'
" 'Michigan! Michigan!'
" 'Football team!' "

Stanfield Wells, a player on that U-M squad, recalled: "Every man-jack aboard who wasn't in the ship's brig marched on the field in their dress blues, with flags flying and horns blaring. They formed a hollow square, whereupon a Chief Bosun's Mate, with a generous charge of Mail Pouch in his right cheek, stepped forward to do the honors."

This is what he said:

"You men are here today for the purpose of engaging in the greatest of all sports, a sport which taxes the quickness of the mind and the eye; a sport which taxes the agility, strength, and endurance of the most perfect man.

"And during the course of the game, keep this fact in mind, that the men who have united in presenting this banner to you are here to cheer you on to victory, regardless of the fact that they represent every state in the Union.

"There are even Pennsylvanians in that number of bluejackets, and they will cheer for you as lustily as those who represent and come from the state of Michigan.

"For this is the keynote of the whole affair. Today we are here as the crew of that great fighting machine which bears the name of the state which your university represents, Michigan. And when this game and this presentation become a thing of the past let your thoughts still dwell upon this occasion, for the enthusiasm of our crew will be as strong for you in your future games as it is today.

"You men, we know, will do your best. That is expected of you. It is no more than your duty to the great university which you represent; but the men who have united in presenting this banner to you expect you to do more than that. They expect you to go the other fellows one better.

WOLVERINE QUIZ

15. Who was responsible for inventing the linebacker position when he moved back from the center of the defensive line?

WOLVERINE QUIZ

16. When did the first radio broadcast of a college football game occur?

"And when you enter your games next year and your eyes, so to speak, rest upon this banner, let it remind you that our crew, no matter where we may be, will have and give their best wishes and loudest cheers for Michigan."

Wells reflected: "Who were we but to do or die after such a stirring interlude, so we went out and won the game for them, 12 to 6."

The upset snapped the Quakers' 24-game unbeaten streak.

WOLVERINE QUIZ

17. Who made up the famous Benny-To-Bennie passing combination of the mid-1920s?

MATCHING MINNESOTA'S MUSCLE The Wolverines' subsequent win over Minnesota set up a rematch in 1910, the highlight of a 3-0-3 season that included ties with Case, Ohio State, and Penn. The Gophers came in for homecoming on the final day of the season, November 19, to battle before 18,000 at Ferry Field.

Many football experts labeled this game, won by Michigan, 6-0, as the most outstanding and toughest of college football's early era. The teams played to a scoreless tie nearly the entire game, the Wolverines stifling the Minnesota Shift offense that had crushed six straight opponents.

With six minutes left on the clock, Yost revealed a shift of his own, with Wells, an All-America end, shifting into the backfield. Wells gunned a pair of newly legalized forward passes to move U-M downfield. Stan Borleske came up with the big catches against the Gophers of Dr. Henry Williams. Finally, Wells followed a block by 6-5, 265-pound, two-time All-America lineman Al Benbrook for the winning touchdown.

Williams, Yost, Stagg, and Illinois' Bob Zuppke were the game's pioneers in the West, and on this day Williams witnessed a new wrinkle — the first use of the forward pass as an offensive weapon.

Clark Shaughnessy, later coach and author, sat on the Minnesota bench that day. He wrote a book, *Football In War and Peace*, and this game appeared in a section devoted to the 12 greatest games in the 1898-1943 period.

WOLVERINE QUIZ

18. What was Fielding H. Yost's coaching record in 25 years at the helm?

"After thirty-five years in football, I look back to the Western Championship game between Minnesota and Michigan, played at Ferry Field, Ann Arbor on November 19, 1910, as the greatest game I ever saw," Shaughnessy wrote. "Against Michigan, in the game, Minnesota was Lee against Grant, Hannibal against Rome. It was a game I have never seen matched for power in the field and drama of opposing tactics."

Neil McMillan Jr., who played the second half for Michigan with fractured ribs, recalled: "That was the only game I ever saw, before or since, where 22 men played top speed every second of the way. There were no 'spectators' on the field that day. It was the toughest he-man battle I ever saw. Never saw such a game as that, never hope to see again."

YEARS IN LIMBO Michigan wouldn't see Minnesota again until 1919. The Western Conference banned Michigan from playing conference teams following that 1910 game with the Gophers. The Wolverines spent the next several seasons concentrating on Eastern foes.

Ernest "Aqua" Allmendinger, was an All-America guard in 1917.

Back home, Michigan music students J. Fred Lawton and Earl V. Moore concentrated on a song they were writing. When they put the finishing touches on "Varsity," they dedicated it to Yost and Michigan's football teams, not knowing the piece would endure to the present day.

U-M posted records of 5-1-2, 5-2, 6-1, 6-3, 4-3-1, and 7-2 over the next half-dozen years. The Wolverines provided plenty of exciting individual games through this period, such as a come-from-behind 11-9 win over Penn in 1911, played in a snowstorm at Ferry Field.

There was revenge the following season, when the Quakers rallied from a 21-0 deficit to lay a crushing 27-21 loss on Yost's men in Philadelphia. In 1913, the Wolverines beat not only Penn but Syracuse and Cornell in going 6-1. By now home games were attracting as many as 25,000 to new concrete stands erected at Ferry Field.

Michigan fans also got to witness All-Americans such as Jim Craig, Miller Pontius, and John Maulbetsch, who scored 32 touchdowns in his 26 games. A symbol of Michigan spirit and a member of the College Football Hall of Fame, Maulbetsch was honored in 1956 when Michigan named a trophy for him. It is given to a Wolverine freshman who best exemplifies desire, character, and capacity for leadership.

In the famous 1914 Harvard game, Maulbetsch used his indomitable battering style to outgain the entire Harvard backfield, managing 133 yards in 33 carries. Although Michigan narrowly lost that day, 7-0, the team — and Maulbetsch — opened more eyes in the East.

All-America running back Johnny Maulbetsch gained 133 yards on 33 carries to outrush the entire Harvard team during a 7-0 loss in 1914.

Author Ring Lardner commented: "After this, if any Easterner tells you that the game played back East is superior to that played in the Midwest, try not to laugh yourself to death. Johnny Maulbetsch of Michigan shot that theory full of holes."

Despite the Easterners' growing respect, Michigan fans began to long for the conference days and the yearly regional rivalries. Athletic director Bartelme found himself begging for games to fill Michigan's schedule, which galled him.

Michigan law professor Ralph Aigler, appointed to the Board in Control of Athletics in 1913, began to rally support for a return to the Western Conference. On November 20, 1917, the conference approved Michigan's application for membership.

Ohio State had been admitted in 1912, so Michigan boosted the conference to 10 teams. It would be known for the first time as the Big Ten. Michigan was back home.

YOST RIDES HIGH Michigan went 8-2 in 1917, outscoring opponents 304-53, with big wins against Nebraska and Cornell and season-ending losses to Penn and Northwestern. The Northwestern game was the first to occur after the Wolverines were readmitted to the conference.

Yost's men were truly back in the conference in 1918, a season shortened by World War I and a nationwide flu epidemic. The Wolverines went 5-0, and they tied for the Big Ten tied championship with a 2-0 mark. Michigan was also recognized in many quarters as being the nation's best team.

Angus Goetz, who later went on to become an orthopedic surgeon, was a member of Yost's squad at the beginning of the year. When three Michigan games were canceled at the start of the season, he began leaning toward giving up football to concentrate on his studies. Yost, however, was looking to an impending game against the Maroons — Michigan's first since the bitter 2-0 loss of 1905 — and embarked on a little arm-twisting.

Ernie Vick, standout center on the championship 1918 squad and an All-American in 1921.

"Coach Yost was a very understanding, and also a very persuasive, man," Goetz recalled in a "This I Remember" segment. "He wasn't going to risk a loss to Chicago. He needed every man on the squad for that big game, he told me. Perhaps that seems strange to some of you younger fans, but back in the days when Stagg was coaching at Chicago, his teams were always near the top in the Big Ten, and the coaching rivalry between him and Coach Yost was extremely great. The next thing I knew, Coach had convinced me to stick with football for the rest of my college days — a decision I never regretted."

Yost didn't regret it, either. Goetz blocked a field goal attempt, scooped up the ball, and ran 60 yards for a touchdown in Michigan's 13-0 win.

SLIPPING BACK U-M's euphoria over a return to conference prominence was short-lived. The 1919 season produced a 3-4 record, Yost's only losing season in 25 years as head coach and Michigan's first losing season in 28 years. The Wolverines responded with records of 5-2 and 5-1-1 in each of the succeeding two seasons, while Yost began paving the way for his eventual exit as head coach.

Bartelme stepped down as athletic director after the

1920 season, and in 1921, Yost became AD, a post he would hold for 20 years. That same season, Michigan bumped Ferry Field's capacity up to 46,000, also foreshadowing big changes in Michigan football in the 1920s.

DEDICATION DAYS The rivalry with a certain team from Columbus, Ohio, began heating up during this period as well. The 1920 Ohio State game was a sellout, and fans even found a new use for the automobile — they drove over a fence in concert to see the Buckeyes beat the Wolverines, 14-7.

Doug Roby, a solid performer for the Wolverines during the early 1920s.

In 1922, the Buckeyes boasted a brand-new stadium and drew a crowd of 71,000 for the dedication game against Michigan. The Buckeyes should have chosen a different opponent, as OSU fans fumed in frustration over a 19-0 loss.

Paul Goebel's field goal put U-M up 3-0, and then halfback Harry Kipke put together one of Michigan's most memorable performances of all time. Kipke scored on a 26-yard run in the second quarter, off Old 83.

"Two Buckeyes reversed but they were a couple of steps too late, and I'll never forget sliding across the goal line with the first touchdown in the history of this magnificent football stadium," Kipke penned in a "This I Remember" segment. "An official came up for the ball and I tossed it to him and said, 'Well, the place is really dedicated now.'"

Kipke later picked off a Buckeye pass and rambled 38 yards for a third-quarter TD, intercepted a fourth-quarter pass, and kicked a final U-M field goal. He also kept the Buckeyes at bay by averaging 47 yards on 11 punts, nine of which went out-of-bounds inside the OSU 8-yard line.

"The Michigan band got on the field and started into 'The Victors' and thousands and thousands simply screamed," Kipke recalled. "Ohio's costly and beautiful

DO-IT-ALL HARRY

Harry Kipke, one of the most versatile Wolverines of all time, scored 14 touchdowns on teams that went 19-1-2 (1921-23) and won two conference championships. He was also a great defensive player, a fine placekicker and the top punter in Michigan history. Kipke topped it off by coaching the Wolverines from 1929-1937 and winning Big Ten championships from 1930-33, with national titles in 1932 and 1933. As a player, Kipke earned All-America honors in 1922 and is a member of the College Football Hall of Fame.

All-American Harry Kipke

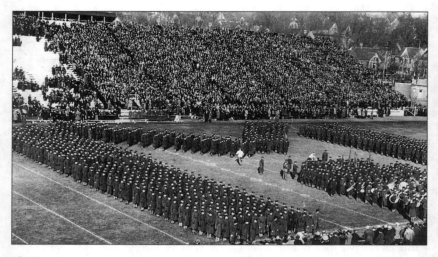

The Quantico Marines came to Ferry Field in force in 1923.

stadium sod was trod underfoot by this gigantic throng of jubilant Michiganders."

So was the Big Ten that year. The Wolverines went 6-0-1, the tie coming in a fierce scoreless struggle against Vanderbilt. Michigan knocked off Illinois (24-0), Michigan Agricultural (63-0), Wisconsin (13-6), and Minnesota (16-7) to capture its second Big Ten title since rejoining the league.

The Wolverines made it two straight Big Ten titles the following year, posting a perfect 8-0 record, including wins over Ohio State (23-0), Iowa (9-3), Wisconsin (6-3), and Minnesota (10-0).

Controversy shrouded the crucial victory over Wisconsin. Michigan's Tod Rockwell scored the game's only touchdown on a punt return after he had been knocked to the ground twice. In those days, a ball carrier's forward progress had to be stopped while he was in the grasp of a defender, so officials let the play stand.

The partisan Wisconsin crowd charged out of the stands and after the officials when the contest concluded. The refs were saved only by a human corridor formed by Wisconsin players. The Wisconsin State Police intervened and whisked away the still-in-uniform officials, who didn't get their street clothes back for a week.

Michigan's undefeated 1923 team shared national acclaim with conference foe Illinois, whom the Wolverines did not play that season. Scribes argued over which was the nation's top team, a segue to the widely recounted meeting in 1924.

Ferdinand A. "Tod" Rockwell, scored a controversial touchdown against Wisconsin that won the Wolverines a championship in 1923.

GHOST GALLS YOST Yost had plenty of fire remaining in him, despite more than two decades in the coaching wars. Jack Blott, a member of the 1922 team, vividly recalled the first fall practice that year. Yost began by preaching to the team about the honor and pride associated with wearing the Maize and Blue.

Suddenly, Yost grabbed the first player he came to, which happened to be Blott. The coach wanted to demonstrate technique. He told Blott to take an offensive stance, then sent the befuddled player sprawling by smacking him on one shoulder with the heel of two large hands. Blott scrambled back into position, but Yost sent him over backwards with a straight-on shove. Blott righted himself and braced for the onslaught. Yost grabbed him and pulled him forward onto his face.

Jack Blott, All-America center in 1923

"He spun around me like a top, first a rising blow with one elbow, then a jolt with his other elbow, one after the other," Blott recalled for a "This I Remember" segment. "Then came front knee blocks and rear knee blocks. Each time I would be under him when we landed. I honestly believe I received more bruises in this five-minute demonstration than I ever received from any opponent. I learned my lesson well — the next year I stayed in the back of the pack the first day of practice."

But the grand old man had nothing more to prove. He'd won eight conference championships and laid claim to six national championships in 23 years as coach, and he'd built a legacy unmatched in football. He also had a new job, Michigan athletic director, that required his time and attention.

So following the 1923 season, he stepped down and named George Little head coach. The Wolverines made a respectable showing in Little's one season, going 6-2 in 1924. But one loss — 39-14 to Illinois and Red Grange — brought Yost out of retirement.

That game also sealed forever the legend of Illinois' "Galloping Ghost." In the dedication game for Illinois' Memorial Stadium, 66,609 watched Grange race 95 yards for a touchdown on the opening kickoff. Before the first quarter ended, Grange had scored three more TDs on runs of 70, 57, and 43 yards. In the third quarter, Grange scored his fifth touchdown on a 13-yard dash, and capped the scoring by firing a 19-yard touchdown pass.

Edliff R. Slaughter earned All-America distinction at a guard spot in 1924.

Although overshadowed completely by Grange's history-making performance, Herb Steger, Michigan's captain, provided an inspirational performance that day. The cry "Fight Like Steger" reverberated around Michigan football for years after.

The 1924 season also featured the first radio broadcast of a college football game, which occurred on October 25. Michigan beat Wisconsin, 21-0, at Ferry Field before 45,000 spectators and the radio audience of station WWJ in Detroit. Announcers Ty Tyson and Doc Holland broadcast the game from the stands and were required to

Herb Steger (right, without helmet) battles in Michigan's stunning loss to Red Grange and Illinois in 1924. Steger kept up the effort against all odds, prompting the cry "Fight Like Steger" to be heard around Michigan for years after that game.

Robert Brown, All-America center in 1925.

purchase tickets. Tyson would go on to broadcast Michigan football for more than a quarter of a century.

BACK IN THE SADDLE Yost was a spectator that day as well. He didn't have to buy a ticket, but Illinois' stunning display had ticketed Yost for two more seasons of coaching. He took his team back in 1925, and one game stood out more in his mind than any other — Illinois.

A record 29 trains were called upon to transport spectators to Champaign that fall, many hauling Illinois fans from Chicago. Railroad officials said that every Pullman car in the country had been engaged to accommodate the Ann Arbor-to-Champaign run.

The Wolverines were determined that Red would fade to black, and that's precisely what happened. Grange managed just 56 yards on 25 carries, and new U-M quarterback Benny Friedman kicked a 24-yard field goal in the third quarter for the game's only points. Mission accomplished — Michigan won, 3-0.

That game, however, only hinted at the enormity of Yost's accomplishments. The Wolverines shut out six other opponents that year, finishing 7-1 and earning a share of the Big Ten title. U-M's only loss was to Northwestern, a crushing 3-2 defeat in mud, driving rain and biting swirls of wind at Grant Park in Chicago (now Soldier Field). The game was nearly called before it began, with one Chicago sportswriter noting no football game had ever been played under such adverse conditions.

Northwestern kicked a 15-yard field goal in the game's opening moments — the only points scored on the Wolverines all season. Those points were enough to keep the Wolverines from a national championship, although many regarded Yost's men as the nation's best.

Following Michigan's 54-0 win over a strong Navy team, Ed Pollock of the *Philadelphia Public Ledger*, wrote: "The mythical national championship in one afternoon

'BENNY TO BENNIE'

Ben Friedman became Michigan's first All-America quarterback in 1925 and earned All-America honors in 1926 as well. One of Michigan's greatest performers of all time, Friedman threw 27 touchdown passes and averaged almost 20 yards a completion. In his three seasons at quarterback, the Wolverines went 20-4 and captured a pair of Big Ten championships. This College Football Hall of Fame member teamed with Bennie Oosterbaan to form the famous "Benny To Bennie" passing combination, the most feared tandem of the 1920s.

Bennie Oosterbaan became yet another Wolverine who coached U-M following a successful playing career. The Muskegon, Mich., native caught 18 career touchdown passes, scored two others, and passed for three TDs on teams that went 20-4 and won two Big Ten championships.

Benny Friedman, left, and Bennie Oosterbaan were an All-America combination for U-M in 1925 and 1926.

A College Football Hall of Fame member, Oosterbaan earned All-America honors in all three of his varsity seasons — 1925, 1926, and 1927. He is one of only two, three-time All-Americans (Anthony Carter being the other) in Michigan history. Oosterbaan also coached the Wolverines to a 63-33-4 record from 1948-1958, including Big Ten championships in 1948, 1949, and 1950 and a national title in 1948.

traveled about a thousand miles. It moved from Franklin Field to hover over Ann Arbor, where Michigan smothered a first-class Navy team, 54-0."

The history books would never record it that way, but Yost appreciated this team perhaps more than any other. He said so in a postseason banquet, showering praise on standouts such as Friedman, Bennie Oosterbaan, Tom Edwards, Bruce Gregory, Harry Hawkins, John Molenda, Wally Weber, Bill Flora, Bill Herrnstein, and captain Bob Brown.

"You are members of the greatest football team I have ever coached," Yost said. "In fact, you are the greatest football team I ever saw in action. I am making this statement cognizant of the wonderful record of the 1901 team and the Point-A-Minute teams that followed."

LAST DANCE Yost's 1925 team outscored its opponents 227-3, captured the ninth Big Ten championship of his coaching career, and featured All-America standouts Friedman, Oosterbaan, Edwards, Hawkins, and Brown.

The elusive Benny Friedman dodges would-be Ohio State tacklers in 1926.

Still, the old man had a final bit of magic to perform.

Yost directed the 1926 team, his last, to a 7-1 record and the 10th conference title in his 25 seasons as coach. Even more impressive, Yost's 10 championships came in the 15 years Michigan was a Western Conference member. The Wolverines shut out Minnesota (20-0) and Illinois (13-0), before losing their only game of the season to the consensus No. 1 team in the country, Navy, 10-0. U-M finished the season by smashing Wisconsin (37-0) and posting thrilling wins at Ohio State (17-16) and Minnesota (7-6), its second win of the season over the Gophers.

The Ohio State game remains one of the most memorable in the rivalry. The Buckeyes charged to a 10-0 lead, only to see the Wolverines tie the game on a

Fielding H. Yost, right, with famous humorist Will Rogers, in a scene from Rogers' last movie, Old Kentucky, *in which Yost made a cameo appearance.*

7-yard TD pass from Friedman to Oosterbaan and a 30-yard Friedman field goal with a minute left in the first half.

Early in the fourth quarter, Friedman took advantage of an Ohio State fumble on a punt. The U-M quarterback fired an 8-yard TD pass to Leo Hoffman on a fourth-down play, and Friedman himself kicked the extra point that proved the difference in the game. It was Ohio State's only loss of the season.

In the second Minnesota game in Minneapolis — with the conference title again on the line — the Gophers chewed up more than 400 yards of offense, enough yardage, in the outgoing Michigan mentor's words, to "lay out a golf course."

The Wolverines hung on anyway for a 7-6 win, and afterward Yost was characteristically pragmatic.

He said, "It isn't the *first* downs that count, y'know, it's the *touchdowns*."

For Yost, winning counted most. He left coaching permanently after the 1926 season, devoting himself to the expansion of Michigan's athletic and physical education programs and the development of athletic facilities, including the new Michigan Stadium. But he also left a record (165-29-10) by which all subsequent coaches would be measured.

A quarter century earlier, Yost vowed he'd take care of the coaching. He also took Michigan's budding football tradition and cast it in stone. In a famous halftime speech, Yost once demanded to know: "Who are they, that they should beat a Meeshegan team?"

Michigan coaches and players have posed that rhetorical question ever since.

Fielding H. Yost, (center), with his 1925 Big Ten championship team. Only a 3-2 loss in the mud at Northwestern kept this team from a national championship. Yost said it was the finest team he'd ever coached.

Tom Edwards, All-America tackle on the 1925 team.

Post-Yost: Wieman & Kipke

1927-1937 Overall record: 55-32-5 (.625 winning percentage)
Coaches: Elton E. "Tad" Wieman (1927-28), Harry G. Kipke
   (1929-37)
Conference Championships: 1930 (8-0-1), 1931 (8-1-1),
   1932 (8-0),1933 (7-0-1)
National Championships: 1932, 1933.

Elton E. "Tad" Wieman, Michigan football coach in 1927 and 1928.

Michigan football was all new in the fall of 1927. Oh, the ringmaster was still around, calling the shots as athletic director. But Fielding H. Yost was out of coaching for good this time. Elton E. "Tad" Wieman, captain of Michigan's championship team of 1918, now prowled the sidelines for the Wolverines.

Even the sidelines were new. What's more, they were surrounded by a sparkling football palace called Michigan Stadium. Michigan's Board of Regents had approved the building of the stadium the previous January, and the constructors of this football shrine went to work.

The sagacious Yost told planners a seating capacity as great as 150,000 might be required in future years. Some proposals called for a double-decked stadium to accommodate such needs.

A compromise of 70,000 seats was reached, although Yost lobbied for, and got, an additional 15,000 bleacher seats installed on the wide concourse at the top of the stadium. Yost also saw to it that the approved design called for footings that ultimately would enable the stadium capacity to exceed 100,000.

The largest college-owned structure of its kind was dedicated solely to football. Some 240,000 square yards of dirt had to be excavated before the four-month job of pouring cement was completed. An additional 440 tons of reinforcing steel went into the construction, and the original seating consisted of 22 miles of California redwood. For good luck, a single four-leaf clover was planted into the 360-by-160-foot turf.

The stadium cost $950,000 to build, and it looked like a million bucks on October 1, when Wieman trotted the Wolverines onto the pristine sod for the opener against Ohio Wesleyan. A new era had begun for Michigan, dramatically embodied in its crown jewel of a stadium.

WIEMAN WINS, WANES That first game at Michigan Stadium drew more than 50,000 on a gloomy, rainy afternoon. Louie Gilbert's 28-yard TD pass to Kip Taylor was the first touchdown scored in the stadium.

Gilbert later fired touchdown passes to Leo Hoffman and Bennie Oosterbaan, scored on a punt return, and added a 90-yard touchdown run to account for all five Wolverine TDs on the day.

On opening day, Ohio Wesleyan didn't dent the new end zone, losing, 33-0. In fact, no opponent scored against Michigan through the first four games. The Wolverines added shutouts over Michigan State (21-0) and Wisconsin (14-0), before taking on Ohio State on the stadium's dedication day.

The governors of Michigan and Ohio joined Yost on the field during pregame ceremonies, before a capacity crowd of 85,000. Five years earlier, the Wolverines had spoiled the dedication day for Ohio Stadium, but they accepted no comeuppance in return.

From his end position, Oosterbaan gunned three TD passes to Gilbert, and Michigan blanked the Buckeyes, 21-0. All-America tackle Otto Pommerening recalled the moment years later, in a "This I Remember" segment.

"Bennie Oosterbaan was captain, and I well remember the first game we played in the huge bowl," Pommerening said. "It was an awe-inspiring place then, even as it is now."

The Wolverines were less awe-inspiring in the final four games of the season, losing at Illinois, 14-0, and dropping their first homecoming game at Michigan Stadium to Minnesota, 13-7. The Wolverines finished the first year in their new stadium 6-2.

That foreshadowed a comparatively dismal 1928 season, in which Michigan lost its first four games and struggled to a 3-4-1 record. The Wolverines did knock off eventual conference champion Illinois, 3-0, when Illini kicker "Frosty" Peters hit the crossbar with a potentially game-tying drop kick from 40 yards out. U-M also upset conference runner-up Iowa at homecoming, 10-7.

"U. of M. has had far better elevens but never one that had more fight, or improved so greatly in a single season," one sportswriter noted.

That wasn't enough. Michigan, despite its big triumphs over the conference kingpins, scored just 36 points that season en route to its first losing record in nine years.

The skid rendered Wieman's coaching stint a brief one. After the season, Yost replaced him with former U-M All-America halfback Harry Kipke, prying him away from the head coaching job at Michigan State.

SHORT-LIVED DEPRESSION Having experienced their own Great Depression in 1928, Kipke's men began to

WOLVERINE QUIZ

19. What was Michigan Stadium's original seating capacity when it opened in 1927?

Otto Pommerening, All-America tackle in 1928.

rebound even as the nation was reeling. They did make a concession to the economic woes of the times, playing doubleheaders to open the 1929, 1930, and 1931 seasons.

In 1929, U-M started the season with same-day wins over Albion (39-0) and Mount Union (16-6) at Michigan Stadium. The Wolverines then topped Michigan State, 17-0, before consecutive losses to Purdue (30-16), Ohio State (7-0), and Illinois (14-0) cut the heart out of a rebuilding campaign. Kipke's crew did draw great encouragement from a 14-12 win over Harvard, before a home crowd that exceeded 85,000.

Equally heartening was the 7-6 Brown Jug win against Minnesota and the legendary Bronko Nagurski. In addition, the passing combo of Harry Newman and Ivy Williamson was set to join the varsity, along with some talented freshmen, including Francis "Whitey" Wistert — the first of three Wistert brothers who became cornerstones of Michigan success.

Nobody around Ann Arbor was going to be depressed for very long.

GLORY DAYS Michigan now entered a sterling four-year span in which it would lose one game, glean four Big Ten champion-ships, and secure a pair of national titles. With their emphasis on defense, the Wolverines shut out 25 opponents in 35 games.

The incredible run coincided with Newman's arrival at quarterback, although he didn't start the first three games of 1930 (wins over Denison and Michigan Normal, and a 0-0 tie with Michigan State). When he did

WOLVERINE QUIZ

20. Who coached U-M to national championships in 1932 and 1933?

'WELL ABOVE THE MASS'

Harry Newman took his place among Michigan's all-time greats by quarterbacking the Wolverines to three Big Ten championships and a national championship in the early 1930s. The Detroiter fired 12 touchdown passes and averaged almost 20 yards a completion on teams that went a combined 24-1-2.

In analyzing Newman's place on the 1932 All-America team, legendary sportswriter Grantland Rice said, "From a fine field, Newman stood well above the mass."

Newman's rushing abilities and kick-return prowess helped propel the Wolverines to greatness, while paving his own way into the College Football Hall of Fame.

Harry Newman

appear in the fourth game of the season, against defending Big Ten champion Purdue, most thought Kipke was saving his first-string quarterback for winnable games later in the season.

Purdue took a 13-0 lead on a pair of first-quarter TDs, and Kipke sent Newman on for his debut. Newman later recalled that moment in a "This I Remember" segment.

"Immediately, I proceeded to become a hero," Newman quipped. "I dropped a Purdue punt. Fortunately, 'Sol' Hudson recovered and gave us an opportunity to go on the offensive."

Given this reprieve, Newman immediately fired a 64-yard touchdown pass to Norm Daniels. Newman, sandwiched between two Purdue rushers, didn't realize what had happened until he scrambled to his feet and, to his amazement, saw Daniels exulting in the end zone with the football.

With time running out in the first half and U-M on Purdue's 5-yard line, the Wolverines ran Old 83 to perfection. Jack Wheeler scored the touchdown, Newman kicked the extra point, and U-M shut out the Boilermakers in the second half for a 14-13 win.

That Michigan defense never let up. It yielded 10 points during the final five games, while the Wolverines swept through Ohio State (13-0), Illinois (15-7), Harvard (6-3), Minnesota (7-0), and Chicago (16-0) to capture their 12th Big Ten title.

The next year revealed more of the same, despite an ankle injury that hobbled Newman much of the season. Once again, U-M featured a suffocating defense, shutting out eight opponents on its way to an 8-1-1 record and a second straight Big Ten championship.

The Wolverines did lose to Ohio State, 20-7, and were tied by Michigan State, 0-0. But they yielded only seven other points, in a 13-7 win over Chicago. The day before a 21-0 win at Princeton, Michigan standouts such as Newman, Williamson, All-America center Maynard Morrison, John Heston, Bill Hewett, Stan Fay, Ted Petoskey, and captain Roy Hudson rode in convertibles down Fifth Avenue in New York. The Michigan Marching Band joined in the gala procession.

That was it for Michigan parades in 1931. At season's end, the Tournament of Roses Association invited Michigan to play in the Rose Bowl. In keeping with Big Ten regulations on postseason games, however, Michigan declined the offer.

NATIONAL CHAMPS Michigan's "Punt, Pass, and a Prayer" approach had its critics, but the Wolverines' defense was

Harry Newman, great Michigan quarterback of the early 1930s.

Maynard Morrison, All-America center in 1931.

such that fans and players never worried about the opponents' having the ball. Petoskey, who along with Newman and lineman Chuck Bernard, was named an All-American in 1932, said any time the Wolverines wanted the ball from an opposing team, they'd take it.

The national championship season of 1932 proved all take and no give. Just two teams scored on the Wolverines, who posted six shutouts and a perfect 8-0 record.

Michigan reeled off wins over Michigan State (26-0), Northwestern(15-6), Ohio State (14-0), and Illinois (32-0) to start the season, then faced what appeared to be a homecoming breather against Princeton. Princeton head coach Fritz Crisler, though, entertained other ideas.

The Wolverines fell behind 7-0 before Princeton's Jack Bales dropped a punt from John Regeczi. The ball bounced off Bales' foot and into his own end zone. He chased it down but was caught by Michigan's Willis Ward. The resulting safety spurred a 14-7 comeback win by the Wolverines.

Wins over Indiana (7-0) and Chicago (12-0) set up a national championship showdown with a powerful Minnesota team. Michigan had held its three previous opponents to negative yardage, but nobody expected

Charles Bernard, All-America center on Michigan's national championship teams of 1932 and 1933.

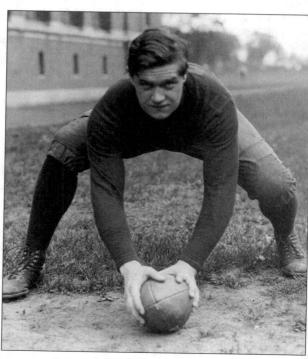

U-M to shut down the Gophers and their great backs, Pug Lund and Jack Manders.

John Regeczi, one of Michigan's all-time great punters.

The Minnesota landscape was bitterly cold that day. The temperature began at six above zero and reached six below by game's end. Brass band instruments were rendered inoperable by the chill. Fans carried pails of hot bricks to the game to keep their feet warm.

"I can still see the Michigan bench with each substitute buried in blankets, jackets, gloves, and hay knee deep attempting to keep warm," noted Russell Oliver for "This I Remember." "I doubt if Kipke could have found a substitute ready even if he wanted to use one."

He didn't need one. Minnesota became the fourth straight Michigan victim to lose yardage overall. In fact, the Gophers never crossed midfield. A Minnesota fumble at its own 30, recovered by Bernard, set up the only score. Newman drove the Wolverines downfield and kicked a field goal to secure a 3-0 Michigan win, the national championship, and a warm glow on the coldest of days.

Newman recalled: "However, with all the happy memories of the football field, the one that stands out above all others concerns what happened in the locker room after the game. That grand old man, Fielding Yost, came charging into the shower room with the battered hat on his head, the chewed up cigar in his mouth, and his heavy overcoat. He threw his arms around as many as he could reach and was soaked to the skin when he came out.

"The enthusiasm of this man I shall never forget."

PLAY IT AGAIN Enthusiasm remained high through the 1933 season, when Michigan stayed atop the college football world. The Wolverines outscored their opponents 131-18, went 7-0-1 and collected a second straight national championship.

Minnesota marred Michigan's otherwise perfect mark, managing a 0-0 tie in Ann Arbor. But the Wolverines, led by Fay, Bernard, Wistert, Ward, Petoskey, Herm Everhardus, John Kowalik, and Bill Renner, shut out five more opponents and extended their undefeated streak to 22 games.

WOLVERINE QUIZ

21. What was Michigan's record in the four straight Big Ten championship years of 1930-33?

Chapter 3: Post-Yost: Wieman & Kipke **45**

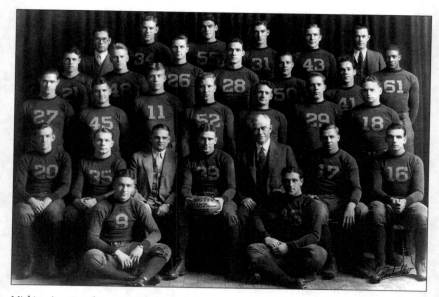

Michigan's national champions of 1932. Front (l to r): Louis Westover and Harry Newman. Second row: Charles DeBaker, Stanley Fay, Coach Harry Kipke, captain Ivan Williamson, Athletic Director Fielding H. Yost, Ted Petoskey, and John Regeczi. Third row: Charles Bernard, John Kowalik, Francis Wistert, Tom Austin, Carl Savage, Willard Hildebrand, and Russell Fuog. Fourth row: John Heston, Gerald Ford, Russell Damm, Cecil Cantrill, Oscar Singer, Abraham Marcovsky, and Willis Ward. Back: student manager Colombo, Harvey Chapman Sr., Roderick Cox, Herman Everhardus, Russ Oliver, and trainer Roberts.

After smacking Michigan State (20-6) and Cornell (40-0), Michigan faced a homecoming crucible against Ohio State. Some 87,000 packed into Michigan Stadium to watch two teams that between them would lose one game in 1933. Detroit writers picked the Buckeyes, and emotions bubbled over.

Wistert, in a poignant "This I Remember," noted there were few pregame pep talks back then. On this day, after almost all the coaches had left the locker room, assistant coach Frank "Cappie" Cappon delivered a memorable one.

"In three short minutes, he managed to raise us to an emotional pitch that was unbelievable," Wistert said. "I glanced next to me at Chuck Bernard. His tears were falling into his helmet. I dared not look any farther, for I was sure the rest were as dewy-eyed as I. When Cappie finished and shouted 'Let's go!', we almost tore off the dressing room door getting out."

The Wolverines and All-America selections Wistert, Bernard, and Petoskey proceeded to tear apart the favored Buckeyes, 13-0, securing a national championship and a fourth consecutive Big Ten crown.

Not that it was easy. The Wolverines barely got past Illinois, 7-6, when Illini placekicker Bart Cummings missed a field goal attempt from the 15 with seconds remaining.

The game was a typically hard-hitting, superb defensive struggle. Or so Wistert was told.

"Grantland Rice came into our dressing room after the game, patted me on the back and mumbled something about the greatest line play he had ever seen," Wistert recalled with bemusement. "I honestly didn't know what he was talking about. A head-on tackle on the opening kickoff fixed me good. Thereafter, my performance had to be by habit and instinct because it was completely involuntary. I couldn't then and to this day [1965] can't remember anything of the game except the opening and closing minutes. That experience might better be related under a 'This I Don't Remember' sobriquet."

Wolverine fans didn't forget 1933, or the years preceding it. The following four seasons, though, were another story.

BOTTOMING OUT Graduation gutted Kipke's defensive demons of 1933. Michigan hadn't lost five games in a season since 1892 and had never lost as many as six. Yet in 1934, the Wolverines went an unthinkable 1-7. They were shut out five times, scored 21 points, and beat only Georgia Tech, 9-2.

That year normally would draw little attention, yet in retrospect, it produced a badge of honor for the Wolverines. The Most Valuable Player of that struggling team was junior center Gerald R. Ford, who would become the 38th president of the United States.

But not even Ford could prevent Michigan's fall from grace.

The Wolverines were pelted by Bernie Bierman's national champion Minnesota team, 34-0. (The win was particularly noteworthy because despite all their great teams, the Gophers had not beaten a Michigan team in Minnesota since 1892.)

Ford took lessons from that game, which he later recalled: "During 25 years in the rough-and-tumble world of politics, I often thought of the experiences before, during, and after that game in 1934. Remembering them has helped me many times to face a tough situation, take action, and make every effort possible despite adverse odds. I remember how Michigan students and people in Ann Arbor met us at the train station that Sunday. There was a rousing parade, and this was a meaningful tribute to the fight the Wolverines had put up against Minnesota."

U-M leveled out at 4-4 in 1935 but again took poundings from the Gophers (40-0) and Ohio State (38-0). Despite its pedestrian outcome, that season

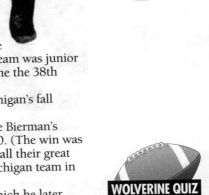

Francis Wistert, the first of the three famous Wistert brothers to play at Michigan.

WOLVERINE QUIZ

22. *What distinguished group accompanied Michigan's football team down Fifth Avenue in New York City the day before U-M's 21-0 win at Princeton in 1931?*

President Gerald R. Ford, during his playing days as a Michigan Wolverine.

WOLVERINE QUIZ

23. Why did Michigan decline an invitation to the 1931 Rose Bowl?

proved special. It marked the moving of the Ohio State game to the last weekend of the regular season, a frenzied tradition that continues each fall.

The drought continued into 1936, when the Wolverines again plummeted to 1-7, beating only Columbia, 13-0. National champion Minnesota shut down Kipke's men, 26-0.

Michigan climbed back to 4-4 in 1937, Kipke's last season as head coach. The architect of the Wolverines' incredible success of the early 1930s had witnessed a dark decline in his team's fortunes and stepped aside for Yost's next protégé.

BETTER DAYS AHEAD Even during the gloom of the late 1930s, signs of future greatness flashed onto the scene. Dr. William D. Revelli began his career directing the Michigan Marching Band in 1935. What Yost was to Michigan football, Revelli would be to the band, guiding it to greatness in his 36-year career as director.

Archie Kodros, an aggressive player for Wolverine teams of the late 1930s.

On the practice fields, some remarkable performers were appearing. Freshmen Tom Harmon, Forest Evashevski, Paul Kromer, Jeep Mehaffey, Jack Meyers, Ralph Fritz, Ed Frutig, Reuben Kelto, and Ed Christy came on the scene in 1937, quietly awaiting their turn to push Michigan back to prominence.

In fact, Harmon noted the varsity was called upon to scrimmage his freshman team that fall. The talented frosh grabbed a 21-0 lead, and the coaches refused to call off the scrimmage. Michigan wound up playing against itself in the dark — Harmon's first inkling that the Wolverines had some good days coming.

Yost sought a man to mold and direct that talent. The man he wanted was Fritz Crisler, who had coached under Stagg at Chicago, worked his wizardry for two years in Minnesota, and then coached Princeton to a 35-9-5 (.765) record through six seasons. Hiring Crisler away would require an attractive package, and Yost put one on the table.

In addition to power and a hefty salary, Crisler was told he could succeed Yost as athletic director after Yost retired in three years. Crisler accepted — and the following decade was golden for the Maize and Blue.

WOLVERINE QUIZ

24. How many shutouts did the Wolverines' great defenses of 1930-33 record?

Crisler's Era of Excellence

Fritz Crisler coached Michigan to a national championship in 1947, but his greatest contribution may well have been his design of U-M's distinctive winged helmet.

Michigan's new coach, Fritz Crisler, pauses with his captain for the 1938 season, Fred Janke.

1938-1947 Overall Record: 71-16-3 (.805 winning percentage)
Coach: Hebert Orin "Fritz" Crisler (1938-47)
Conference Championships: 1943 (8-1), 1947 (10-0)
National Championship: 1947

Fritz Crisler wasted no time in making an impact on Michigan football. In fact, one of his first accomplishments was to create one of the most recognized symbols in all of sport — Michigan's winged helmet.

The new coach not only wanted to dress up the helmet, he sought a method whereby pass receivers could be more easily spotted. There were few home and away uniforms in those days, and many teams blended together in drabness.

The distinctive helmet, with its defiant wings and stripes, has set Michigan apart from other teams for nearly 60 years.

Crisler's new team went looking for respect in his debut. For four straight lackluster seasons, the Wolverines had lost their opening game to upstart Michigan State.

Tom Harmon, Forest Evashevski, and the other freshmen of 1937 witnessed a 19-14 loss, stealing glimpses at frustrated teammates who had never beaten MSC. They quietly vowed it would not happen to them.

It didn't. Crisler's first game was a 14-0 win against the visitors from East Lansing, and it was followed by a 45-7 pasting of Chicago. The Wolverines then lost a typically tough game at Minnesota, 7-6, for their only defeat of the season.

U-M did tie Northwestern, 0-0, but recorded key wins against Illinois (14-0), Penn (19-13), and Ohio State (18-0). The victory over the Buckeyes, capping a 6-1-1 season, marked a crucial turning point for Michigan football. The previous four seasons, Ohio State had rolled over the Wolverines, 34-0, 38-0, 21-0, and 21-0.

Crisler's willingness to veer from the norm became apparent as he prepared for the OSU game. He gave his players the week off from scrimmages and contact work, meeting instead to discuss strategy. Some of the assistant coaches worried he was being too lax.

Ralph Heikkinen, an All-American on that team, noted in a "This I Remember" segment: "No doubt their fears must have been confirmed when they learned that on the Friday night before the game, which we spent in Toledo en route to Columbus, a few of our players actually volunteered to appear on stage in a vaudeville

Crisler taught this talented quartet in 1938 — (l to r) Forest Evashevski, Bob Westfall, Tom Harmon, and Fred Trosko.

act which was part of the entertainment at a movie house to which many of us had gone since tickets were provided to the squad by its proprietor and it was a way of killing time."

Never fear — Michigan saved its best act for last. Harmon rushed for two touchdowns and passed for another, while U-M's defense picked off three Buckeye passes and yielded 109 total yards in posting the 18-0 shutout.

The Wolverines were back in the hunt, following the 1938 campaign with a 6-2 season in 1939. A pair of numbing upset losses (16-7 at Illinois and 20-7 at home against Minnesota) took some of the joy out of the season, but the nucleus of Crisler's crew created plenty of moments to remember.

HARMONIZING Harmon proved the centerpiece of those memories. The dashing running back began to blossom into full stardom for the Wolverines, accounting for four of Michigan's 12 touchdowns in an 85-0 humbling of Crisler's alma mater, Chicago. (It would be Chicago's final season of Big Ten football competition.)

But Harmon was just getting started. In a matchup against Iowa and eventual Heisman Trophy winner Nile Kinnick, Harmon stole the show. Kinnick grabbed the early spotlight, firing a 70-yard touchdown pass before Harmon delivered a knockout punch in what would be Iowa's only loss of the season.

Harmon scored all of Michigan's points on four touchdowns and three conversions, guiding the team to a 27-7 victory. He blunted an Iowa scoring attempt by picking off a pass at the Michigan 5 and sprinting a school-record 95 yards for a touchdown.

Such exploits swept Harmon to All-America status and a runner-up finish to Kinnick in the Heisman balloting. Harmon rushed for 884 yards in eight games during 1939, averaged 6.8 yards per carry, passed for 488 yards, and scored 14 touchdowns. He led the nation in total offense and scoring.

He needed to lead a scoring surge after conference champion Ohio State grabbed a 14-0 lead in the first 12 minutes of the season finale. Harmon passed to Evashevski to get one TD back, and then U-M tied it on a touchdown following a Ralph Fritz fumble recovery. The game remained tied until the final 50 seconds, when holder Fred Trosko scampered 32 yards off a fake field goal to give U-M a rousing 21-14 comeback victory.

FLYING HIGH The glow of victory burned well into 1940, one of the most luminous seasons in Michigan history. Crisler eventually called his 1947 national champions his

'OLD 98'

Tom Harmon is the most celebrated star in the galaxy of Michigan football. This College Football Hall of Fame member became Michigan's first Heisman Trophy winner in 1940 a year in which he appeared on the cover of *LIFE* magazine. A tailback in Fritz Crisler's single-wing offense, Harmon accounted for 49 touchdowns in 24 games. He produced 3,438 yards in total offense, returned punts and kickoffs, placekicked, punted, and played terrific defense on teams that went 19-4-1.

A two-time All-American (1939 and 1940), Harmon and his number, 98, will never be forgotten by Michigan fans.

Tom Harmon was Michigan's first Heisman Trophy winner and the most celebrated Wolverine of all time.

The 1940 Wolverines. Fritz Crisler said it was his craziest team, but Tom Harmon reckoned it might have been his best.

best team, while referring to the 1940 squad as his "craziest."

These were characters, all right, from their impromptu stage appearances to their incessant ribbing of Harmon over the attention lavished upon him.

They were also great football players, who went 7-1, fell one point shy of an undefeated season, and came within one rain-soaked afternoon of a national championship. The 1940 season also began a streak of 11 straight during which the Wolverines finished in The Associated Press Top 10, a feat matched just once. (by Oklahoma, from 1948 to 1958.)

U-M began the campaign in historic fashion, becoming the first college football team to travel across country by airplane for a matchup with California's Golden Bears. U-M boarded three DC-3s for the flight from Ypsilanti to Berkeley. Once aboard, Harmon found himself next to Bennie Oosterbaan, the receivers coach (and former standout end) who would eventually take over for Crisler.

As Harmon remembered it, "We were ready for takeoff and Oostie was holding onto the arms of the seat so hard, his knuckles were white. I said: 'What's the matter, Ben?' He said: 'Nothing, why?' I was happy to know that Oostie figured that if the plane did go down, the seat and he would still be airborne."

Harmon ran wild against Cal, spearheading an attack that produced 408 yards and 23 first downs to Cal's 56 yards and three first downs in a 41-0 Michigan win.

Harmon sprinted 95 yards for a TD on the opening kickoff. His dazzling display continued with a 70-yard punt return, a 7-yard touchdown dash, and a TD pass thrown to Dave Nelson. The play that lives forever in the highlight reels, though, is Harmon's 86-yard touchdown run from scrimmage, when even the Golden Bears' 12th man couldn't stop him.

"I was in the clear by the 45-yard line and I was running easily toward the Cal goal line," Harmon recalled. "Suddenly I see this guy come out of the stands, under the goal posts and heading for me! I didn't know what he was up to, but it didn't take me long to find out. At about the 2-yard line, he took his shot at me. Fortunately, he missed. The local boys in blue escorted him off the field."

The boys in Maize and Blue left California awash in press clippings, mostly involving Harmon. Headlines screamed, "Harmon 41, Cal 0," and "Harmon Is The Team For Michigan."

When the U-M star trotted onto the field for Monday's practice, his teammates fell to their knees in mock obeisance. Center Bob Ingalls turned to the others and said, "OK, boys, we can practice now ... here's the team."

WOLVERINE QUIZ

27. When did Fielding H. Yost step down as Michigan athletic director?

TEARS IN THE RAIN The team stayed loose and the press clippings piled up after a 21-14 win against Michigan State, followed by consecutive shutouts of Harvard (26-0), Illinois (28-0), and Penn (14-0). Michigan carried a 5-0 record into Minnesota for a battle of unbeatens, one that would decide the national title.

The Gophers had won four Big Ten and three national titles in the six preceding years. Even the Minnesota weather conspired to aid the home team.

Evashevski's "This I Remember" put it this way: "Harmon and I were awakened with the roar of thunder about 2 a.m. the Saturday of the big game and we lay without speaking, listening to the storm rage outside. We listened with great concern because we both knew the Great Evener was at work and that a slippery field would place Tom Harmon on an equal plane with Minnesota backs."

It did precisely that. Michigan outgained Minnesota threefold in the sea of mud, but scored just once, on a Harmon TD pass to Evashevski. Harmon's extra-point attempt sailed wide. Minnesota later slogged 80 yards for a touchdown, and the extra point proved the difference in a spirit-crushing 7-6 Michigan loss. The Wolverines put the ball inside the Gophers' 5-yard line four times, but couldn't cover the narrow tract of land separating joy from misery.

"As coaches helped tired players off with their muddy jerseys, tears flowed unashamedly," Evashevski recalled. "Perhaps that is why there is always a great depth of feeling among teammates and a rapport which lasts a

WOLVERINE QUIZ

28. In what year was Michigan's first night game played?

lifetime because in situations like this, grown men can bare their emotions without ever a feeling of shame or guilt. I don't remember what was said or done in the locker room other than that. The only memory I have is aching and crying."

Minnesota won the national championship, and Michigan players were understandably despondent on the train trip home. To their surprise and delight, a huge throng met the train back in Ann Arbor, screaming support.

BOUNCING BACK Michigan didn't forfeit its season in the Minnesota mud. Rather, the Wolverines bounced back to trip Northwestern, 20-13, and prepared to invade Columbus for the season-ender against Ohio State.

The Buckeyes worried Crisler, despite his team's depth. Remember, this was his craziest team.

Harmon recalled: "Now, when you played for Fritz Crisler, you were expected to eat, drink, sleep, and talk football all your waking hours. As Fritz walked through the train on the way to Columbus hearing all this talk about dates, parties, and everything *but* football, he got so mad that as we came into Toledo, he hauled us all off the train and gave the student managers a fit trying to locate two buses to take us to a hotel. When he finally got us there, he calmly read the riot act to us for two hours. He wanted to know who we thought we were — we were playing Ohio State, and the Buckeyes would kill us tomorrow unless we got serious about this game."

When his tirade didn't quell the non-football chatter, Crisler's anger rose. It was then that Evashevski stepped in, asked the coaches to leave, and told his teammates: "This game is the last one a lot of us will play for Michigan. We intend to win it and ... if anyone goofs off, he'll have to pay to me!"

The Wolverines paid the Buckeyes — in spades. On a dark and rainy afternoon in Columbus, Michigan routed Ohio State, 40-0, out-gaining OSU 447 yards to 122. In his last Michigan game, Harmon performed magnificently. He rushed for 139 yards on 25 carries, completed 11 of 22 passes for 151 yards, returned a punt 35 yards, returned two kickoffs and picked off a pair of passes. In all, Harmon handled the ball 52 times and amassed 392 all-purpose yards. He scored three touchdowns, passed for two more to Evashevski and Edward Frutig, kicked four extra points, and averaged 50 yards on three punts.

When the soon-to-be Heisman recipient left the game in the fourth quarter, the Ohio Stadium crowd came to its feet. A standing ovation for a Wolverine! Harmon himself stood strong for Crisler, calling him the greatest college football coach ever and ranking the 1940 U-M

WOLVERINE QUIZ

29. What famous U-M supporter began his illustrious broadcasting career in 1945?

WOLVERINE QUIZ

30. In what year did the first live telecast of a Michigan football game occur?

squad among the best of all time.

"We didn't win the national championship because I goofed in the mud at Minnesota and we lost, 7-6, … but, in my mind, this should have been the national championship team," Harmon said. "They were just great!"

NO LETDOWN Yost retired as athletic director in 1941 following a 40-year association with Michigan. As athletic director, he had spearheaded an aggressive building program that included Yost Field House, the Intramural Sports Building, the University Golf Course, and Michigan Stadium.

As he had been promised, Crisler was tapped to be AD. In addition to his new job, he would have to rebuild a football team stripped of Harmon, Evashevski, Frutig, et al. But he stayed focused, exacting a 6-1-1 season out of the 1941 Wolverines.

Bob Westfall, who rushed for 688 yards and scored seven touchdowns that year, recalled it this way in a "This I Remember" segment: "I know that many will take exception to this next statement, but I firmly believe that from a coaching standpoint, the revitalizing and reshaping of the 1941 team was possibly Crisler's finest hour. He not only faced a rebuilding program in which he had to rely heavily on sophomores, but he also had to convince this squad that they, individually, and Michigan as a team, could function in championship style despite the loss of Harmon and Company."

Fritz Crisler and Tom Harmon display the Heisman winner's ripped No. 98 jersey, following Harmon's final game. The 40-0 win over Ohio State capped a sterling career for the dynamo from Gary, Ind.

Chapter 4: Crisler's Era of Excellence **57**

Bob Westfall carries against Illinois in 1940. Many thought Michigan would decline after the immense loss of talent after that season, but Westfall was among those who made certain it didn't.

Rallying from a 7-0 deficit, the Wolverines knocked off Michigan State in the opener, 19-7. That made a huge difference in the season, Crisler said.

"The new team was born in the first period of the Michigan State game," Crisler told *The Detroit News*. "State scored a touchdown in the first two minutes, and I felt that Michigan's future depended upon immediate reaction. When the boys struck back furiously, instead of staggering under the blow, I saw the elements of greatness. I was sure that we would be all right, and I was not disappointed."

He was hardly disappointed in the four shutouts his team posted. Only at homecoming, a 7-0 loss in another battle for supremacy with Minnesota, did 85,000

Fritz Crisler relied on Bob Westfall during the 1941 season, and the future College Football Hall of Famer didn't disappoint. He rushed for 688 yards and seven touchdowns in an All-America season.

Wolverine fans feel deflated.

Westfall recalled: "The ensuing battle was one of the fiercest, most bitterly contested games in Michigan's history. ... There were the plays that missed by inches that might have turned the tide, but the one I remember most vividly was when I fumbled and lost the ball on Minnesota's 5-yard line, when our blocking was so complete that I literally could have crawled across the goal line."

Westfall earned All-America honors that year, and stood tall, even in a 20-20 tie with Ohio State. He finished his career with 1,864 rushing yards and 13 touchdowns for teams that went 19-4-1.

WAR ERA BATTLES

WAR ERA BATTLES Even with World War II gripping the nation, Crisler's teams refused to release their grasp on winning. The Wolverines ranked ninth nationally and went 7-3 in 1942. Among their victories was a 9-0 win over Great Lakes Naval Training Station, one of the era's great service teams, and a 32-20 pasting of Notre Dame at South Bend. The Irish had led 14-13 at the half, but U-M left them shell-shocked with three touchdowns in the first eight minutes after intermission.

The victory both boosted and deflated Michigan's season. George Ceithaml would later remember: "It was a tremendous Michigan victory over a determined, hard-hitting Notre Dame team. Michigan's victory was not without a price, for on the following Saturday at Columbus the team, drained of its emotion, lost the Big Ten title."

That 21-7 loss broke the hearts of such 1942 stars as Albert Wistert, Julius Franks, Tom Kuzma, Bob Wiese, and Paul White. All-Americans Franks and Wistert could only watch the following year when their teammates fulfilled their dream.

Years later, Wiese marveled via "This I Remember" at what Crisler wrought in those days:

"In the early 1940s it (the single-wing formation with the spinning fullback series) became Michigan's main formation and with good faking and deception, it was hard for any team to stop it," Wiese said. "Fritz installed it at Michigan, and it was perfected on the practice field by running the plays over and over. Fritz would stand behind the defensive player where the play was aimed. If he could see the ball being handled from that spot, he would call the play over. We kept practicing until he couldn't see who had the ball."

Albert Wistert, the second of Michigan's famous Wistert brothers. He said equipment manager Henry Hatch once offered him his older brother Francis' uniform number No. 11, and the younger Wistert spent the rest of his career trying to live up to it. He didn't do badly, earning All-America recognition in 1942 and eventual entry into the College Football Hall of Fame.

Julius Franks earned All-America recognition for the Wolverines in 1942.

The 1943 team rocketed back to the top of the Big Ten, posting an 8-1 record and outscoring opponents 302-73. The Wolverines, led by White, Wiese, Bill Daley, Elroy "Crazylegs" Hirsch, Bob Nussbaumer, Merv Pregulman, Fred Negus, and Art Renner crushed Minnesota (49-6), Illinois (42-6), and Ohio State (45-7) on the way to Michigan's 16th Big Ten title.

Hirsch, though historically associated with Wisconsin, was assigned by the Marine Corps to Michigan for training under the Navy V-12 program. Daley, a fullback from Minnesota, also marched in to lead Michigan with 817 yards and nine touchdowns in six games before leaving for service duty. Hirsch led the team in kickoff and punt returns, passing, interceptions, and touchdowns (11).

They helped boost the Wolverines to No. 3 in the nation that year, but a revenge-minded Notre Dame team kept them from the top. Michigan's only loss came to Heisman Trophy winner Angelo Bertelli and the Irish, 35-12.

U-M lost out to a Heisman winner in 1944 as well, falling to Les Horvath and Ohio State, 18-14, in a thriller that decided the Big Nine championship (Chicago officially left the conference that year). The nation's eighth-ranked team at 8-2, the Wolverines came within three minutes of claiming a second consecutive conference crown.

Bill Culligan scored from 1 yard out to put Michigan ahead of the Buckeyes, 14-12, capping an arresting 83-yard fourth-quarter drive. Horvath finished his Heisman year — and Michigan— by dashing in with the

Fritz Crisler's crew in 1942 included captain George Ceithaml, left, assistant coach Bennie Oosterbaan, and All-American Albert Wistert, kneeling.

game-winner.

Don Lund played a key role on those teams of great victories and near-misses. His Michigan program remembrances, though, drifted to Crisler himself.

"Indomitable. That's the word I think of when I think of Fritz Crisler," Lund related. "He was my football coach at Michigan in 1942-43-44, and no man I have ever known commanded as much awe as he did. When he spoke, you listened.

"He was not a great halftime orator. He didn't plead for performance. He demanded excellence. We might come in leading 28-0, but to Fritz, it was always nothing-to-nothing. Nobody could let up. He made everyone keep pushing. He kept demanding perfection."

Michigan numbered among its meager total of defeats six losses to the eventual national champion-ship teams between 1940 and 1946: Minnesota (1940, '41), Ohio State (1942), Notre Dame (1943), and Army (1945, '46).

TAKE TWO While demanding, Crisler always provided. In 1945, Crisler introduced two-platoon football in the first meeting between Michigan and Army. The game was played at Yankee Stadium in New York and pitted the defending national champion Cadets of Coach Red Blaik against a Wolverine team loaded with freshmen, who were allowed to play during World War II.

When Michigan's first drive of the game ended and Army took possession, Crisler sent on eight substitutes. Until that moment, no team had taken advantage of the 1941 rule change that allowed such substitutions. Michigan bowed 28-7 that day to the great Glenn Davis and Doc Blanchard (who were on their way to a second straight national title), but the days of ironman football bowed to the Wolverines' mastermind.

U-M ended the season ranked sixth nationally, but an early season loss to Indiana (13-7) proved enough to prevent a Big Ten title.

Meanwhile, over at radio station WPAG in Ann Arbor, a former Michigan track star by the name of Bob Ufer was heard broadcasting games for the first time. Michigan football would surge several decibels over the following 36 years.

SADNESS BEFORE SPLENDOR Yost died in 1946, at the age of 75. He'd seen and created many magnificent moments in Michigan football history, but he would miss two of U-M's finest seasons. Maybe the Wolverines accomplished them in his honor — or maybe he did witness the 1947 and 1948 seasons and somehow intervened on behalf of his beloved Meeshegan.

First, though, Crisler guided U-M through one more near-miss season in 1946. The Wolverines went 6-2-1 and were ranked sixth in the nation, but they saw their confer-ence hopes slip away in a 13-9 loss to Illinois. Even in the heartache of that year, the caldron of greatness simmered.

WOLVERINE QUIZ

31. What was the nickname of Michigan's national championship team of 1947?

Michigan lost to Army, 20-13, in what many consider one of the greatest games ever played. The Cadets, led by 1945 Heisman winner Blanchard and 1946 Heisman winner Davis, pushed their winning streak to 22 games in the classic tussle. The Wolverines led early, on a 13-yard Bob Chappuis-to-Howard Yerges touchdown pass, and mounted a valiant drive at the end. An Army interception at its own 11 halted Michigan's comeback attempt.

Michigan endured a tie with Northwestern and lost to Illinois in the wake of the defeat to Army. Then all the talent that had returned from or flooded in after the war — Chappuis, Yerges, Bruce Hilkene, Dom Tomasi, Gene Derricotte — suddenly jelled.

The Wolverines finished 1946 on a tear, smashing Minnesota, 21-0; Michigan State, 55-7; Wisconsin, 28-6; and Ohio State, 58-6. It looked like the start of something big, and it was. Michigan's winning streak eventually stretched to 25 games.

CRISLER'S LAST — AND BEST

The 1947 Michigan team provided the real-life manifestation of every football fan's often unfulfilled dreams. Known as "The Mad Magicians" for their ball-handling wizardry, the '47 Wolverines featured a dream backfield of Chappuis at tailback, Yerges at quarterback, Jack Weisenburger at fullback, and Bump Elliott at wingback.

Bob Mann and Dick Rifenburg provided the pass-catching exterior of an offensive line that featured captain Hilkene and Bill Pritula at tackle, Tomasi and Stu Wilkens at guard, and J.T. White at center. Other standouts included the third of the famous Wistert brothers, Alvin, great linebackers Dick Kempthorn and Dan Dworsky, along with Derricotte, Hank Fonde, Pete

Gene Derricotte was one of many Wolverines who saw greatness blossoming during the 1946 season.

Michigan's "Dream" backfield of 1947 included (left to right) Howard Yerges, Bob Chappuis, Bump Elliott, and Jack Weisenburger.

Elliott, Quentin Sickels, Joe Soboleski, Len Ford, and Scotty McNeill.

In addition to tremendous talent, there existed an intangible quality in that group of men. Bump Elliott alluded to it when asked to "Remember."

"A number of our players had been battle-tested in World War II," Elliott said. "Some had faced death many times. There was talk that these players might not respond well to the discipline necessary to make a great football team; that they had 'had it,' and football was just a game after all. Nothing could have been farther from the truth.

"Let me cite one concrete example. Chappuis had been an Air Force pilot. On his 21st mission over Italy, he was shot down and barely escaped capture by the Germans. For months he hid behind the enemy lines, helped by Italian partisans, his life in danger every moment before he finally escaped. Yet in the dressing room before a game, Bob was as pale and tense as the rest of us; when he took the field he was prepared to give everything he had."

The Wolverines crushed their first four foes, roaring past Michigan State, 55-0; Stanford, 49-13; Pittsburgh, 69-0; and Northwestern, 49-21. When Chappuis made the cover of *Time* magazine, the entire nation marveled over Michigan's magicians.

The start was a blessing and a curse. Writers had the Wolverines in the Rose Bowl already (a bowl agreement was reached with the Pacific Coast Conference in 1946)

Dan Dworsky had designs on a national championship in 1947. He went on to become a renowned architect and the designer of Crisler Arena.

Dick Kempthorn (38) spearheaded a rugged U-M defense in the national championship year of 1947.

Dick Rifenburg could catch a pass with the best of them, and crack a joke when the moment was ripe.

Howard Yerges was the quarterback for "The Mad Magicians," whose on-field excellence left opponents tied in knots.

and were drawing comparisons to the "Point-A-Minute" teams. Crisler grew wary of overconfidence. The players called a team meeting the week of the Minnesota game to quash any big-headedness. The tone of that meeting was deadly serious, bordering on grim.

That group, like its 1940 predecessors, didn't lack for characters. At the end of the meeting, Rifenburg broke the tension.

"I'm not getting enough publicity," he deadpanned.

Nobody lacked ink after Michigan pulled off a 13-6 homecoming win over the Gophers. Minnesota wasn't the juggernaut it had been but still led 6-0 nearing halftime. Michigan had the ball close to midfield, and Yerges announced the Wolverines hadn't trailed at halftime the entire year and weren't about to start. The next play, he said, had to go all the way.

Chappuis recalled: "Knowing that Minnesota had been giving a terrific pass rush all afternoon, I turned to Bump and said, 'I don't have much time to look for you, do you have any idea where you might be?' He said, 'Just throw it toward the corner and I'll see if I can get there.'

"I faded back to pass, and as I turned to look downfield, all I saw was (Leo) Nomellini and (Clayton) Tonnemaker so I let fly toward the corner. I never did see the play, but as I lay on the ground, I could tell by the roar of the crowd that Bump had 'gotten there.' "

That TD pass spurred the Wolverines' comeback win, and Elliott 'got there' again the following week. His 60-yard punt return made the difference in Michigan's 14-7 win at Illinois.

The Wolverines had survived back-to-back scares. There would be no more.

After a 35-0 rout of Indiana, U-M had a chance to clinch the conference crown and a Rose Bowl berth against highly regarded Wisconsin. To do so, Michigan would have to beat the Badgers at Madison in a sea of mud, conditions that had smudged the records of other talent-laden U-M teams. Would "The Mad Magicians" resort to smash and slog?

Hardly.

The Wolverines led early, 7-0, and faced a fourth-and-one inside Wisconsin's 5. The situation called for a straight dive, and when Yerges called for a pass, Chappuis recalled thinking "mad" was an appropriate description.

"I was tempted to speak up in the huddle and question 'Yergs' on his play selection," Chappuis noted. "But Fritz Crisler's teams were always well-disciplined, and one of his rules was that once the quarterback stepped into the huddle no one but the quarterback was allowed to say anything.

"We broke the huddle, the ball was snapped, I threw

Gene Derricotte intercepts a Wisconsin pass in the 1947 victory that sealed the conference championship and a trip to the Rose Bowl. Pete Elliott (45) was also right there.

the pass which was caught for a touchdown. Who caught it? — Howard Yerges. From then on out we rolled. We ran practically every play in the books without a flaw and that, coupled with a great defensive effort, allowed us to win 40-6, and we were Rose Bowl bound."

BOWLED OVER No one could touch this team. Not Ohio State, which fell 21-0. Certainly not Southern Cal in the 1948 Rose Bowl, which reprised Stanford's effort by getting mauled, 49-0. The repeat of the 1902 score

Fritz Crisler fretted about Michigan's mental preparedness for the 1948 Rose Bowl. Here he meets with the players for the final time, prior to the Wolverines' 49-0 bombardment of Southern Cal.

Fritz Crisler (top) conducted the runaway national championship train in 1947, getting plenty of impetus from the likes of Dick Rifenburg (middle) and Bruce Hilkene.

caused one smart-aleck copy editor to set the headline: "MICHIGAN FAILS TO IMPROVE!"

The Wolverines rolled up 491 yards of offense. Chappuis completed 12 of 22 passes for 139 yards and two touchdowns and added 91 rushing yards on 13 carries. Weisenburger blasted for 91 yards on 20 carries, with three touchdowns, and "Automatic" Jim Brieske added to his season total of 52 extra points.

Chappuis, who finished second in the Heisman Trophy balloting, ran the single-wing attack to perfection and earned Rose Bowl MVP honors. The battered Pacific

TRIPLE-THREAT

Bob Chappuis was one of Michigan's greatest all-purpose backs, playing in 1942 then returning from World War II to star in 1946 and 1947. In three varsity seasons, Chappuis recorded 3,468 yards of total offense, accounting for 27 touchdowns on teams that went 23-5-1. He was a marquee player on the 1947 national championship team, earning All-America honors that year. He is a member of the College Football Hall of Fame.

Bob Chappuis

Gene Derricotte holds for "Automatic" Jim Brieske, who converted 107 of 120 extra-point attempts during his career.

Coast delegation didn't shut down the bowl this time, but it might have been tempted.

Braven Dyer, a leading West Coast writer, quipped: "Well, it wasn't as bad as we expected. It was worse. The academic big-wigs of the Pacific Coast Conference who perpetuated this unholy union with the Big Nine a year ago should be made to line up on the Rose Bowl turf next January and pay for their perfidy."

Michigan, meanwhile, was repaid for its perfection. In a special post-bowl Associated Press poll, media representatives were asked to choose a national champion between the undefeated teams of Michigan and Notre Dame. The Wolverines drew 226 votes, the Irish 119, and 12 called it a draw.

Crisler called it a career. He continued as athletic director but left coaching at the top of the mountain. Whenever football historians debate over the greatest college football teams of all time, the 1947 "Mad Magicians" are invariably mentioned.

"The 1947 team was one of the best I've seen in college football," Crisler reflected later. "It was a great pleasure to be associated with it and see those players move on to become doctors, lawyers, architects, coaches, teachers, and administrators. It was a remarkable group of people who came as close to perfection on the football field as any coach could expect.

"After they had graduated it seemed like a good time to step down as head coach. There was not much that could happen afterward which would be more rewarding for a coach."

Bennie's Boys

1948-1958 Overall record: 63-33-4 (.650 winning percentage)
Coach: Bennie Oosterbaan
Conference Championships: 1948 (9-0), 1949 (6-2-1), 1950 (6-3-1)
National Championship: 1948

Bennie Oosterbaan spent 20 years as an assistant coach at U-M and turned down several other job offers to become the Michigan head coach.

Bennie Oosterbaan had been an assistant under Fritz Crisler, Harry Kipke, and Tad Wieman, an apprenticeship of 20 years spent on the Michigan sidelines.

Considered one of the nation's great pass receivers during his playing days at U-M in the 1920s, Oosterbaan had been one of the Western Conference's best all-around athletes. He had led the conference in scoring in basketball during the 1928 season, then joined the baseball team and led the league in hitting.

Oosterbaan could have gone on to play either professional baseball or football after graduating, but refused. A winner of the Western Conference Medal of Honor for proficiency in scholarship and athletics, Oosterbaan eschewed all other job opportunities to remain in Ann Arbor.

Crisler wanted to devote more time to running Michigan's athletic programs and was also disheartened at the prospect of having to go out and actually "recruit" players for his teams.

"It was only a matter of time before the college would seek the man, instead of the man seeking the college," Crisler said. "And, personally, I would never be able to recruit."

Relinquishing control of one of the nation's elite collegiate football powers, Crisler expressed the utmost confidence in Oosterbaan, calling him "the one man who could retain our single-wing, and the finest football mind I know."

WISTERT AT TACKLE Oosterbaan's first line was anchored by a 32-year-old former Marine whose surname was synonymous with Michigan football. Alvin Wistert became the third member of his family to don No. 11 (a numeral that would later be retired in honor of Francis "Whitey" Wistert, Albert "The Ox" Wistert, and Alvin "Big Moose" Wistert).

Not only did "Big Moose" meet the Wistert standard, he exceeded it by becoming the only Wistert brother to be named All-American twice (1948-49). All three brothers were later inducted into the National Football Foundation Hall of Fame as well as the Michigan Hall of Honor.

BENNIE'S FAST START Oosterbaan's first test as Michigan's head man was not an easy one — a road trip to East Lansing to face Biggie Munn's up-and-coming Michigan State unit.

WOLVERINE QUIZ

Michigan State had a reservoir of extra emotion to draw upon, having been thumped 55-0 by Michigan at Ann Arbor the year before in Munn's debut. In addition, the '48 game marked the dedication of MSU's newly enlarged Macklin Stadium. Despite the Spartans' extra motivation, the Wolverines prevailed in Oosterbaan's debut by a 13-7 score.

Michigan State's touchdown, a disputed one, was the only score the Wolverines surrendered in their first four games under Oosterbaan. Shutouts over Oregon (14-0), Purdue (40-0), and third-ranked Northwestern (28-0) followed.

32. Who was the oldest player ever to play football at Michigan, and how old was he when he played?

ANOTHER CLASSIC WITH THE GOPHERS Playing before the largest crowd ever in Minneapolis (65,130), Michigan got two first-half touchdowns from fullback Tom Peterson and a game-clinching TD reception by Dick Rifenburg in cruising to a 27-14 victory over Minnesota.

"No one — absolutely no one outside of the Michigan camp— gave Michigan a chance to beat the highly favored Gophers," halfback Wally Teninga recalled in a "This I Remember" essay. "The victory was Bennie's. We worked extremely hard that week. We knew what had to be done and everyone made that special effort— that

Halfback Leo Koceski caught this TD pass from Walt Teninga against Northwestern in 1948.

OH, BROTHER

There may never be another set of brothers to play college football that matches the exploits of Michigan's famed Wisterts. Francis, Albert and Alvin all played tackle, wore No. 11, and earned first-team All-America honors.

Alvin "Big Moose" Wistert was the last of three Wistert brothers to play for Michigan.

Francis "Whitey" was a member of the 1933 U-M team that won Big Ten and national championships. Albert "The Ox" starred for Fritz Crisler in the early 1940s and was picked as an All-American in 1942. Alvin "Moose" Wistert was the oldest man ever to play football for Michigan. He was a standout tackle at the age of 32 after serving in the Marines during World War II. All three brothers have been enshrined in the National Football Foundation Hall of Fame as well as the Michigan Hall of Honor.

incremental effort that augers success."

Illinois also put up a game fight, but U-M prevailed, 28-20, for its 20th consecutive victory. Harry Allis kicked all four of Michigan's extra points and hauled in a 45-yard pass from Chuck Ortmann to lead the way.

CHAMPIONS AGAIN After decisive wins over Navy (35-0) and Indiana (54-0), Michigan clinched a share of the Big Nine conference title.

In the season finale at Columbus, Ohio State gave the Wolverines a great test, but U-M prevailed 13-3 behind the fine play of Teninga and quarterback Pete Elliott.

The victory over the Buckeyes gave Michigan a 9-0 record in Oosterbaan's first season. The Wolverines had outscored their opponents 252-44 to win their second consecutive conference title, the school's 18th overall.

Michigan also extended its winning streak to 23 games and only the Western Conference's two-year no-repeat rule prevented the Wolverines from going back to Pasadena. Runner-up Northwestern represented the conference at the Rose Bowl and beat California.

TOPPING THE POLLS AGAIN When the final Associated Press poll came out on November 29, 1948, Michigan

Versatile Wally Teninga was a fine ball carrier and defender as well as an accomplished punter.

had finished at the top, giving the Wolverines back-to-back national titles.

Oosterbaan helped the Michigan football program make history by being named College Football Coach of the Year. Crisler and Oosterbaan made U-M the first school to have two different coaches consecutively honored as the best in the land.

THE BIG HOUSE GETS BIGGER Two consecutive national titles can do wonders for a team's popularity, and mighty Michigan braced for a surge in attendance. Permanent steel stands added to the top of the concrete and brick bowl that is Michigan Stadium boosted capacity from 84,401 to 97,239 for the 1949 campaign. During this construction, engineering reports confirmed the structure's footings were so deep they could easily support a second deck around the stadium. Some say Yost had planned things that way, while others maintained the footings had been required because of the high water table under the stadium.

The Michigan State Spartans gave U-M a scare in the 1949 opener, and it took the unheralded passing combination of Bill Putich and Irv Wisniewski to pull out a 7-3 victory. Wisniewski hit Putich on a long pass for the game's only touchdown. The reception came on Putich's only play of the afternoon, earning him the nickname "One-Play Putich."

Stanford was expected to give Oosterbaan's boys a stiff challenge but the Indians fell in Palo Alto, 27-7, Michigan's 25th straight victory.

ARMY ENDS THE STREAK The third Michigan-Army game also marked the end of U-M's 25-game winning streak as the Cadets romped over the Wolverines in Ann Arbor, 21-7.

Ace passer Chuck Ortmann suffered a slight concussion from a kick to the head on the second play from scrimmage, and Michigan completed just three passes in 23 attempts for 16 yards.

Oosterbaan termed Ortmann's injury "one of the breaks of the game." But Army Coach Earl "Red" Blaik's sentiment was shared by a good number of Michigan fans when he said, "It wasn't just a bad break. It was truly a tragedy." Blaik added that his Cadets had played "way over their heads."

BRIDESMAIDS IN WHITE Michigan carried a 15-game Western Conference winning streak to Evanston, Ill., the following week to meet Northwestern. The Wildcats had tied U-M, 14-14, in 1946, a week before the Wolverines' last conference loss.

In 1949, Michigan State, one of the Wolverines' chief rivals, was admitted to the Western Conference — transforming it from the Big Nine back into the Big Ten. But the Spartans didn't compete for the championship until 1953 because of scheduling conflicts.

WOLVERINE QUIZ

33. What distinction did Bennie Oosterbaan earn in his first season as the Michigan head coach, and how was the honor historic?

Halfback Chuck Ortmann played through many injuries in his career, yet was still a standout passer and punter.

The debut of white road jerseys did not spur Oosterbaan's eleven to victory, however. Reliable placekicker Harry Allis missed the conversion kick on Michigan's second touchdown of the game, allowing Northwestern to escape with a 21-20 victory.

Suddenly, the tables had turned on the Wolverines. Minnesota, traditional spoilers of Michigan winning streaks, came to town for homecoming riding a four-game winning streak. The Gophers were a touchdown favorite against the Wolverines, losers of two straight.

"Michigan Mighty Again" screamed *The Michigan Daily* headline after the Wolverines' 14-7 win over the Gophers. "Bennie's Beleaguered Boys became Bennie's Beautiful Blockers" noted the game story while "Mediocre Michigan (became) Mighty once again."

Ortmann was brilliant. The oft-injured halfback rushed for 115 yards, completed nine of 17 passes for 92 yards, and scored the Wolverines' first touchdown.

Chuck Lentz tied a conference record with three interceptions in a great defensive performance and went on to set a Western Conference standard with seven interceptions during the season.

NEW SATURDAY TRADITIONS BORN During Michigan's 20-12 win over Purdue in 1949, airplanes carrying banners made their debut over Michigan Stadium, another game-day tradition that has carried on to the present. Planes were required to fly 1,000 feet above the stadium and the pilots were required to wear parachutes. A typical banner cost about $450. Two weeks later, 1,850 area high school bandsmen joined the 120 members of the university band for the first incarnation of Band Day, an event *The Michigan Daily* called "one of the most spectacular displays ever to grace the stadium."

The group of almost 2,000 musicians spelled out B-A-N-D-S and then S-O-U-S-A while performing Sousa's "Stars and Stripes Forever." *The Daily* marveled at how "the high school musicians were able to follow (U-M band) director William D. Revelli perfectly after only one practice session."

FIT TO BE TIED As usual, the Michigan-Ohio State game saw the Big Nine Championship hang in the balance. Leo Koceski hauled in a pass from Wally Teninga to put the Wolverines ahead 7-0, but the Buckeyes fought back.

OSU scored in the fourth quarter to close the margin to a single point, setting the stage for the most controversial play of the season. Jim Hague's extra-point kick sailed wide. However, the officials ruled Michigan offside and allowed Hague to redeem himself.

The 7-7 tie gave the Buckeyes a share of the 1949 conference title with U-M and a trip to Pasadena because of the two-year no-repeat rule. Ohio State celebrated the tie wildly, while the Wolverines treated it as a defeat. Michigan's overall record went in the books at 6-2-1.

THE LONG WAY BACK TO PASADENA Top-ranked Army pounded the Wolverines, 27-6, at Yankee Stadium, sending Michigan to its second defeat in its first three games of the 1950 campaign. After a homecoming win over Wisconsin, Michigan traveled to Minnesota as a two-touchdown favorite but returned with a 7-7 tie. "Michigan didn't lose, but Minnesota won" read the lead the next day in *The Michigan Daily*.

U-M's Rose Bowl hopes were practically gone after losing to Illinois, 7-0, in a blinding snow and ice storm. Playing in the inclement weather, as it turned out, was to be a good rehearsal.

During a season in which just about everything had gone wrong, things started falling into place for Oosterbaan's squad.

Michigan downed Indiana and Northwestern to set up the season finale with Ohio State. Meanwhile, Illinois still had the inside track to the Rose Bowl after downing the Buckeyes. U-M's trip to Columbus was billed as an offensive showdown between Ortmann and Buckeye great Vic Janowicz, the conference's top yardage gainer and eventual 1950 Heisman Trophy winner.

ROSES THAT BLOOMED IN THE SNOW On Thanksgiving weekend, a massive storm pummeled the Midwest, nearly forcing the contest to be canceled. As it was, the game started late while crews cleared six inches of snow

WOLVERINE QUIZ

34. What team ended Michigan's 25-game unbeaten streak during the 1949 season?

WOLVERINE QUIZ

35. The week after the 25-game unbeaten streak ended, U-M also lost its 15-game Western Conference unbeaten run to which opponent?

off the Ohio Stadium yard lines.

"No member of the football team believed a football game would be played that Saturday," recalled fullback Ralph Straffon. "I can remember the wind whistling through the ear holes of our plastic helmets. We had to tape the ear holes closed in order to hear the signals."

Janowicz gave the Buckeyes a 3-0 lead on a 40-yard field goal four minutes into the game, but the terrible conditions had all but halted the offenses. With 47 seconds left in the first half, Janowicz again figured in the scoring but not in a way he would have wanted.

U-M had already blocked one Janowicz punt to cause a safety. Now with time winding down, linebacker Tony Momsen crashed through the middle of the Ohio State line. Momsen stuffed Janowicz's kick at the Buckeye 2-yard line and pounced on the loose ball in the end zone, scoring the game's only touchdown. Michigan owned a 9-3 triumph, in what came to be known as "The Snow Bowl."

On one of the worst days ever for football, Michigan edged Ohio State, 9-3, to capture the 1950 Big Ten title and a berth in the Rose Bowl.

Ortmann played all 60 minutes and punted 24 times, tying the modern NCAA mark. The 45 punts by the two teams still stands as the modern conference standard.

Late in the game, Leo Koceski informed the U-M offensive huddle that Northwestern had shocked an overconfident Illinois team 14-7 in Evanston. The jubilant Wolverines warmed up in the locker room after the game with a chorus of "California, Here We Come."

DUFEK LEADS ROSY COMEBACK

The Wolverines beat California, 14-6, in the 1951 Rose Bowl game before 98,939 fans in Pasadena.

The Golden Bears dominated the first half and led 6-0 on a 39-yard touchdown pass. Michigan turned the game around after halftime, taking the lead on Don Dufek's 1-yard touchdown plunge in the fourth quarter. Dufek put the game on ice with a 7-yard scoring run off a Cal turnover moments later.

The 1950 season saw the Wolverines post a 6-3-1 record, win their fourth straight conference championship (their 20th overall), and earn a No. 9 ranking. It marked the 11th straight season during which Michigan finished in The Associated Press Top 10.

NOT READY FOR PRIME TIME

Oosterbaan's teams during the early 1950s were not up to the standards of his first three squads. The win over Ohio State in '51 left the Wolverines 4-2 and in fourth place in the Big Ten, but they finished 4-5 overall — the program's first losing campaign in 15 years. The good news was that end Lowell Perry earned All-America honors.

In 1952, the Wolverines finished with a disappointing 5-4 mark, while still featuring some fine talent, including halfback Ted Kress and linebacker Roger Zatkoff. So dominant was Zatkoff at his position from 1950 to 1952, that an annual team award bearing

Rugged Don Dufek, shown here in action in 1948, scored both of Michigan's touchdowns in the 14-6 win over California in the 1951 Rose Bowl.

Roger Zatkoff was one of the top linebackers to play at U-M. The team's linebacker award has been named in his honor.

U-M PIONEERS TELEVISION AGE

In 1947, television became the newest medium for Michigan loyalists to follow their team. U-M's 55-0 thrashing of Michigan State to open the season marked the first appearance by a U-M football squad on the small screen. WWJ-TV in Detroit carried all six Michigan home games during Fritz Crisler's final season, as well as all the home contests in 1948 and 1949.

In 1950, the NCAA stepped in and forbade the telecasting of college football games, citing an adverse effect on attendance. Paradoxically, Michigan averaged nearly 94,000 fans for its six home games in 1949, a record that stood for 26 years.

Home games were shown on closed circuit television in Detroit theaters in 1950, but the NCAA put the kibosh on the closed circuit telecasts and assumed absolute control over college football on television in 1951. An experimental series of games was aired by NBC that season, including U-M's 7-0 loss at Illinois and its 7-0 win against Ohio State in Ann Arbor in Woody Hayes' first game against Michigan.

his name was established in 1991 to honor Michigan's top linebacker.

IN THE SPARTANS' SHADOW Before the start of the 1953 season, Fritz Crisler, Michigan athletic director, chairman of the NCAA rules committee, and the man who had pioneered two-platoon football as U-M head coach, announced the game's return to one-platoon. The overriding reason was the high cost of maintaining two separate squads.

Michigan looked ready to storm back to the top of the Big Ten in 1953, rolling to victories in its first four games before being blanked by Minnesota, 22-0. U-M then enjoyed a 24-14 homecoming win against Pennsylvania before falling to Illinois, 19-3.

The Wolverines played Michigan State at East Lansing for only the sixth time in 46 games on the season's penultimate weekend. Before a sellout crowd of 51,421 at Macklin Field Stadium and a national television audience, the defending national champions edged a stubborn Michigan club, 14-6.

A 20-0 victory over Ohio State helped the 1953 Wolverines end the season on a high note and with a 6-3 overall record.

AN END TO REMEMBER Ron Kramer came to Michigan from East High School in Detroit in the fall of 1953 and sold programs at Michigan Stadium while sitting out his freshman year. When he stepped onto the practice field for the first time in the fall of 1954, photographers and reporters surrounded Kramer to talk to him about his upcoming career as a Michigan football player.

"It didn't take me long to realize that most of the other freshman football players were as nervous and unsure of themselves as I," recalled halfback Terry Barr in a "This I Remember" essay. "I said most, because there was one player (Ron Kramer) who acted as if he already belonged.

"You just can't imagine how comforting it was over the next four years when bending over in the huddle I could look up, see Ron, and know that he was on my side."

Did Kramer ever perform. He could play both offensive and defensive end, run with the ball, and punt or placekick. Sometimes Kramer did all of these things in the same game. Oosterbaan, however, pointed to Kramer's blocking and tackling as his greatest contributions.

Twice Kramer was picked as a consensus All-American in football (1955-56), and he also left U-M as the school's all-time leading scorer in basketball with 1,124 points. Kramer, whose No. 87 has been retired by the Wolverines, is regarded as one of U-M's all-time great athletes.

He caught 53 passes for 880 yards, scored nine touchdowns, and was the punter and placekicker on nationally ranked teams that went 20-7 from 1954 to 1956.

"To top off his marvelous physical gifts of size and speed and strength, plus an uncanny coordination, Kramer was one of the fiercest competitors I've ever seen," Oosterbaan said. "Nothing was impossible for him. The impossible was only a challenge."

ANOTHER CLOSE CALL WITH OSU The Wolverines were picked to finish in the lower division of the Big Ten in 1954, but they had lost only twice going into the

One of the greatest players in Michigan history, Ron Kramer was appreciated most by Coach Oosterbaan for his blocking and tackling prowess.

... EVERYTHING BUT SELLING POPCORN

Ron Kramer was a two-time All-American in football and collected three letters in three different sports at U-M — football, basketball, and track. Not only did the East Detroit native lead the Michigan football team in scoring for two years, he did the same on the basketball team. He was a devastating blocking and tackling force on the gridiron but could also run the ball, punt and placekick. Kramer totaled 1,119 points in his Michigan basketball career and was named the team's Most Valuable Player as a junior. After leaving Michigan, Kramer went on to a successful professional football career with the Green Bay Packers and the Detroit Lions.

WOLVERINE QUIZ

36. Who set a Western Conference record with seven interceptions during the 1949 season?

The first Michigan Stadium crowd of more than 100,000 saw the Wolverines lose to Michigan State, 9-0, in 1956.

season finale.

The Big Ten race and Rose Bowl berth came down to the game against Ohio State in Columbus, where the Buckeyes triumphed, 21-7, before 78,447 at Ohio Stadium.

Late in the third quarter with the game tied 7-7, U-M drove to the Buckeyes' 1-yard line, where Dave Hill was stopped at the goal line on a disputed fourth-down play. OSU took the ball and drove 99 yards in 11 plays, scoring on an 8-yard pass play. Howard "Hopalong" Cassady added another touchdown for the Buckeyes, who would finish the season 10-0 and be named national champions.

THE HAWKEYES' ALBATROSS While Ohio State would supply Michigan with a number of disappointments, the Wolverines similarly inhabited the nightmares of the Iowa football team. Time and again, the Hawkeyes seemed ready to topple mighty Michigan, only to be the victims of an improbable comeback.

U-M roared into the 1955 homecoming game with Forest Evashevski's Iowa team ranked No. 1 in the nation and sporting a 5-0 record. The Hawkeyes, however, jumped out to a 14-0 lead.

A Lou Baldacci plunge from 1 yard out and a 34-yard pass from Tony Branoff to Tom Maentz got U-M on the board in the third quarter. Iowa retaliated, scoring before the end of the third quarter to take a 21-13 lead.

In the fourth quarter, U-M put up 20 unanswered points. Ron Kramer collected a 65-yard touchdown pass from Jim Maddock, Maentz hauled in a 60-yard TD strike from Maddock with four minutes left, and Branoff scored on a 30-yard touchdown run for some insurance in a big Michigan victory. It marked the third year in a row that Michigan had come from behind to beat Iowa.

The win was the Wolverines' last bit of glory that season. Illinois upset Michigan at Champaign, 25-6, the following week to knock U-M from the No. 1 ranking. Ohio State dashed Michigan's conference title and Rose Bowl aspirations two weeks later with a punishing 17-0 decision in Ann Arbor. Michigan State, whose only loss of the season had been to the 7-2 Wolverines, received the Rose Bowl berth.

AND AN EXTRA SEAT FOR FRITZ Before the 1956 season, a new press box had been built at Michigan Stadium and seating capacity raised to 101,001. The odd seat was for Athletic Director Fritz Crisler, a tradition that would continue. (Present-day capacity is 102,501.)

The Wolverines fell to Michigan State, 9-0, in the second game at their expanded home, the first time a crowd of more than 100,000 attended a game at Michigan Stadium. Ron Kramer was hindered by a broken hand he had suffered a week earlier against UCLA.

Michigan unleashed a powerful offensive attack in a

WOLVERINE QUIZ

37. *What famous sporting venue was the site of the 1950 game between Michigan and Army?*

Halfback Terry Barr makes a leaping reception. Barr could also pass the ball and was an outstanding defensive back.

WOLVERINE QUIZ

38. What multi-sport standout played end for Michigan from 1954-56?

48-14 dismantling of Army before 93,402 at Michigan Stadium. Terry Barr, another in a long line of outstanding Michigan halfbacks, rushed for 65 yards on five carries, scored a touchdown, and completed a 57-yard pass to Ron Kramer.

Minnesota came up with a new twist, a no-huddle offense that befuddled the U-M defenders. "The whole defense was a sieve, except for Terry Barr, who was playing safety and many times I thought he was actually a linebacker," Kramer recalled. The Gophers won, 20-7.

A week later Michigan trailed Iowa 14-3 at halftime. Predictably the Wolverines came back for a 17-14 victory, the fourth straight season U-M had rebounded to beat the Hawkeyes.

Michigan closed out a successful 7-2 campaign in '56 with a 19-0 win at Ohio State in the collegiate finale for Barr and Kramer.

TWO-POINTER ARRIVES; BENNIE DEPARTS Oosterbaan's 1957 unit went 5-3-1, tying Iowa before more than 90,000 fans in Ann Arbor and a national television audience. But Michigan State and Ohio State cast a pall over the season by trouncing the Wolverines, despite an All-America campaign by halfback Jim Pace.

All-America running back Jim Pace (43) blasts through the Indiana line for a 31-yard gain in 1957.

The two-point conversion was introduced into college football in 1958. Crisler had spearheaded this action in an effort to reduce the number of tie games.

U-M still battled MSU to a 12-12 tie, a relative high point

for the Wolverines in a dismal season.

Michigan finished 2-6-1, the school's worst showing since a 1-7 mark in 1936. Captain John Herrnstein closed out a solid career, the third member of his family to don the Maize and Blue. Al Herrnstein (1901-02) and Bill Herrnstein (1923-25) each starred for some of Fielding Yost's best teams.

Oosterbaan stepped down as head football coach at the end of the season but continued to serve Michigan in a number of capacities, including color commentator on radio broadcasts and director of alumni relations for the athletic department.

WOLVERINE QUIZ

39. For whom is the '1' on the end of the Michigan Stadium capacity figure the reserved seat?

Bump Gets His Break

1959-1968 Overall Record: 51-42-2 (.547)
Coach: Chalmers W. "Bump" Elliott
Conference Championship: 1964 (9-1)

Newly appointed head coach Bump Elliott told Michigan fans it would take three to five years for him to build a championship program.

Even before Bennie Oosterbaan opted to retire from the rigors of college coaching, rumors circulated around Ann Arbor that Nebraska assistant coach and former U-M standout Pete Elliott would succeed Oosterbaan.

Instead, his brother Chalmers W. "Bump" Elliott, who served as Oosterbaan's assistant in 1957 and 1958, was elevated to the post and became the Big Ten's youngest coach.

After graduating from Michigan in 1948, Elliott had served as an assistant at Oregon State (1948-51) and Iowa (1952-56) before returning to Ann Arbor to work for his former coach. When Elliott ascended to the top job, he warned everyone that it would take him as long as five years to get the program back to the top of the conference. His prophecy turned out to be accurate.

Elliott instituted a three-platoon system for the 1959 season in an effort to get experience for more players and kick-start the rebuilding process.

SLOW START, STRONG FINISH George Mans, in a "This I Remember" essay, described the 1959 team as a "tough and spirited outfit." The Wolverines were indeed resilient, coming back from three losses in their first four games — including a 34-8 pounding in Ann Arbor by Michigan State — to finish the season with a bit of a flourish.

George Mans, captain of the 1961 team, was a member of the famed 1959 "Raiders" defensive unit that was charged with containing the Big Ten's top offensive threats.

"I was a member of the 'Raiders' unit, which was the defensive specialty unit," Mans recalled. "We took great pride in our role and had our best moments against two great fullbacks, holding both Bill Brown of Illinois and Bob Ferguson of Ohio State under 75 yards."

Inspired by the throttling of Brown in Champaign, the Wolverines upset the Illini, 20-15, only to slip and fall the following week at Indiana, 26-7, in Michigan's final appearance at old Memorial Stadium. Ohio State brought one loss into the '59 finale. And despite Wolverine halfback Dennis Fitzgerald being sidelined by an injury, Elliott's upstart youngsters were game for a challenge.

By the end of the game, Woody Hayes had been reduced to slamming his coat on the ground and tossing a folding chair into the Michigan Stadium stands. U-M won, 23-14.

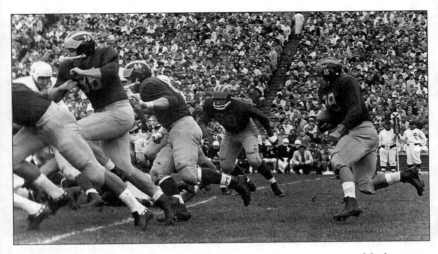

1-1 IN FOURTH-QUARTER DRAMATICS

Although 4-5 was not the kind of record the '59 Wolverines would brag about, the strong finish provided hope. U-M opened the 1960 season with a 21-0 trouncing of Oregon, then dropped a 24-17 thriller at Michigan State. The Michigan highlight of the day was Fitzgerald's 99-yard kickoff return for a touchdown.

This unit was stronger than the year before, but one that could still not find a way to win consistently. Minnesota, which would capture the national championship that year, spoiled U-M's homecoming, 10-0.

The next week, Wisconsin nipped the Wolverines, 16-13. U-M quarterback Dave Glinka recovered a

One of the last Michigan players to play without a face mask, halfback Dennis Fitzgerald was a load for opposing defenses to bring down.

Dave Glinka (bottom) and Jerry Smith (51) combine to bring down a Minnesota ball carrier in Minnesota's 10-0 win at Michigan Stadium at homecoming 1960.

*40. Who set a
Michigan record by
returning a kickoff
99 yards for a
touchdown against
Michigan State in
1960?*

blocked field goal attempt in the final seconds and completed a pass to Bob Johnson. Unfortunately, Johnson was run out of bounds at the Badgers' 6-yard line as time expired.

Johnson, who had been a member of the Michigan Marching Band before opting to play football, was again the receiver on a trick play seven days later against Illinois with the Wolverines trailing 7-0.

"We faced a fourth-and-seven against the largest defensive line in the Big Ten," Glinka recalled. "We lined up in punt formation, the ball was snapped, but I intercepted it and threw a 17-yard pass to Johnson. A few plays later, Bill Tunnicliff scored and we went for two points and made it (to win), 8-7."

STALLED IN THE REBUILDING ZONE Ohio State scored a fourth-quarter touchdown in the 1960 closer to pull out a 7-0 win that gave U-M a 5-4 record. Michigan would return several top players for the '61 season. Unfortunately, it would be a year that, like many in Elliott's tenure, had potential for greatness but disappointed Michigan's legion of fans.

Blowouts of UCLA (29-6) and Army (38-8) to begin the 1961 schedule heightened expectations, but Duffy Daugherty's Spartans came through once again and hung a 28-0 shutout on the Wolverines in Ann Arbor.

Two weeks later, U-M grabbed a 20-8 lead over Minnesota before a late fumble deep in Michigan territory allowed the Gophers to pull out an exciting 23-20 victory, virtually eliminating the Wolverines from Big Ten title contention. U-M was still a respectable 6-2 entering its home finale with OSU.

The high-powered Buckeyes captured the conference title, embarrassing U-M, 50-20. However, the Ohio State Faculty Senate voted to decline the Rose Bowl invitation. Among the jilted Buckeyes were assistant coach Bo Schembechler and junior lineman Gary Moeller.

"The only thing that stood out from this romp was Woody Hayes' effort to pour on the scoring," Glinka recalled. "Leading 35-12, Hayes left his first team in as Bob Ferguson scored his fourth touchdown of the afternoon with four minutes remaining.

"Joe Sparma then completed a 70-yard pass and with six seconds left. OSU scored its final touchdown and Hayes elected to go for the two-point conversion."

STRUGGLING FOR POINTS, WINS The Wolverines lost 21 seniors from the 1961 squad that had gone 6-3 and the 1962 team would show it. After a 1-1 start, another 28-0 setback at the hands of Michigan State set the tone for the remainder of the schedule.

Quarterback Dave Glinka and his teammates suffered a 50-20 lambasting by Ohio State in 1961, but the Buckeyes were not allowed to make the trip to Pasadena.

"Things only got worse as the season went along," recalled Glinka. "Injuries began to take their toll on experienced players. This meant even more young players would be called upon to play."

Michigan failed to score in three successive games — Michigan State, Purdue, and Minnesota — and posted a 2-7 record, the school's worst showing in 26 years. Ohio State capped the season by serving up a 28-0 drubbing in Columbus.

End Jim Conley suffered through a 3-4-2 season in 1963 but captained the 1964 squad to Michigan's only Rose Bowl appearance under Bump Elliott.

ON THE BRINK OF GREATNESS Michigan's 1963 unit posted a disappointing 3-4-2 record in a season with few highlights.

In the second week of the campaign, Navy quarterback Roger Staubach riddled the U-M defense during the Middies' 26-13 victory in Ann Arbor. Staubach went on to win the Heisman Trophy, and many felt his aerial antics at Michigan Stadium propelled him to the award.

The Wolverines showed signs of life the following Saturday, battling Michigan State to a 7-7 draw to snap the Spartans' four-game winning streak over Elliott and Michigan.

Elliott picked up his second homecoming win in five seasons with Michigan's 27-6 dismantling of Northwestern, setting the stage for another matchup with Pete Elliott's Illinois team. The game turned out to be a pivotal one in the Bump Elliott era at Michigan.

"We had been suffering through a mediocre year trying to rebuild the Michigan tradition," All-Big Ten end Jim Conley recalled in a "This I Remember" segment. "Rumor had it that Bump Elliott was on his way out. No one on that team wanted that to happen — we loved him.

"The Illini of 1963 were undefeated and heading for the Rose Bowl. We entered Champaign as a heavy underdog and won, 14-8. In the process we sent seven regulars to the sideline. From then on, we knew we could win."

In their seven-year series, Bump held a 6-1 record over brother Pete. (Still, the Illini captured the Big Ten title in 1963 and posted a victory over Washington in the 1964 Rose Bowl.)

The assassination of President John F. Kennedy caused the Michigan-Ohio State game in Ann Arbor to be postponed a week. When it was finally played, the game attracted only 36,000 fans. The Buckeyes prevailed in a snowy 14-10 battle.

3-0, AND ON THEIR WAY Mass substitution had been approved for 1964, and coaches were able to insert as many players as they wished when the clock stopped and two while the clock was running.

The season got off the a fine start when U-M bombed

WOLVERINE QUIZ

41. What quarterback got his 1963 Heisman Trophy season rolling with a big showing against Michigan?

WOLVERINE QUIZ

42. What caused the Michigan-Ohio State game of 1963 to be postponed for a week?

Rick Sygar (18) and Rick Volk (49) teamed up to give Michigan a formidable defensive backfield in 1964. Here, the duo combine to break up a pass at Michigan State during a 17-10 Wolverine win.

WOLVERINE QUIZ

43. What player known as "The Preacherman" played quarterback on Bump Elliott's Rose Bowl champion team in 1964?

Air Force, 24-7, and Navy, 21-0, (Staubach was slowed by an injured heel). Defensive back Rick Volk ended Staubach's day in the third quarter with a solid hit near the sideline. The Wolverines then went looking for their first win over Michigan State after six losses and two ties.

"I knew we were ready to play when MSU took the field," Conley said. "They ran through our team, which was taking calisthenics. The next thing I knew, Rick Sygar had decked one of their players, who apparently had run a little too close to him. The melee ended abruptly, but the end zone crowd was less than gracious when we left the field for our pregame talk."

Trailing 10-3 in the fourth quarter, quarterback Bob Timberlake hit Sygar with a 5-yard touchdown pass, but the extra point failed. Later, on a halfback option, Sygar connected with John Henderson for a 31-yard touchdown pass that propelled U-M to an important 17-10 win.

TIMBERLAKE RAMBLES, BUT U-M FALLS The lone disappointment of 1964 came when Purdue quarterback Bob Griese led the "Spoilermakers" to a 21-20 upset of the fifth-ranked Wolverines at Ann Arbor. Griese threw for two touchdowns and also kicked all three extra points.

Halfback Rick Sygar was known as a ferocious competitor who did whatever it took to give the Wolverines an advantage on offense or defense.

Three lost fumbles helped doom the Wolverines. Afterward, Purdue Coach Jack Mollenkopf called the U-M team "probably the finest Michigan team since the Crisler era. It could easily win the remainder of its games."

Timberlake scored a pair of TDs, one of them an improbable 54-yard scamper for the game's final score. But he came up a yard short on U-M's two-point conversion with seven minutes to go.

"To my amazement, our off-side lineman had leveled their defensive backs," Timberlake said. "The goal line beckoned 54 yards ahead. My juices flowed. I stretched my long legs and crossed the goal line. It was the first and only time I had scored for Michigan while standing up.

"But my glory was tarnished. Not only did I fall short in the run for two points, causing us to lose, but I was cheated out of any remaining plaudits by the Monday movies.

"The pictures clearly showed that Tom Mack, a lowly tackle, had appointed himself my personal escort for the last 40 yards of the run. And as I pressed ahead full throttle, he sauntered alongside, barely extending himself, looking for any 300-pound middle guard who might have been gaining ground on us."

THE CHARGE TO CALIFORNIA Elliott's troops bounced back from the Purdue loss to edge Minnesota, 19-12, and then drilled Northwestern (35-0), defending league champion Illinois (21-6) and Iowa (34-20).

Known as "The Preacherman", Bob Timberlake quarterbacked the Wolverines to a 9-1 record in 1964 and a win over Oregon State in the Rose Bowl.

The Wolverines were back in position to return to Pasadena, a locale they had not visited since the end of the 1950 season. They had climbed back up to No. 6 in the AP poll, one spot ahead of Ohio State, also 7-1. U-M had the nation's best rushing offense, while the Buckeyes had the country's best rush defense entering the season finale.

"The enthusiasm and electricity on campus were overwhelming. We covered the huge tree in front of the Sigma Chi house with cartons of toilet paper — it looked like a snow storm in bloom," recalled defensive end Bill Laskey. "I don't think any of us slept a quiet night, and I

Michigan head coach Bump Elliott called the Wolverines' 10-0 win at Ohio State in 1964 "my happiest moment in football."

MVP Mel Anthony gets a personal escort from lineman Tom Mack for the final yards of his 84-yard TD run in the 1965 Rose Bowl.

know that few of us made many classes."

On a cold and windy day on the banks of the Olentangy River, Michigan cashed in on an 18-yard TD pass from Timberlake to Jim Detwiler in the second quarter and a 27-yard field goal by Timberlake in the fourth.

The 10-0 triumph ended the Wolverines' four-game losing streak to Woody Hayes and gave U-M its first conference title in 14 years. "This is my happiest moment in football," said Bump Elliott, whose Wolverines awaited No. 8 Oregon State in the Rose Bowl.

ANTHONY RUNS THROUGH THE BEAVERS All did not proceed according to plan once the Wolverines arrived in Pasadena. The Wolverines took full advantage of the California hospitality — and the free ice cream — while basking in the season's success. Running back Mel Anthony put on 10 extra pounds and watched as the rest of the team struggled through practices.

"Our timing was off. A few days before the game, the coaches became concerned and brought it to our attention," Anthony recalled in a "This I Remember" segment. "We decided to have our own meeting and Conley took charge. We agreed, openly or silently, our priorities were out of hand. We rededicated ourselves to winning a football game against Oregon State."

Michigan spotted the Beavers a 7-0 lead before getting their legs. Anthony set a Rose Bowl record with an 84-yard touchdown run and Carl Ward scrambled 43 yards to give U-M a 12-7 half-time lead. Anthony ran for

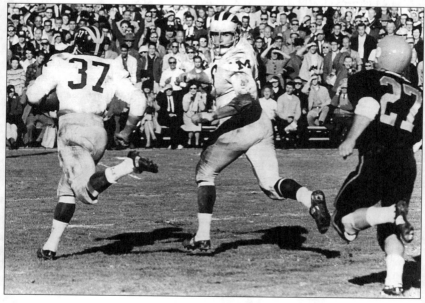

The 1964 Big Ten
champion and 1965
Rose Bowl champion
Michigan football
team.

two more touchdowns in the third quarter, and
Timberlake scored on a 24-yard run in the fourth quarter
for a decisive 34-7 Michigan victory.

Anthony was named Rose Bowl MVP after rushing for
123 yards and three touchdowns on 13 carries. Conley
made sure that Elliott received the game ball.

"The thing I remember most about our ball club in
1964 was the esprit de corps and closeness we all had
for each other," Laskey said. "We were like a team of
'no-names,' every one of us willing to make any sacrifice
for the other."

The victory gave U-M a 9-1 season record and a No. 1
ranking by some experts. But the team finished No. 4 in
both the AP and UPI polls.

BACK TO REALITY An opening 31-24 win at sweltering
North Carolina and a 10-7 edging of California allowed
1965's team to temporarily meet fan expectations.

Once the Wolverines entered the Big Ten season,
though, little seemed to go Michigan's way.

"Michigan had been picked by some preseason polls to
be national champs," offensive tackle Tom Mack recalled.
"Consecutive losses to Michigan State, Purdue, and
Minnesota totally destroyed our once optimistic team.

"Worse, for the seniors it meant relegation to the
bench as the coaches gave more and more under-classmen
playing time in preparation for next season."

A 50-14 triumph over Wisconsin soothed some of the
ache for the upperclassman, and allowed Elliott to empty
his bench while holding a lead. The Wolverines trounced
Illinois a week later, 23-3, in Bump Elliott's final
coaching matchup with brother Pete. Losses to
Northwestern (34-22) and Ohio State (9-7) left the team
with a 4-6 record.

Offensive lineman
Tom Mack saw three
straight losses crush
the morale of the
1965 Michigan team
in its defense of the
Big Ten title.

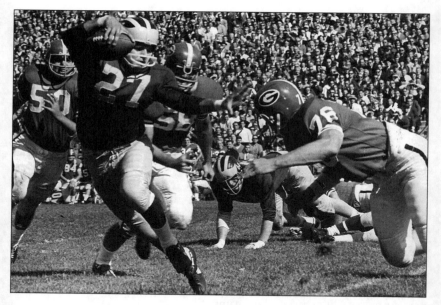

Quarterback Dick Vidmer avoids a Georgia tackler during the third game of the 1965 season. The 15-7 loss snapped an eight-game U-M winning streak.

Dick Vidmer got an earful from Coach Elliott for calling an audible in a 28-21 loss to Illinois in 1966.

MID-SEASON SLIDES PLAGUE U-M

Michigan State won three in a row from the Wolverines from 1966 to 1968, and each defeat seemed to deepen Michigan's frustrations. Fans, players, and coaches were forced to endure losing streaks in each of those years.

In a "This I Remember" essay, quarterback Dick Vidmer recalled U-M's 20-7 loss at Michigan State in '66, "The game itself was brutal, almost surreal. I have never played in or seen such a contest. No one had a sense of physical limits. Every play was a collision that shook the field. We lost the game, but no respect."

U-M improved to 4-3 with wins over Minnesota (49-0) and Wisconsin (28-17), and had a 21-14 lead on Illinois with the ball near the Illini goal line. After the Wolverines were stuffed twice at the 2-yard line, Elliott called for a safe pass to the short side. Vidmer, however, tried to go to Jack Clancy on the wide side and watched as Illinois' Bruce Sullivan intercepted the ball and sped 98 yards for a touchdown.

On the sideline, Elliott went ballistic. "The first and only time I heard him curse," Vidmer recalled. The Illini went on to win, 28-21.

DETWILER MUSHES PAST OSU

U-M's offensive line came together just in time for the '66 finale at Ohio State, which made a hero out of halfback Jim Detwiler.

"The offensive line took complete charge of the line of scrimmage," Detwiler recalled. "Running tailback from the I-formation, which was new for us for that game, I carried the ball what seemed to be more times than I had all season. I had never gained more than 100 yards in a game before, but I surpassed that total in the first half.

"Had I been in good condition I might have doubled the 140 yards I gained, but in the third quarter my legs turned to mush and the coach wisely benched me. Living up to his reputation of being a gentleman and a nice guy, Bump told the press that he pulled me because I had a touch of the flu."

The 17-3 win over the Buckeyes capped a 6-4 season. Michigan slipped to 4-6 in 1967, losing to Michigan State and Ohio State. The stage was set for Elliott's last season at the helm and nearly his most triumphant.

Dennis Brown quarterbacked the Wolverines to eight straight wins in 1968, Bump Elliott's final season as Michigan's head coach.

BUMP'S FINALE The weather was the only thing perfect about Elliott's last season-opener as Michigan head coach. Under sunny skies and in 80-degree temperatures, Cal delivered a 21-7 jolt to the Wolverines. Predictions that had U-M finishing seventh in the Big Ten looked to be quite accurate.

Michigan stormed back, however, winning its next eight in a row, including a crowd-pleasing 28-14 victory over Michigan State on a sparkling day at Michigan Stadium.

"The game was typical in every respect, great intensity, great emotion and plenty of hard hitting," quarterback Dennis Brown recalled in a "This I Remember" piece. "It was the game that means the most to me and I believe to most members of the '68 team."

Carl Ward gets big yardage in a homecoming victory over Minnesota in 1966.

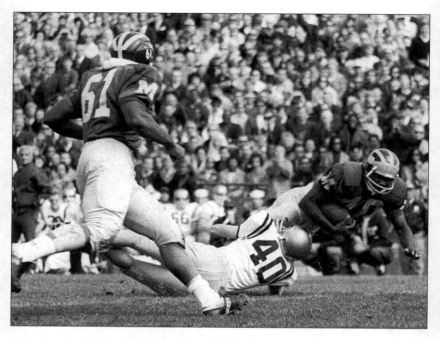

WOLVERINE QUIZ

Ron Johnson stretches for a few extra yards in Michigan's 32-9 win over Navy in 1968.

44. Who was the Most Valuable Player of the 1965 Rose Bowl?

JOHNSON 34, WISCONSIN 9 Ron Johnson set 10 Big Ten rushing records in the Michigan victory over the Badgers on November 16, 1968, before a regional television audience. He rambled for a remarkable 347 yards and five touchdowns, scoring on jaunts of 35, 67, 1, 60, and 50 yards on a rain-soaked afternoon at Michigan Stadium. His yardage established a new modern college single-game rushing record.

"Johnson gave the greatest one-man performance I have ever seen," Elliott said.

"The more I carry the ball, the better I feel," Johnson said afterward. "This is a great football team to play on. We've come a long way this season, and you can be sure we'll be ready for Ohio State next Saturday."

The Buckeyes came in 8-0 and ranked No. 2 in the nation to Southern Cal, while U-M was 8-1 and fourth in the country.

Woody Hayes' super sophomores of 1968, led by quarterback Rex Kern, blasted Michigan, 50-14, in a raucous Ohio Stadium. Hayes left his starters in until 3:16 remained and the Buckeyes led 44-14. After a final OSU touchdown, Hayes decided to go for two, but the Wolverines held.

"The Buckeyes were bigger, faster, and there were more of them, and thank God it wasn't on television," said *The Michigan Daily* the day after the shellacking. (The game had been televised on closed circuit television

RUNNING TO GLORY

Ron Johnson turned in the most outstanding single-game performance of any Michigan ball carrier but also had one of the greatest careers of any Wolverine. The captain of the 1968 team rushed for 347 yards and scored five touchdowns (the most for a Wolverine since 1917) on a rainy day against Wisconsin in 1968. Johnson also set the Big Ten single-season rushing record (1,021 yards) in 1968, along with the conference season scoring mark (92 points). He was named the Big Ten's Most Valuable Player in 1968 and the state's Amateur Athlete of the Year.

Standout running back Ron Johnson was Bump Elliott's favorite captain, for more reasons than his 347-yard rushing performance against Wisconsin.

at the Events Building, now known as Crisler Arena.)

Many of the players from that 8-2 squad of 1968 would get another chance, but Elliott had coached his last game.

He accepted an offer from Athletic Director Don Canham to become an associate athletic director, giving way to a fiery young coach from Miami (Ohio), Glenn E. "Bo" Schembechler.

Even the most optimistic of Michigan fans couldn't have dreamt what the following two decades would hold.

WOLVERINE QUIZ

45. What team did Ron Johnson run through for 347 yards in 1968?

Bo Fashions A Dynasty

1969-1989 Overall Record: 194-48-5 (.796)
Coach: Glenn E. "Bo" Schembechler
Conference Championships: 1969 (8-3), 1971 (11-1),
*   1972 (10-1),1973 (10-0-1), 1974 (10-1), 1976 (10-2),*
*   1977 (10-2), 1978 (10-2),1980 (10-2), 1982 (8-4),*
*   1986 (11-2), 1988 (9-2-1), 1989 (10-2).*

Bo Who?

That was the question around Michigan when athletic director Don Canham tabbed the Miami (Ohio) University head coach to lead one of the nation's most respected football programs. Most U-M fans had little idea who Bo Schembechler was or how to pronounce his last name.

Recommendations from New York Jets owner Sonny Werblin and Washington Redskins coach George Allen were the clinchers for Canham. Neither NFL man had met Schembechler, but both had heard their coaching staffs talk about what a well-drilled team Miami was. Werblin didn't even know Schembechler's name.

Schembechler came up from Oxford, Ohio, engaged in a one-day interview with Canham, and returned home. Later that week, Canham offered the job to the 39-year-old coach, who accepted it without asking how much he would be paid. Schembechler went on to coach the Wolverines for 21 seasons, each without a contract.

New head coach Bo Schembechler pointed the way and captain Jim Mandich made sure the 1969 Wolverines followed their new leader.

GETTING TO KNOW BO If one were to take a poll of the players on that 1969 team, it would be a safe bet that most — if not all — of them would be able to recall vividly their first meeting with the new head coach.

Dan Dierdorf, destined to be one of the best offensive linemen in football, stuck his hand out to introduce himself to Schembechler in the football building. Schembechler went past the handshake and after Dierdorf's prodigious midsection.

"You are fat!" Schembechler bellowed. End of meeting.

While Bump Elliott's spring practices took on a more relaxed atmosphere in contrast to his fall workouts, Schembechler immediately turned up the heat in his first sessions during the spring of '69.

"The defense was scrimmaging the offense one spring afternoon," defensive back Tom Curtis wrote in a "This I Remember" article. "I jumped in front of a receiver to make an interception. After catching the ball, I sort of danced in the other direction and lateraled the ball to Henry Hill as I was being tackled.

"I thought it was a great play — might even make Bo remember how good an option quarterback I was in high school. He reacted more like Ohio State's Rex Kern had just thrown the winning touchdown over my head. He raced over to me and screamed, 'Curtis, if I ever see you do that again, you'll be sitting on the bench.' "

WOLVERINE QUIZ

46. *Where was Bo Schembechler coaching when he was named the head football coach at Michigan?*

PLAYING ON CANHAM'S CARPET Ron Johnson's remarkable rushing performance against Wisconsin in 1968 would be the last game played on grass in Michigan Stadium until 1991. Canham had artificial turf installed for the '69 campaign, and the Wolverines laid out Vanderbilt (42-14) and Washington (45-7) on the plastic pasture before succumbing to Missouri (40-17).

Schembechler ranted, threw players out of practice, and worked the Wolverines harder than they had ever been worked. In a time of great racial tension and division in the nation, and particularly in Ann Arbor, Schembechler was proud to say he treated all of his players equally — "like dogs."

"I don't know of any team in the history of football who worked harder than that Michigan team of 1969," Dierdorf recalled in a "This I Remember" essay. "Bo prodded, pushed, whipped, and molded us into one heck of a football team. I know that I have never played on a team that had more character and pride."

Much of that pride was shattered in Schembechler's first meeting with Michigan State. The Wolverines were favored, but MSU posted a 23-12 win at East Lansing. Spartan Head Coach Duffy Daugherty had installed a new veer offense and began the surprises with an onside

WOLVERINE QUIZ

47. *What player had three interceptions and a 60-yard punt return in the 24-12 win over Ohio State in 1969?*

Defensive back Tom Curtis made this interception against Washington in 1969, but one he made in spring practice got him in big trouble with Schembechler.

WOLVERINE QUIZ

48. What future Big Ten head coach took over for Bo Schembechler in the 1970 Rose Bowl game?

kick to start the game.

Schembechler left half of his team home from a road trip to Minnesota the next week in response to his team's lethargy. Although quarterback Don Moorhead played with a severely bruised hip, the Wolverines turned their season around when they came back from a 9-7 half-time deficit to win convincingly, 35-9.

Blowouts of Wisconsin (35-7), Illinois (57-0), and Iowa (51-6) kept U-M in title contention, pending a meeting with defending national champion and top-ranked Ohio State, coached by Schembechler's mentor, Woody Hayes.

BEAT THE BUCKS! The chant began in the Michigan locker room after the romp over Iowa, and gained fervor around Ann Arbor through the week. A mid-week snow forced the U-M coaches and freshmen to clear the playing field for practice, but it didn't slow the Wolverines.

Schembechler ordered the score of the previous year's humiliation — 50-14 — taped to the players' uniforms during practice. The upperclassmen needed no reminder of Hayes' insertion of starting fullback Jim Otis for a late two-point conversion attempt (that failed) after the Buckeyes had scored half a hundred.

End Jim Mandich, captain of the '69 squad, was especially animated in the locker room at Columbus after the defeat in '68.

"Remember the feeling inside of you today," Mandich said, "the shame, the pain, and the humiliation. And when you're training for the coming season, remember this day and run that extra mile and do all the extra little things necessary to ensure that this will not happen again.

"If there is anyone in this room who is not prepared for the total commitment we need to avenge today's humiliation, don't show up for winter workouts. We will not lose to Ohio State next year."

After beating Iowa, the '69 Wolverines were on their way to the Rose Bowl — OSU could not go because of the no-repeat rule — and every one of Schembechler's players shared the sentiments that Mandich had espoused a year earlier.

"Beat the Bucks! Beat the Bucks! Beat the Bucks!" was the frenzied chant of the Michigan team in the locker room in Iowa City. Schembechler could do nothing to calm his troops down, nor did he feel like it.

"The practices that week were war-like," offensive guard Richard Caldarazzo said. "In fact, after Tuesday's full-team scrimmage, the coaches were worried that we would peak too early in the week and be flat on Saturday. However, they decided to let us go and hope we would maintain that emotional level but also attain higher levels each day."

The No. 1 Buckeyes had not lost a game in two years, winning 22 straight. They were 17-point favorites against Michigan, and there was no doubt they were the best team in college football in 1969.

The only question was whether Hayes' group was the greatest college football team ever assembled.

49. What Michigan and Big Ten record did placekicker Dana Coin set during the 1971 season?

Players and coaches are delirious on the Michigan bench in the final seconds of the Wolverines' 24-12 upset of Ohio State in 1969.

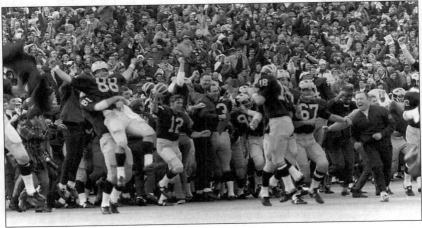

While Michigan's players entered the contest with supreme confidence, their hard-bitten leader felt pangs of self-doubt. Woody Hayes had groomed Schembechler to be a football coach, and now the student had to face his mentor.

"What I hadn't told anybody was how nervous I was, facing my old coach for the first time," Schembechler wrote in his autobiography. "Was I capable of beating Woody Hayes? I had given each of my players a shadow to out-perform; mine was the man with the square shoulders and the slicked-back hair. I was about to fight my football father."

Long before kickoff, Hayes looked to gain the psychological advantage on his pupil. When the Wolverines came out of their Michigan Stadium locker room to warm up, Hayes' Scarlet and Gray legions already were practicing on Michigan's side of the field. Following a terse conversation with his protégé, Hayes ushered his troops to the other end of the stadium.

"Our team took the field both wild with emotion and motivated by a sense of mission," Mandich recalled. "There was no way — no way — we were going to leave the field without victory in our hands."

OSU struck first on a 1-yard plunge by fullback Jim Otis but missed the point-after kick. Garvie Craw got the touchdown back for U-M, and Frank Titas' conversion put Michigan on top. The Buckeyes' Rex Kern hit Jan White with a 22-yard strike on the first play of the second quarter, but the rest of the game was all Maize and Blue.

Craw and Moorhead each scored on short runs to put the Wolverines ahead 21-12. Michigan scored another touchdown just before halftime. The touchdown, however, was nullified by a penalty, and Tim Killian kicked a 25-yard field goal to make the score 24-12.

Defensive back Barry Pierson had a career day, picking off three Ohio State passes — Kern was eventually pulled for backup Ron Maciejowski after throwing five interceptions — and ran back a punt 60 yards to set up a touchdown. U-M's Tom Curtis added two interceptions.

"Despite what people may think, Michigan did not play a perfect game that day," defensive back Bruce Elliott said. "To the contrary, there were a great number of mistaken assignments on defense. However, our overpowering feeling of confidence and enthusiasm made up for our errors, and the overall plan was carried out to perfection."

The Michigan Stadium crowd was boisterous the entire game, finally serenading the Ohio State coach in the final minutes: "Good-bye, Woody. Good-bye,

Woody. Good-bye, Woody. We hate to see you go."

Any discussion of the greatest Michigan victories always starts with the 24-12 upset of the Buckeyes in 1969.

NO BOWLING FOR BO Perhaps the strain of the first 10 months at Michigan was too much for Schembechler. Maybe the high of beating the greatest team ever fielded by his mentor simply overcame him. In the hours before his first Rose Bowl as a head coach, Schembechler's heart could take no more.

His first heart attack was a mild one, but the timing of it was major, coming on the eve of the Rose Bowl. Assistant coach Jim Young, whose defense had performed so brilliantly against the Buckeyes, suddenly had to direct the entire Michigan program in its first Rose Bowl appearance in five years.

Along with mentally and emotionally dragging the Wolverines through his first season, Schembechler had called every offensive play for quarterback Don Moorhead. The offense sputtered with Schembechler and running back Glenn Doughty, who had a knee injury, both out of the game. Pierson was missing from the defensive backfield as well, having suffered a broken arm before the team left for California.

Running back Billy Taylor fights for extra yardage in Michigan's 1970 Rose Bowl loss to Southern California.

"Ironically, on our way to the Rose Bowl on game day, I felt we'd kick the living daylights out of USC because we'd want to win it for Bo," recalled defensive back Frank Gusich. "But during pregame warm-ups, I knew we were in real trouble; our leader was not there,

and we were just flat."

The Wolverines fell 10-3 to Southern Cal, Michigan's first loss in the Rose Bowl. While Young credited the Trojans with being physically stronger on defense than Ohio State, he admitted the Wolverines were not the team they might have been with Schembechler on the sidelines.

THE 10-YEAR WAR INTENSIFIES For eight of the next nine seasons under Schembechler, Michigan football consisted of two distinct parts of the schedule: the first 10 games of cannon fodder for U-M's relentless running game and suffocating defenses and the finale with Woody Hayes' Ohio State teams to determine the Big Ten championship and Rose Bowl representative.

The 1970 squad opened with victories over Washington and Texas A&M and two weeks later gave Schembechler the first of his eight straight wins over Michigan State, 34-20 at Ann Arbor.

Four easy victories later, Schembechler took his 9-0 team into Ohio Stadium for the first time, and Hayes and the Buckeyes were ready. A record crowd of 87,331 cried for revenge, and the fired-up Buckeyes were happy to oblige. U-M had its chances to steal the game, but the determined Buckeyes held on, scoring 10 points in the fourth quarter to secure a 20-9 victory.

Paul Staroba rambles across the new artificial turf at Michigan Stadium.

The loss to OSU dropped Michigan to 9-1 for the season

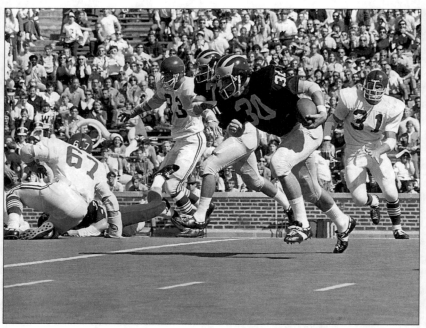

TWO IN THE TRENCHES

Dan Dierdorf and Reggie McKenzie ushered in an era of outstanding offensive line play at Michigan. Dierdorf was a consensus All-American in 1970 and is considered one of the best tackles to play college football. McKenzie was a 1971 All-American, perhaps the best pulling guard ever at U-M, and helped the Wolverines smash all of the team rushing records in his three seasons.

Dierdorf was twice named the NFL's most outstanding offensive lineman with the St. Louis Cardinals before going on to a successful career in sportscasting. Dierdorf was inducted into the Pro Football Hall of Fame in his hometown of Canton, Ohio, during the summer of 1996. During his illustrious career with the Buffalo Bills, McKenzie helped clear the way for O.J. Simpson.

with a No. 9 national ranking and steeled the Wolverines for one of the school's most magnificent seasons.

MELLOW, BUT NOT YELLOW There was no secret to the success of Schembechler's teams. A maniacal work ethic, pounding running game, and impenetrable defenses made the Wolverines a feared opponent.

Schembechler's team marched over and through every opponent in sight. Northwestern, a 21-6 victim in the 1971 opener, was the only team to score on U-M in the first four weeks of the season. In the same span, Michigan scored 161 points.

The Wolverines dominated the Spartans at East Lansing, 24-13, in the fifth week of the season. Michigan put up 35 points on both Illinois and Minnesota, and then surpassed 60 in wins over Indiana and Iowa.

"The 1971 season was a special one for all of us," recalled placekicker Dana Coin in a "This I Remember" article. "As seniors, we had the opportunity to lead a group of sophomores and juniors that were recruited by Bo and his staff for *his* program. They were already indoctrinated to Bo's successful and stern philosophies. Our job was to prove that they indeed worked."

The team was led by a rugged group that dubbed themselves the "Mellow Men of Michigan": running back Billy Taylor, guard Reggie McKenzie, linebacker Mike Taylor, safety Thom Darden, defensive end Butch Carpenter, and split end Mike Oldham. To be a Mellow Man, a player had to own three jazz record albums.

The Wolverines survived a scare at West Lafayette from Purdue's "Spoilermakers," 20-17, on Coin's last-second field goal to clinch the Big Ten title and set the stage for another grudge match with the Buckeyes.

Quarterback Tom Slade was used chiefly as an extra blocker in Michigan's punishing running game of 1971.

Before the 1971 season, William D. Revelli surrendered the baton of the Michigan Marching Band to long-time assistant George Cavendar after 36 years of unequaled excellence. Cavendar's eight-year tenure would include adding women to the traditionally all-male ensemble.

Billy Taylor (42) carries around right end as Fritz Seyferth (32) gets ready to deliver his famous block during the 1971 Ohio State game. Quarterback Larry Cipa (13) also throws a block during Taylor's famous, game-winning run.

This time, U-M was heavily favored and striving for something rarely found in or out of football — perfection.

FRITZ BLOCKS OUT THE BUCKS Ohio State was a battered team, having lost 11 starters to injuries, but Woody Hayes was determined to ruin Michigan's season the way the Wolverines had foiled his great '69 squad. For three quarters, Hayes was on schedule to pull the upset of the season.

U-M lost its 3-0 lead when Tom Campana weaved 85 yards on a punt return to give Ohio State a shocking 7-3 advantage. The Michigan Stadium crowd of 104,016 was stunned into silence and stayed that way until the game's final five minutes.

"What I remember most was the confidence we had in the offensive huddle on our last possession," said offensive lineman Jim Brandstatter. "Nobody panicked, nobody yelled. We knew what we had to do and quietly went to work."

Larry Cipa had replaced the injured Tom Slade at quarterback after the hard-nosed blocker had suffered a hip injury. Cipa misfired on his first six pass attempts, and then connected with Bo Rather for 22 yards on a key third down. On fourth-and-one at the OSU 24, fullback Fritz Seyferth dove over right guard for a first down, setting the stage for his most glorious Michigan moment.

Taylor took a pitch to the right from Cipa, and there was Campana waiting to make the play. Suddenly, Seyferth buried the OSU defender with a perfect block. Taylor raced 21 yards down the western sideline, his index finger in the air, to put U-M ahead 10-7 with 2:07 remaining. The packed house went crazy.

Ohio State had one final chance, but Thom Darden

came up with his second interception of the game to secure the win. Hayes went wild, arguing with referee Jerry Markbreit that Darden had interfered with OSU receiver Dick Wakefield. Hayes was assessed two 15-yard penalties after destroying the sideline markers.

"You have just completed the greatest single season in Michigan football history," Schembechler told his team in the locker room.

The foursome of Darden, guard Reggie McKenzie, Billy Taylor, and linebacker Mike Taylor all received All-America honors in 1971.

AFTER 70 YEARS, STANFORD GETS EVEN An 11-0 Michigan team met Stanford in the 1972 Rose Bowl for the first time since 1902, when the Wolverines rolled to a 49-0 triumph in the inaugural game. The Wolverines looked to return to the days of yore after the disappointment of two years earlier and grabbed a 10-3 lead on Seyferth's 1-yard plunge early in the final quarter.

Although U-M's defense held, Stanford faked a punt from its own 33-yard line to gain a first down, en route to a tying touchdown. Coin tried to answer, but his 46-yard field goal fell short. Then Ed Shuttlesworth tackled Jim Ferguson in the end zone for a safety on an attempted return to give Michigan a 12-10 leadwith 3:18 to go.

The Wolverines appeared to have won the game with the odd two-pointer, but Stanford quarterback Don Bunce passed the Indians down the field to the U-M

The Michigan defense celebrates Thom Darden's game-clinching interception against OSU in 1971. Woody Hayes drew two 15-yard penalties and ripped up the sideline markers while protesting the play.

Fullback Fritz Seyferth edges the ball over the goal line for Michigan's go-ahead touchdown in the 1972 Rose Bowl game with Stanford.

14-yard line with 14 seconds remaining. The diminutive Rod Garcia trotted out and booted a 31-yard dagger through the heart of the Wolverines, giving Stanford a 13-12 win, the second straight year the Indians were upset winners in the Rose Bowl.

THE BRIGHT LIGHTS OF PASADENA After struggling to down Northwestern 7-0 in the 1972 opener, Schembechler's team headed back to California to meet UCLA at the Los Angeles Coliseum for a night game, Michigan's first one in 28 years. Along with playing a good opponent, the Wolverines faced a mental challenge, having lost in their previous two Rose Bowl appearances (1970 and 1972).

"Coach Schembechler defied the [Rose Bowl] jinx and practiced the team in the Rose Bowl the night before the game. There was never a time that a Michigan team could have been more inspired and fired up by the speeches Bo had made throughout the entire week of preparation," defensive back Randy Logan recalled.

Mark Harmon, the son of U-M Heisman Trophy winner Tom Harmon, could not duplicate Stanford's magic. Michigan drilled the Bruins, 26-9, giving up the most points the Wolverines would allow in their first 10 games.

The Big Ten had rescinded its no-repeat rule, meaning that Schembechler's team could head right back to Pasadena for the '73 Rose Bowl. U-M stayed on track by handling Michigan State, 10-0, and edging Purdue, 9-6, on a last-minute field goal by Vietnam War veteran Mike Lantry.

CLOSE, BUT NO ROSES In the season finale at Columbus, Ohio State freshman sensation Archie Griffin dashed 30 yards for a touchdown to give the Buckeyes a 14-3 lead in the third quarter, even though the Wolverines were dominating. Fullback Ed Shuttlesworth came back with a 1-yard TD run on fourth down, and Dennis Franklin found Clint Haslerig with a two-point conversion pass to cut the OSU lead to 14-11.

Randy Logan's late interception put U-M in position for the go-ahead points. On third-and-goal at the OSU 1-yard line, the Michigan linemen were sure Harry Banks had given the Wolverines the lead. The officials, however, disagreed.

Franklin tried to sneak in on fourth down, but the Buckeye defense held.

Schembechler could have opted for a tying field goal that might have sent Michigan to the Rose Bowl. When asked why he chose to go for the touchdown, the U-M coach flatly stated, "Because we thought we could score. We should have scored."

The 1972 team finished the season 10-1 and ranked No. 9 in the nation.

HUNG BY A TIE Top-ranked Ohio State came to Ann Arbor to meet fourth-ranked U-M under familiar circumstances in 1973. The winner would go to the Rose Bowl and win the Big Ten title. The loser would have to wait 364 days for revenge.

Michigan had humbled 10 victims, including Stanford and Michigan State, entering the Ohio State game and had established itself as one of Schembechler's most powerful teams. The Buckeyes were 9-0, the only time in the Hayes-Schembechler era both teams entered the game undefeated.

"Practice during the week prior to the game is both guarded and intense," recalled defensive back Don Dufek of facing Ohio State. "Every detail is thoroughly gone over and emotions build to a crescendo by week's end. Those games of 1973-74-75 were noted for their conservative offense and staunch defense."

In another epic battle between the Big Ten superpowers, the Buckeyes raced to a 10-0 half-time lead. The resilient Wolverines, however, responded in the fourth quarter with a 30-yard Mike Lantry field goal and a dazzling 10-yard scoring run by Franklin on a fourth-down play.

Late in the game Lantry had two opportunities to win

WOLVERINE QUIZ

52. What was Bo Schembechler's record in his 10 meetings with his mentor, Woody Hayes of Ohio State?

WOLVERINE QUIZ

53. Who was Michigan announcer Bob Ufer emulating whenever he called the Wolverines "Meeshegan"?

Fullback Ed Shuttlesworth crashes through the Ohio State line in the 10-10 tie with the Buckeyes in 1973.

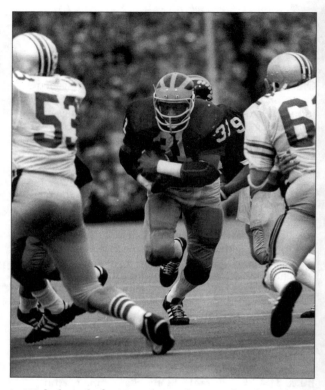

WOLVERINE QUIZ

54. Who kicked the game-winning field goal in Michigan's 20-17 win over Iowa in 1983?

it. With the aid of a 20-mph wind, Lantry barely missed a 58-yarder with 1:06 remaining.

Woody Hayes inserted little-used quarterback Greg Hare to try to pass the Buckeyes down the field, but Tom Drake intercepted at the OSU 40. Michigan was out of time-outs, though, and Franklin had suffered a broken collarbone just after his touchdown run.

Lantry lined up for a 44-yarder to win the game with 0:28 on the digital scoreboard, but pushed the kick off to the right. The 10-10 tie left Michigan and Ohio State deadlocked for the conference title.

The Big Ten athletic directors, in a shocking 6-4 vote, elected Ohio State as the conference representative to the Rose Bowl, even though U-M outgained the Buckeyes 312 yards to 247, and picked up 16 first downs to OSU's nine. Franklin's injury was pointed to as a reason for sending the Buckeyes, but Schembechler was not buying that.

"I'm very bitter and resentful. Petty jealousies were involved. They just used the injury to Dennis Franklin as a scapegoat," Schembechler said. "I'm very disappointed in the administration of the Big Ten. It hasn't been very tough, and it hasn't been very good."

PUT THE A.D. AT QB! Michigan donned white pants for a 27-16 win at Stanford, which put the 1974 team at 4-0 before the Wolverines' first serious order of business arose. Michigan State athletic director Burt Smith had helped send Ohio State to the Rose Bowl a year earlier with what U-M backers saw as the deciding vote in a 6-4 decision.

Smith's vote gave the Wolverines a little added fire when the Spartans headed to Ann Arbor. Bumper stickers around the Michigan campus suggested "Burt Smith For Quarterback." Schembechler's troops made their point, racing to a 21-0 half-time lead before winning, 21-7.

The Wolverines rolled to victory in their first nine games for the fifth straight season to maintain an unbeaten streak that reached 21 games. Again, Hayes' Buckeyes were all that stood between Dennis Franklin and Pasadena.

Franklin hit Gil Chapman with a 37-yard touchdown pass and Lantry kicked a 37-yard field goal to put the Wolverines ahead 10-0 in the first quarter. Czech-born kicker Tom Klaban booted four field goals, though, to give the Buckeyes a 12-10 lead that would stand up. Still, Michigan made a final charge before Lantry narrowly missed a 33-yard try with 18 seconds left in the game.

OSU's Archie Griffin, soon to be awarded the first of his two Heisman Trophies, extended his own modern-day record by gaining more than 100 yards in his 22nd straight game with 111 yards on 25 carries.

The Big Ten athletic directors convened the next day near Chicago's O'Hare Airport and sent Ohio State to the Rose Bowl for the third year in a row.

Inspired by Schembechler, the conference later adopted a multipoint tie-breaking procedure to determine the Rose Bowl representative and take the selection process away from the athletic directors.

Franklin and the seniors of the 1974 team graduated with a three-year record of 30-2-1, three shared Big Ten titles, and no bowl appearances. Defensive back Dave Brown was named All-America for the second time in '74.

THE PEACH FROM FLINT Franklin's graduation left a highly touted freshman from Flint at the controls of Schembechler's option attack, a football/baseball standout from Southwestern High named Rick Leach. Legendary U-M announcer Bob Ufer dubbed him "The Peach."

Leach responded, with the help of All-American tailback Gordon Bell and a sturdy defense, by leading the Wolverines to key wins over Wisconsin, Missouri,

At the prodding of Bo Schembechler, the Big Ten changed a musty conference rule before the 1975 season when it voted to allow teams that had not won the league championship to accept postseason bowl invitations. The Wolverines have been to a bowl game every year since.

Michigan State, and Purdue. In a 28-0 win over the Boilermakers, Leach hit Jim Smith with an 83-yard touchdown pass, the longest in school history.

In the season finale with the 11-0 Buckeyes to decide the Big Ten title and Rose Bowl berth, a touchdown by Leach put the 8-0-2 Wolverines ahead of Ohio State, 14-7, before the Buckeyes rallied for two fourth-quarter scores to pull out a thrilling a 21-14 victory. The loss ended Michigan's home unbeaten streak, dating to 1969, at 41 games.

Leach would lead Michigan to four bowl games, the first being an Orange Bowl matchup with Barry Switzer's tough Oklahoma team. Like Michigan, the 10-0 Sooners had posted a stellar record over the previous three seasons (31-1-1).

The game was a tight affair. Gordon Bell finally got U-M into the end zone from 2 yards out with 7:06 remaining. Leach, who sat out the third quarter with a concussion, failed to reach the end zone on the two-point conversion. Oklahoma had the upper hand in a 14-6 win, though, and captured the national title by virtue of Ohio State's shocking loss to UCLA at the Rose Bowl earlier in the day.

A MAN FOR ALL SEASONS

Rick Leach is considered one of the top all-around athletes in Michigan history. Michigan's starting quarterback from 1975-78, Leach was named the All-Big Ten quarterback three times. He finished third in the Heisman Trophy balloting as a senior, when he was named the conference's Most Valuable Player. The left-hander from Flint set all of U-M's career passing, total offense, and touchdown records, and also excelled for the Michigan baseball team. One year, Leach quarterbacked the first half of the spring game, then ran over to Ray Fisher Stadium and homered in the second game of a doubleheader. He won the Big Ten batting crown as a junior and was named an All-American in both football and baseball as a senior. Leach was a first-round draft choice of the Detroit Tigers.

Freshman quarterback Rick Leach led the Wolverines into the 1976 Orange Bowl, where Oklahoma held on for a 14-6 win and the national championship.

BO'S '76 POWERHOUSE Michigan's option offense under Leach was nearly unstoppable. The Wolverines entered 1976 as the top-ranked team in the nation and backed it up with 352 points in their first eight victories, an average of 44 points per game.

In the ninth game of the season, U-M walked into Ross-Ade Stadium a 27-point favorite. Led by tailback Scott Dierking, Alex Agase's Purdue Boilermakers handed Michigan a 16-14 setback. Good-bye, No. 1.

"It was at this point that the 1976 team demonstrated its true character," linebacker Calvin O'Neal said. "We could have just given up and played out the string. But Bo and our team were too tough to let that happen."

Michigan responded by thumping Illinois, 38-7, to set up the annual showdown with the Buckeyes. After a scoreless first half against Ohio State, Leach got the option rolling with Russell Davis doing the inside work and Rob Lytle using his speed to get wide.

U-M scored third-quarter touchdowns on drives that consumed 80 and 52 yards and ran more than 11 minutes off the clock. The Wolverines clinched the Big Ten title, winning in Columbus for the first time in 10 years.

"Michigan will get my vote as the No. 1 team in the

Russell Davis paced the Wolverines' ground attack in a 22-0 drubbing of the Buckeyes at Columbus in 1976.

country," OSU coach Woody Hayes admitted after the 22-0 thrashing. "Any team that beats us as soundly as they did deserves to be No. 1."

"With less than five minutes to play, we were driving toward Ohio State's goal line," recalled split end Curt Stephenson. "In the huddle, Bill Dufek blurted out 'Smile guys, we're on TV.' We all looked up and saw the Goodyear blimp directly overhead. That made the entire huddle laugh.

"We approached the line of scrimmage chanting 'Rose Bowl, Rose Bowl, Rose Bowl.' The Ohio State players could hear us, but they could do nothing to stop us. That was probably the most fulfilling five minutes I've ever spent with my teammates."

The Wolverines headed for Pasadena ranked second to Pitt and just ahead of upcoming foe Southern Cal. Vince Evans ran and passed the Trojans by U-M, though, 14-6, leaving the Wolverines ranked third in the nation.

Lytle, O'Neal, end Jim Smith, and offensive guard Mark Donahue, were chosen All-Americans, an honor Donahue would receive again in '77.

ROCKING THE AGGIES While Ohio State and Michigan were flogging the rest of the Big Ten through the 1970s, U-M also was making mincemeat of its non-conference opponents. After losing to Missouri in 1969, Schembechler did not lose another non-conference game in the regular season for the next 10 years.

Texas A&M, though, was not the average intersectional punching bag. The 1977 meeting with the Aggies was supposed to be a serious test for the Wolverines, but Leach and defensive coordinator Bill McCartney's "Monsters" were brilliant.

Bill McCartney was the coordinator of some of Michigan's stingiest defensive units before becoming head coach at Colorado.

"I can't recall a better defensive performance than the one we put on that day," defensive lineman Chris Godfrey said of the 41-3 victory. "From start to finish, we were relentless. We all felt cornered and related in kind. All day long, the only points they received were from a long field goal by a bare-footed kicker (Tony Franklin)."

The win catapulted Michigan to the top of the national polls, setting the Wolverines up for a fall. Three games later, 20-point underdog Minnesota slew the Wolverines in Minneapolis, 16-0, Michigan's first shutout in 10 years.

U-M rebounded as it had a year earlier after the loss at Purdue to down Ohio State, 14-6, repeat as Big Ten champions and claim the Rose Bowl berth. Touchdown runs by Roosevelt Smith and Leach paved the way to an emotion-charged victory on the 50th anniversary of Michigan Stadium's dedication. The Buckeyes dominated play and had several golden scoring opportunities but

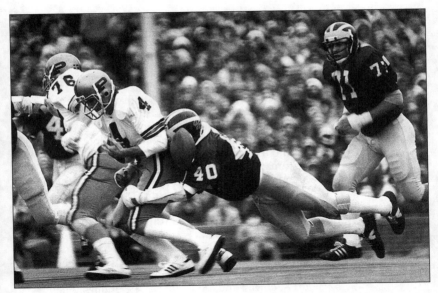

continuously were repelled by Michigan's stellar defense.

Although the fourth-ranked Wolverines headed back for Pasadena as heavy favorites against Pacific 8 champion Washington, they dug themselves a 24-0 hole by the third quarter. Leach engineered a furious comeback in the final period, but the Huskies hung on for a 27-20 win. A potential game-winning pass from Leach bounced off the shoulders of freshman Stanley Edwards and into the arms of a Washington defender in the final moments.

Linebacker Ron Simpkins played from 1976-79, graduating as U-M's all-time leading tackler with 516 career stops, a record he still holds.

THE RETURN OF THE IRISH Rick Leach had made a mental note of this game during his freshman year. In the fall of 1978, Michigan traveled to Notre Dame to renew a rivalry that had been dormant since 1943. Even a severely sprained ankle, suffered the Monday before the game, could not keep the senior quarterback out of the lineup.

All Leach did was run for a touchdown, throw two scoring strikes to tight end Doug Marsh, and fling a bomb to Ralph Clayton during the 28-14 U-M triumph on a gorgeous afternoon at South Bend. Curtis Greer put the finishing touches on the victory with a sack of Notre Dame quarterback Joe Montana for a fourth-quarter safety.

THE END OF THE 10-YEAR WAR Despite a midseason setback to archrival Michigan State — Michigan's first loss to the Spartans in nine years — the Wolverines marched to their third straight Big Ten championship, culminating in season-ending victories over highly touted Purdue, 24-6, and Ohio State, 14-3.

The victory over the Buckeyes would mark the end of

the 10-year rivalry between Hayes and Schembechler, and gave the protégé a 5-4-1 edge over his mentor in their head-to-head meetings. (Hayes resigned after the 1978 Gator Bowl, a game in which he punched a Clemson player while on the sidelines during the Buckeyes' 17-15 loss.)

In the 65th Rose Bowl, USC tailback Charles White scored what became known as the "phantom touchdown" in the second quarter.

Although umpire Don Mason saw White fumble the ball into the arms of Jerry Meter, head linesman Gil Marchman ruled that White had given Southern Cal a touchdown. The score was the difference in the game, won by the Trojans 17-10 despite Michigan's dominance.

U-M ended the '78 season with a 10-2 record and a No. 5 national ranking, the 10th straight top-10 finish for Schembechler's teams.

NO. 1, ALWAYS AND FOREVER The 1970s were the days of three-yards-and-a-cloud-of-dust football in the Big Ten, with Michigan and Ohio State as the unquestioned leaders. As the decade waned, however, even Schembechler began to embrace the forward pass.

A big reason Schembechler began to feel some affection for throwing the ball was a lithe receiver from Riviera Beach, Fla., by the name of Anthony Carter. It

A.C. — ALWAYS NO. 1

For sheer excitement on the football field, few in the history of college football could match Michigan's No. 1, Anthony Carter. The Riviera Beach, Fla., native almost left U-M in his freshman year because he was homesick, but he returned to become the school's greatest wide receiver and return man. Carter was the eighth Big Ten player to be named an All-American three times (1980-82) and was the first receiver to go over 3,000 yards in receptions. He graduated as Michigan's all-time modern-era leader in touchdowns (40), points (244), receptions (156), yards (3,017), and touchdown catches (37), the latter a Big Ten record.

Carter was a captain of the 1982 team and finished fourth in the Heisman Trophy balloting, the top vote-getter outside of quarterbacks and running backs. For all of his career accomplishments, he

Anthony Carter earned All-America honors three times.

may best be remembered for catching a 45-yard pass from John Wangler on the final play of the 1979 Homecoming game to give the Wolverines a 27-21 win over Indiana in his freshman season.

did not take long for Carter to leave an indelible mark on the 100th year of Michigan football.

U-M hosted Indiana in the 1979 Homecoming game and struggled with a feisty group of Hoosiers. The Wolverines appeared doomed to a 21-21 tie until John Wangler unleashed a 45-yard pass over the middle to Carter on the game's final play.

Carter sidestepped one Indiana defender on his right and almost got knocked over by another on his left, but he kept his balance at the 10-yard line and made his way into the end zone. The clock read 0:00. Michigan 27, Indiana 21.

Schembechler's 1979 team finished the season at 8-4, including disappointing losses to Purdue, No. 1-ranked Ohio State, and North Carolina in the Gator Bowl.

A CLASSIC BEGINS THE '80s

The 1980 meeting between the Wolverines and Notre Dame was a bona fide classic. With Michigan trailing 14-0, John Wangler went into the game with a bad knee that had only partially mended from the previous season's Gator Bowl.

Two Wangler touchdown passes tied the game by halftime, and the second half was a wild, see-saw contest. Craig Dunaway caught a Wangler touchdown pass — which had been tipped by intended receiver Butch Woolfolk — with 41 seconds left to put U-M ahead 27-26.

But the Irish pulled out one of their greatest miracles. A stiff wind that had been blowing all day suddenly died, and kicker Harry Oliver — who had never kicked a field goal longer than 38 yards — willed a 51-yard boot over the crossbar to give Notre Dame a 29-27 victory.

A GREAT 1-2 TEAM

Eventual Heisman Trophy winner George Rogers' South Carolina team came to Ann Arbor and hung a 17-14 loss on the Wolverines, making the 1980 squad the first to start out 1-2 under Schembechler.

"I'll never forget the locker room after the (South Carolina) game," recalled defensive lineman Mike Trgovac. "Bo told us we got some bad breaks but that he still had confidence in this team. He said we were the best 1-2 team in the nation. When we came out for our next home game, our fans supported us. They gave us a thunderous ovation, and by the middle of the season, we started to turn things around."

After a 27-23 win over Michigan State, U-M rolled through the rest of the Big Ten and headed into season-ending showdowns with Purdue at Ann Arbor and Ohio State at Columbus. Defensive coordinator Bill McCartney installed a "Six-Penny" defense that featured six defensive backs to throttle Boilermaker quarterback Mark Herrmann at every turn.

WOLVERINE QUIZ

55. Who did Michigan defeat in 1986 to make Bo Schembechler the school's all-time winningest coach?

Andy Cannavino (41) captained the 1980 Michigan defense that went the last 22 quarters of the season without allowing a touchdown.

The outstanding defensive scheme and U-M's offensive production turned the game into a 26-0 rout. The following week, Wangler hit Carter with a 13-yard touchdown pass and McCartney's "Monsters" on defense propelled Michigan to a 9-3 win over the Buckeyes, sending the Wolverines back to Pasadena to face Washington.

"Going into the (Rose Bowl) game, we had held our opponents 18 quarters without a touchdown," Trgovac said. "We said to ourselves we wouldn't give up a touchdown in this game — and we were obsessed with the thought.

"On the opening drive, Washington shocked us. They took the ball down to our 3-yard line. After a time-out, Coach McCartney got us together and said, 'We've come too far and worked too hard to give up a touchdown now.' On fourth down, (Touissant) Tyler went over the top, but the ball didn't — and this time the referee saw it. They didn't score a touchdown, and we played solid defense the rest of the way."

Butch Woolfolk ran for 182 yards and a touchdown, Wangler completed 12 of 20 passes for 145 yards, and Anthony Carter snared a 7-yard touchdown in the third quarter while keeping the Huskies off-balance all day. The defense was stout, and Schembechler finally got his first bowl win in eight tries, 23-6.

Bo Schembechler and Anthony Carter talk to Merlin Olsen of NBC Sports after Schembechler's first Rose Bowl victory, a 23-6 decision over Washington in 1981.

Michigan's 1980 team finished the season 10-2 and ranked No. 4 in the nation.

Despite impressive victories over Notre Dame, Michigan State, and Illinois, the 1981 team fell victim to Wisconsin, Iowa, and Ohio State to finish with an 8-3 regular-season record. The highlight of the season came when U-M spotted the Illini a 21-7 lead at Ann Arbor before quarterback Steve Smith directed the Wolverines to 63 unanswered points in a 70-21 rout.

The Wolverines finished the year on a high note with a 33-14 pounding of UCLA at the Bluebonnet Bowl in Houston on New Year's Eve.

THE VOICE OF MICHIGAN FALLS SILENT Before Bob Ufer spent 37 years broadcasting Michigan football games, he was one of the outstanding quarter-mile runners in the world. He broke eight varsity track records at U-M, was an All-American and set a world record in the 400-yard dash that stood for five years.

Ufer had graduated from Michigan in 1943 and entered the WPAG booth in 1945. His voice became the soundtrack of fall Saturdays for thousands of Wolverines fans.

To Ufer, Woody Hayes was "Dr. StrangeHayes," Ohio State fans were the "Scarlet and Gray legions" and Russell Davis "went in there like a bat outta, well, you

Long-time Michigan radio announcer Bob Ufer delivered an inspiring speech at a 1981 Rose Bowl game.

know where bats come from." In tribute to Fielding Yost's West Virginia accent, Ufer always referred to his school as "Meeshegan."

His unmatched enthusiasm and outright bias for Michigan outraged opponents, but those were not the ears Ufer aimed to please. In a speech before the 1981 Rose Bowl game, Ufer reminded the Wolverines that "you have 60 minutes to play but a lifetime to remember. And, by God, you will remember tomorrow when you give the nation's finest coach his first Rose Bowl victory."

Cancer forced Ufer from the booth early in the 1981 season. The Michigan band spelled out "UFER" on the field at halftime of the Iowa game. It was Ufer's last appearance at Michigan Stadium, and the Wolverines lost that day, 9-7. Ufer died a week later.

THE 'LITTLE EIGHT' START CATCHING UP Michigan won or shared nine Big Ten titles from 1969 to 1980, while Ohio State won 10. The Wolverines appeared in six Rose Bowl games during that stretch, while OSU attended six. Michigan's 96-10-3 regular-season record in the '70s was the nation's best.

The turn of the decade, however, brought a new balance to the conference. Iowa went to the 1982 Rose Bowl and became the 11th Big Ten team to lose the game in 13 years. Four different schools went to Pasadena over the next four years.

After a 1-2 start, the 1982 team righted itself and rolled through its next seven games. A four-play goalline stand at Illinois propelled the Wolverines to a 16-10 win over the Illini. Anthony Carter garnered 123 receiving yards, including touchdown passes of 48 and 62 yards, in a 52-21 win over Purdue the following week. It was his final Michigan Stadium appearance, and it clinched U-M's berth in the 1983 Rose Bowl. The following week, the Buckeyes thumped the Wolverines at Columbus, 24-14.

In Pasadena, quarterback Steve Smith and offensive lineman Rich Strenger each left the game with injuries, and UCLA's brilliant quarterback Tom Ramsey led the Bruins to a 24-14 victory, leaving Michigan with an 8-4 record and a No. 15 national ranking.

BO MEETS BO Mike White's Illinois team, powered by junior college transfers, won the Big Ten outright in 1983, the first team other than Michigan or Ohio State to do so in 17 years. They upended the Wolverines, 16-6, marking U-M's first loss at Champaign in 26 years.

The '83 season, however, had its share of triumphs. Michigan blasted Michigan State at East Lansing, 42-0, its 13th win over the Spartans in 14 meetings. U-M edged Iowa, 16-13, on Bob Bergeron's last-second field goal and beat Ohio State at Michigan Stadium in a 24-21 thriller to earn a berth in the Sugar Bowl with Southeastern Conference champion Auburn.

Steve Smith scurried in from 4 yards out to put Michigan ahead 7-0 eight minutes into the New Year's Day game. Multisport standout Bo Jackson eventually wore down the U-M defense with 130 rushing yards, although he never dented the end zone. Auburn's third field goal of the second half, with 27 seconds left, gave the Tigers a 9-7 win.

Whatever could go wrong did for the Wolverines in 1984. The season started with great promise when U-M toppled defending national champion and top-ranked Miami, 22-14, in a sweltering season-opener at The Big House. Hurricane quarterback Bernie Kosar was intercepted six times, three of them by Miami native Rodney Lyles.

There were several key injuries during the season, including a broken arm for quarterback Jim Harbaugh, and the Wolverines sputtered to a 6-5 record, 5-4 in the conference. Both marks were Schembechler's low points.

The Wolverines accepted an invitation to play undefeated, untested and top-ranked Brigham Young in the Holiday Bowl at San Diego. BYU quarterback Robbie Bosco shook off a badly sprained knee to lead the Cougars to a 24-17, come-from-behind win and an eventual national title. After the Wolverines lost a 17-10 lead in the final quarter, Schembechler called the Cougars "the worst holding football team I've ever seen."

Bob Perryman rushed for three touchdowns in Michigan's 22-14 victory over defending national champion and top-ranked Miami to open the 1984 season.

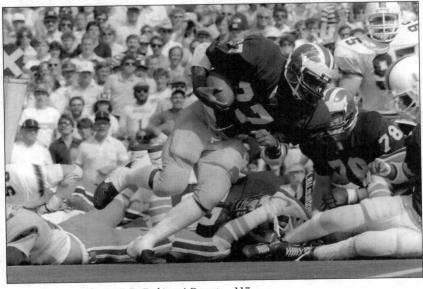

CALLING THE SHOTS

Jim Harbaugh was one of the best passers and team leaders ever to play quarterback at Michigan. With Harbaugh out of the lineup with a broken arm, the 1984 Wolverines struggled to a 6-6 record. During the next two seasons, U-M was 21-3-1 with a 27-23, come-from-behind win over Nebraska in the 1986 Fiesta Bowl and an appearance in the 1987 Rose Bowl. Harbaugh led the nation in passing efficiency in 1985 and set the school's single-season passing record of 2,729 yards in 1986, when he was named the Big Ten's Most Valuable Player. Harbaugh was the first Michigan quarterback to throw for more than 300 yards in a game and was named first-team All-America as well as Academic All-Big Ten. He was a first-round draft choice of the Chicago Bears in 1987.

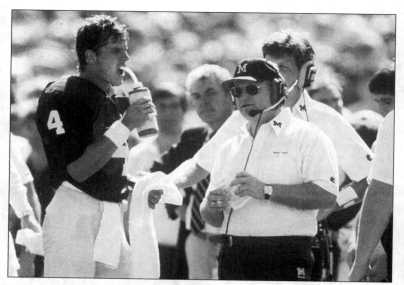

With a healthy Jim Harbaugh (4) back at quarterback, the 1985 Wolverines posted a 10-1-1 record and were ranked No. 2 in the nation.

REDEMPTION IN TEMPE Had the game passed Schembechler by? Was Michigan losing its place among college football's elite? Michigan's 6-6 season of '84 had college football fans asking these questions.

Schembechler downplayed the chatter and got his team prepared for the 1985 schedule. A 20-12 win over Notre Dame to start the season did not hurt. "It means we're decent," Schembechler said dryly. "We're not the dog people think we are."

In fact, this team had plenty of bite. Gary Moeller's defense, healthy and stifling, ended up leading the nation with an average of 8.9 points allowed per game.

The big matchup of the season occurred at rainy Kinnick Stadium in Iowa City. Hayden Fry's top-ranked Hawkeyes, led by quarterback Chuck Long, trailed No. 2 Michigan until the final seconds of the game, when Iowa's Rob Houghtlin booted his fourth field goal on the game's final play to give the Hawkeyes a thrilling 12-10 victory.

Highlights of the season included impressive performances against Michigan State (31-0) and Purdue (47-0). Jim Harbaugh showed his grit in the home finale with Ohio State, unleashing a 77-yard bomb to John Kolesar just as he was buried by a blitzing Buckeye. Kolesar dashed in for the touchdown, clinching a 27-17 win over OSU and a Fiesta Bowl berth.

The Wolverines fell behind Tom Osborne's Nebraska squad 14-3 at halftime, but U-M forced three Cornhusker turnovers in the third quarter. Gerald White dove in from a yard out, Harbaugh did likewise and Pat Moons kicked a 19-yard field goal to put U-M up 20-14. Harbaugh scored again and the defense hung on to post an impressive 27-23 win.

Harbaugh and offensive lineman John "Jumbo" Elliott were named All-Americans, the first of Elliott's two All-America seasons.

A Michigan team that before the season had not been picked to finish among the 20 best in the country or

Captain Eric Kattus (81), Paul Jokisch (84), and Jim Harbaugh (4) lead the Wolverines out for the 1986 Fiesta Bowl clash with Nebraska. U-M scored three touchdowns in the third quarter to pull out a 27-23 victory.

The 1985 Michigan defense yielded a stingy 8.2 points per game, which led the nation in that statistical category, and was far greater than even that impressive number reveals. The offenses U-M faced that year scored an average of 27.8 points per game, leaving a defensive points differential of 19.6, the best defensive differential in major college football in 50 years (from 1946-1995).

Jim Harbaugh delivered on his guarantee of a win at Ohio State in 1986, sending Michigan to the Rose Bowl for the first time in four seasons.

even among the top four in the Big Ten posted a 10-1-1 record and was ranked No. 2 in the final polls. Even though U-M did not win the conference title, the '85 squad is considered one of Michigan's finest teams.

BO KEEPS HIS PROMISE The sign in the locker room still read "Those Who Stay Will Be Champions," but the 1986 team included fourth-year players who had never been to the Rose Bowl. This group did not want to be the first seniors under Schembechler to miss the Pasadena trip.

Lou Holtz made his debut at Notre Dame against U-M in 1986 and saw his team roll up 455 yards on the Wolverines without being forced to punt. Jamie Morris, however, scored three touchdowns — one on a reception from the Wishbone formation — and a last-second field goal attempt for the Irish hooked wide left in a 24-23 Michigan win.

U-M was unbeaten and ranked fourth when undefeated and No. 8 Iowa came to Ann Arbor. The Wolverines were still bitter from Rob Houghtlin's last-second field goal a year earlier.

Captain Andy Moeller, a linebacker and the son of

U-M's defensive coordinator, Gary, pounced on a fumble at the Michigan 49-yard line with 1:57 remaining to give sophomore kicker Mike Gillette a chance to win the game for the Wolverines. The Hawkeyes called a time-out with five seconds left. When play resumed, the cool Gillette drilled the 34-yard field goal to give U-M a 20-17 victory.

Schembechler's last realistic chance for a national championship would fall by the wayside, however, when the 9-0 and second-ranked Wolverines dropped a 20-17 decision to Minnesota at Michigan Stadium. The loss prompted All-American quarterback Jim Harbaugh, the nation's most efficient passer, to guarantee a win the following week at Ohio State with a Rose Bowl berth on the line.

As he did throughout his Michigan career, Harbaugh delivered. Although U-M fell behind 14-3 in the first half at Columbus, Morris dashed for 210 yards and two touchdowns while Harbaugh threw for 261 yards in engineering a Wolverine 26-24 victory. The win was Schembechler's 166th at Michigan, which surpassed Fielding H. Yost's school record, set over 25 seasons.

Those who had stayed were finally going to Pasadena.

Before the Rose Bowl, the Wolverines made the school's first trip to Hawaii to wrap up the 1986 regular season and defeated the Rainbow Warriors, 27-10. The hero was punter Monte Robbins, who unloaded a school-record 82-yard punt with U-M backed up in its own end zone.

In the 1987 Rose Bowl, Michigan jumped out to a

U-M'S MIGHTY MITE

Never named an All-American, Jamie Morris was one of the most durable backs to carry the ball for Michigan. The 5-7 Morris was recruited by Bo Schembechler to be a kick returner, but begged for the chance to be a tailback. All Morris did was set school records for career rushing attempts (809), yards (4,393), and most games with 150 or more yards rushing (eight), all marks that still stand. Although Morris relied mostly on his quickness and cutting ability, he could use his low center of gravity and strength to move the pile downfield. He is Michigan's all-time leader in total offense (6,201 yards) and took part in 960 plays, also a U-M record. Morris is second on the Michigan career lists for kickoff returns (52) and third in kickoff return yardage (1,052).

Jamie Morris rushed more times (809) for more yards (4,393) than any other player in Michigan football history.

15-3 lead on John Cooper's Arizona State squad, but the Sun Devils dominated the second half for a 22-15 victory.

BRUCE GETS A PARTING SHOT The '87 Wolverines suffered losses to Notre Dame and Michigan State and went into the meeting with Ohio State at 7-3. The Buckeyes seemingly had even bigger problems. OSU Coach Earle Bruce had been fired the week before The Big Game, his team 5-4-1, 3-4 in conference play. If Ohio State President Edward H. Jennings wanted to motivate his team for the season finale, however, he had found the perfect tool.

The Buckeyes' devotion to Bruce showed as much on the field as it did on their "EARLE" headbands. Matt Frantz, who missed a last-second field goal in Michigan's win at Columbus a year earlier, connected on a 26-yarder with 5:18 left to give the Buckeyes a 23-20 victory.

Defensive tackle Mark Messner, shown here rushing against Michigan State in 1988, is Michigan's all-time leader in sacks (36) and tackles-for-loss (70).

Rick Bay, who had wrestled and coached at Michigan, quit as the Ohio State athletic director in protest of Jennings' firing of Bruce. He and Bruce each received game balls from the Buckeyes afterwards.

MOELLER GETS A BOWL WIN The Wolverines had to make their first trip to the Hall of Fame Bowl without Schembechler, who had to undergo heart surgery for the second time two weeks after the loss to Ohio State. The

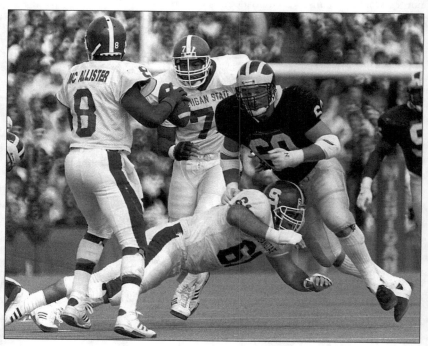

good news for Bo was he would be able to return to the sidelines in 1988.

Offensive coordinator Gary Moeller, the first Michigan assistant to hold such a title after he switched from defensive coordinator in 1987, took control of the team and called one of the riskiest plays in Michigan history.

Alabama trailed 21-3 before mounting a second-half comeback that gave the Crimson Tide a 24-21 lead. On fourth down at the Alabama 20 with 50 seconds left, Demetrius Brown threw a looping pass to John Kolesar in the corner of the end zone. Kolesar made a sliding reception, barely inbounds, to give U-M a 28-24 victory.

"It's still Bo's team," said Moeller, whom Schembechler was clearly grooming as his successor. "I talked to him (by telephone), and he said 'You did a great job.' "

Jamie Morris concluded his career with a personal-best 234 yards and the title of all-time leading Michigan rusher with 4,393 yards. He dedicated his performance to his absent coach: "I cherish the moments that I had playing for Bo Schembechler."

The Wolverines posted an 8-4 mark in 1987, and were ranked 19th in the country. Defensive lineman Mark Messner, U-M's all-time leader in sacks and tackles-for-loss, was chosen as an All-American in 1987 and '88.

CANHAM RETIRES, BO MOVES IN
Schembechler returned for the '88 season with the added responsibilities of athletic director after the retirement of Don Canham. In 20 years at the helm of U-M sports, Canham helped revolutionize college fund-raising and marketing while helping Michigan become one of the country's finest all-around athletic programs.

Schembechler's return was punctuated by agonizing losses at Notre Dame (19-17) and to Miami (31-30) at Michigan Stadium. Jimmy Johnson's Hurricanes scored 17 points in the final 5:23 of the game to retain their No. 1 ranking in one of U-M's most bitter losses. The loss ruined a great performance by quarterback Michael Taylor, who threw for 335 yards and three touchdowns.

Don Canham was one of the nation's most innovative athletic directors while at the helm of the Michigan sports programs.

Like so many of Schembechler's teams, the 1988 unit grew stronger as the season went on. In the season's final game, the Rose Bowl-bound Wolverines built a 20-0 lead at Ohio State, but the Buckeyes were to rally, setting the stage for one of the rivalry's wildest finishes.

Leroy Hoard put Michigan ahead 27-24 with his second touchdown of the game. The Buckeyes answered with a go-ahead touchdown with two minutes to go. John Kolesar returned the ensuing kickoff 59 yards, then caught a 41-yard touchdown pass from Demetrius Brown to put U-M on top, 34-31. Marc Spencer's interception sealed the win.

MICHIGAN 'HOARDS' THE ROSES Powerful sophomore Leroy Hoard gained 113 of his 142 yards in the second half against Southern Cal in the 1989 Rose Bowl, including dashes of 61 and 31 yards that set up his touchdown runs. Hoard helped Michigan come back from an 11-point half-time deficit to post a 22-14 victory in one of U-M's finest performances.

Hoard's second score came on a fourth-and-goal dive from the 1-yard line with 1:52 to play and U-M leading 15-14. Schembechler had called a time-out, informed his players that there would be no field goal try, and ordered Hoard to get the six. He promised his coach he would.

BO BIDS FOOTBALL FAREWELL If the strain of being both football coach and athletic director was wearing on Schembechler, the 1989 Wolverines certainly did not show it.

After Rocket Ismail's two kickoff returns led Notre Dame to a 24-19 win in the opener, U-M went on a roll.

A week later, the Wolverines scored 10 points in the last 90 seconds to pull out a 24-23 win over UCLA at the Rose Bowl thanks to two fill-in players. Elvis Grbac got his first start at quarterback — in place of the sore-armed Michael Taylor. J.D. Carlson squibbed a perfect onside kick to Vada Murray and knocked through the winning field goal with one second left.

The 1989 Michigan team, Schembechler's last, takes the field under the traditional "Go Blue" banner.

A tough 10-7 win at Michigan State was highlighted by All-America defensive back Tripp Welborne stuffing Spartan fullback Blake Ezor on a fourth-and-goal at the U-M 1-yard line. Todd Plate made two interceptions and Hoard ran for 152 yards in Michigan's 28-18 victory

BO KNOWS FOOTBALL

Overstating Bo Schembechler's importance to the Michigan football tradition is virtually impossible. In 21 seasons under Schembechler, the Wolverines were the winningest program in the Big Ten, with a record of 194-48-5. Only Amos Alonzo Stagg (244 at Chicago) and Woody Hayes (205 at Ohio State) won more games at a single Big Ten school.

When he retired from coaching after the 1989 season, Schembechler had the most victories of any active college football coach (234, including six seasons at Miami of Ohio) and was fifth on the all-time list. Schembechler's teams won or shared 13 Big Ten titles and were ranked in the Top 10 at season's end 16 times.

over Ohio State, sending Bo to Pasadena one last time.

Schembechler resigned on December 13, 1989, with one game left in his 21st season as the Michigan head coach. He was college football's winningest active coach with a lifetime record of 234-64-8, entering his final game. The statistics that made him quit, however, were one heart attack, one near heart attack, and two bypass operations.

"The toughest thing I ever had to do was give up my football team," a dewy-eyed Schembechler said at the resignation announcement. "I don't want to run my luck too far. I don't know how I'll react next fall when football season rolls around. I'll probably miss it, but that's the way it goes."

The Wolverines were 10-1 and ranked third in the nation when they met former Schembechler assistant Larry Smith and his Southern Cal team in the 1990 Rose Bowl. The game was tied 10-10 when U-M punter Chris Stapleton sprinted around the left side for 24 yards on a fake. But Bobby Abrams was whistled for holding.

Schembechler was incensed by the penalty, which he was initially told was for blocking below the waist. He threw down his play charts and nearly fell over the cable for his headphones, drawing another 15-yard penalty.

The Trojans drove 75 yards for a touchdown and prevailed 17-10, putting a frustrating end to Schembechler's illustrious coaching career. Despite the bowl angst, two decades of Schembechler football had turned Michigan into one of the most feared football teams in the land.

Remaining The Victors

1990-95 Overall Record: 53-17-3 (.747)
Coaches: Gary Moeller (44-13-3, 1990-94) and Lloyd Carr
  (9-4, 1995)
Conference Championships: 1990 (9-3), 1991 (10-2), 1992 (9-0-3)

Gary Moeller was handpicked by Bo Schembechler to succeed him as head coach for the 1990 campaign.

Bo Schembechler groomed Gary Moeller to be Michigan's head football coach. Moeller came to U-M with Schembechler from Miami (Ohio) in 1969 and was the defensive coordinator of units that led the nation in scoring defense in 1974 and 1976.

Moeller became head coach at Illinois for the 1977 season, but his stint in Champaign was short-lived. The Illini won six games over the next three years, and Moeller was dismissed. Schembechler welcomed him back to U-M in 1980 and made him defensive coordinator in 1982.

"In my judgment, over the last few years, Gary Moeller has been the finest football coach in the United States of America that wasn't a head coach," Schembechler said in 1990. "I could've gone anywhere I wanted to and gotten a coach. I didn't interview anybody, and I didn't think about anybody else."

Michigan fans were excited about the prospect of the Wolverines' continuing with their high-powered offense of the previous decade. Not only had Moeller coordinated the nation's stingiest defensive unit in the mid-1980s, but he had had moved flawlessly to the other side of the ball to direct U-M's efficient passing attack from 1987 up until Bo's retirement. When the torch was passed from Bo to Mo after the 1990 Rose Bowl, the Wolverines were ready to tackle a new decade of challenges with a new leader.

A TEST OF TOUGHNESS In Moeller's first game as U-M head coach, Notre Dame grabbed a 10-3 lead after one quarter at South Bend, but Elvis Grbac hooked up with Desmond Howard on scoring plays of 44 and 25 yards — sandwiched around an Allen Jefferson 1-yard score — to put the Wolverines ahead 24-14. A tipped pass from Raghib Ismail to Lake Dawson led to one Notre Dame touchdown, and sophomore quarterback Rick Mirer drove Notre Dame 76 yards for the winning score in a 28-24 Irish victory.

U-M bounced back to win its next three games convincingly before playing host to Michigan State. The Wolverines had ascended to the nation's No. 1 ranking, but MSU was ripe to knock off its top rival at Ann Arbor

WOLVERINE QUIZ

56. What sophomore tailback opened the 1990 season with two games of more than 200 yards rushing?

on national television.

After the Spartans took a 21-14 lead early in the fourth quarter on a 26-yard run, Howard ran back the ensuing kickoff 95 yards to tie the score. Tico Duckett scored from 9 yards out to put the Spartans back on top, 28-21, setting the stage for a controversial finish.

Grbac drove the Wolverines 71 yards in the final two minutes, connecting on a 7-yard scoring pass to Derrick Alexander with six seconds left. Moeller chose to go for the win, but Grbac's pass to Howard fell incomplete when MSU defensive back Eddie Brown grabbed Howard in the end zone.

"I can't understand how a receiver is lying on the field with a defender on top of him and there is no flag," said an incredulous Grbac, echoing U-M sentiments from coast to coast. "I can't understand how a referee at this level can't make the call."

Moeller berated the Big Ten officials in a manner that would make his predecessor proud, but there was no penalty called. David Parry, the Big Ten supervisor of officials, called Moeller the next day to apologize for the no-call. MSU coach George Perles enraged the Michigan delegation after the game by saying, "We won because we were the tougher team."

STOPPING COOPER IN COLUMBUS A 24-23 homecoming loss to Iowa dropped U-M's record to 3-3, bringing about the first signs of impatience from the Michigan faithful in the Moeller era.

Jon Vaughn led the nation in rushing early in the 1990 season, gaining 489 yards in Michigan's first two games.

Michigan Stadium had an artificial turf surface from 1969 through the 1990 season. A new grass field was installed before the 1991 campaign.

The Wolverines, however, got rolling on offense and played better defensively over the next four weeks. U-M traveled to Columbus with an outside shot at the Big Ten championship in a game that resembled the defensive tussles between Schembechler and Hayes during the '70s.

With the game tied at 13 and OSU needing a win to stay in contention for the Rose Bowl berth, Coach John Cooper elected to go for a fourth-and-one on the Buckeyes' own 29-yard line. The Wolverines stonewalled quarterback Greg Frey on the option, setting up J.D. Carlson's 37-yard field goal to win on the game's final play.

"On that fourth-and-one, I had my fingers crossed and everything," Carlson said. "I was hoping. When the defense stuffed them, I knew I'd get a chance."

The win over Ohio State, along with Minnesota's upset of Iowa that night in Minneapolis, caused the first four-way tie for the Big Ten championship. Iowa, Michigan, Michigan State, and Ohio State shared the title, with the Hawkeyes going to the Rose Bowl by virtue of the conference tie-breaker system.

U-M went to the Gator Bowl in Jacksonville, Fla., and completely manhandled Mississippi, 35-3. Howard showed more of his upcoming brilliance with six receptions for 167 yards and two touchdowns. Grbac passed for 296 yards, and tailback Ricky Powers also gave a preview of coming attractions with 112 yards on 14 carries. So dominant was the offensive line of Steve Everitt, Greg Skrepenak, Dean Dingman, Tom Dohring, and Matt Elliott that it earned a collective game Most Valuable Player award.

Mo's first season also was the last year the floor of Michigan Stadium featured artificial turf. The plastic covering was ripped out in favor of Prescription Athletic Turf, a type of grass field developed at Purdue and installed at Iowa and Ohio State.

HOWARD BREAKS OUT EARLY

HOWARD BREAKS OUT EARLY The 1991 Wolverines proved to be Michigan's best unit of the period. A strong running game centered on tailback Ricky Powers while Elvis Grbac and Desmond Howard became a feared passing tandem. The defense revolved around stalwart inside linebacker Erick Anderson.

The nation got an eyeful of Howard during the first two weeks of the season. Michigan trailed Boston College, 10-0, before Howard caught a TD pass from Grbac, returned the second half kickoff 93 yards for a score, and then caught two more touchdown passes in the Wolverines' 35-13 victory.

Amazingly, Howard was just warming up. He ran a reverse 29 yards for a touchdown the following week against Notre Dame to help U-M build a 17-0 lead. The Wolverines were nursing a 17-14 cushion when Moeller went for broke on fourth-and-one at the Irish 25.

Grbac dropped back for an unexpected pass, pump faked, and heaved the ball to the back of the end zone. Howard outraced the Notre Dame defense and, stretching

Erick Anderson became the first Michigan player to lead the Wolverines in tackles for four straight seasons. He capped his career by winning the Butkus Award as the nation's top linebacker in 1991.

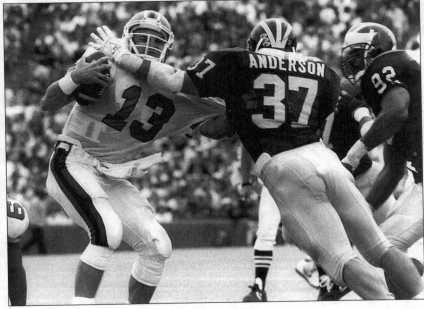

THE CATCH LEADS TO THE TROPHY

Desmond Howard brought speed and an ability to make the diving catch to the wide receiver position. He became the first receiver in Big Ten history to lead the conference in scoring with 90 points during the 1991 season. Howard set or tied five NCAA records and 12 Michigan modern era single-season records that year, including most points (138), most touchdowns (23), and most consecutive games with a touchdown reception (19). Howard won the 1991 Heisman Trophy by one of the largest voting margins in the award's history, garnering 85 percent of the first-place ballots. His spectacular diving touchdown catch at Notre Dame helped the Wolverines beat the Irish, 24-14, and set the stage for his award-winning season. He was recognized as college football's player of the year by the Maxwell Club and received the Walter Camp Trophy. He was also named Big Ten Athlete of the Year. Howard was a first-round draft pick of the Washington Redskins in 1992.

Desmond Howard caught two touchdown passes in Michigan's 45-28 win at Michigan State in 1991 en route to winning the Heisman Trophy.

as far as he could, made a remarkable diving catch.

"As it hung up there, the one thing I thought was I had to get to the ball," Howard said. "It happened so quickly; all I was thinking is 'You've got to get it and pull it in.' "

U-M won, 24-14, the Wolverines' first victory over the Irish in five years, and the Heisman Trophy became Howard's to lose.

Bobby Bowden's high-powered Florida State offense came to Ann Arbor two weeks later and emerged with a 51-31 victory in a wild affair. There would be no more losing for the rest of the 1991 regular season. The Wolverines rolled through the Big Ten, and Howard capped his storybook season with a 93-yard punt return for a touchdown in Michigan's 31-3 hammering of Ohio State. Two weeks later, he followed in the steps of Tom Harmon and became the second Michigan player to receive the Heisman Trophy.

Howard and Grbac set NCAA records for touchdowns by a quarterback-receiver tandem in a single season (19) and a career (31). Howard established or tied 12 Michigan records and five NCAA records en route to winning the Heisman, the Maxwell Award, and consensus national player of the year honors.

WOLVERINE QUIZ

57. *What was unusual about the Most Valuable Player award at the 1991 Gator Bowl?*

HUSKIES MUSH MICHIGAN'S ROSES Erick Anderson was as consistent on defense, if less dramatic, as Howard was on offense. Anderson became the first Michigan player to win the Butkus Award as the country's top collegiate linebacker, and offensive tackle Greg Skrepenak was a finalist for the Lombardi and Outland awards.

All of the Wolverines' honors and accolades meant nothing in the 1992 Rose Bowl, where U-M ran into a Washington team looking for a share of the national championship. The Huskies put defensive pressure on U-M like no other team the Wolverines had seen and rolled to a 34-14 win, Michigan's worst bowl loss.

"A very fine performance by Washington and a very poor performance by Michigan," Moeller said of the game. "That is one of the best football teams we have ever played. But I do say we are a better football team than that. We obviously didn't show it today."

The Huskies finished the season 12-0 and were named national champions by The Associated Press.

WOLVERINE QUIZ

58. *A week before his famous catch against Notre Dame, Desmond Howard scored four touchdowns against which team?*

INJURIES EXPOSE YOUNG TALENT Grbac suffered an injured ankle in U-M's 17-17 tie at Notre Dame to open the 1992 season, giving Michigan fans a peek at future Michigan thrower Todd Collins. In his first start, Collins tossed a school-record 29 completions in a 35-6 drubbing of Oklahoma State. The following week, he

BIGGER THAN JUMBO

Offensive tackle Greg Skrepenak was the biggest player ever to wear a Michigan uniform, and the 6-6, 322-pound native of Wilkes-Barre, Pa., was also among the best in a long line of great offensive linemen at U-M. An All-America choice in 1990 and 1991, Skrepenak set a school record with 48 consecutive starts on the offensive line. He was the captain of the Michigan offense in 1991, after being named co-MVP of the 1991 Gator Bowl with fellow offensive linemen Dean Dingman, Tom Dohring, Matt Elliott, and Steve Everitt. In that game, the Wolverines compiled a school record 715 yards of total offense while blowing out Mississippi, 35-3.

Offensive tackle Greg Skrepenak set a Michigan record with 48 starts on the offensive line. He was a finalist for the Outland and Lombardi awards as a senior.

tied a Michigan standard with four TD throws in a 61-7 drilling of Houston.

Similarly, an ankle injury to Ricky Powers gave more playing time to emerging sophomore Tyrone Wheatley, who capitalized on the opportunity. Wheatley set a U-M record by averaging 7.3 yards per carry in 1992, rushing for 1,357 yards and 13 touchdowns.

As the season went on, the Wolverines simply refused to lose. Pete Elezovic kicked a 39-yard field goal to give Michigan a 22-22 tie with Illinois that clinched a Rose Bowl berth. A week later, Grbac was injured on the only touchdown run of his career and Collins led the team to a sloppy 13-13 tie at muddy Ohio Stadium.

"When an official falls down covering a punt, that should tell you something," seethed Moeller, who called the field conditions "a joke," adding, "That field was slick."

WHEATLEY RUNS TO ROSES Michigan had won or shared five straight Big Ten titles and six of the previous seven entering the 1993 Rose Bowl. The Wolverines had won a record 19 straight conference games before tying Illinois and Ohio State, so there was little left to accomplish, save winning in Pasadena. What better opponent than Washington, providers of so much New Year's Day

misery one year earlier?

Grbac fired an early salvo, gunning a 49-yard pass up the middle to tight end Tony McGee to give U-M a 10-7 lead. Wheatley extended that margin with a 56-yard TD jaunt. Washington came back with two second-quarter touchdowns to take a 21-17 half-time lead, and the Pasadena paralysis seemed to be setting in again.

This Wolverine team, however, stood strong. Wheatley took the first snap of the second half a Rose Bowl-record 88 yards to regain Michigan's advantage.

The Huskies responded with a touchdown and a field

Tight end Tony McGee lunges for the game-winning touchdown in Michigan's 38-31 victory in the 1993 Rose Bowl.

LEADING THE HIT PARADE

Erick Anderson was never flashy at inside linebacker, but he was the first player to lead the Wolverines in tackles for four straight seasons. Anderson collected 428 career stops, second on Michigan's all-time list to Ron Simpkins (516). In 1991,

Anderson became the first U-M player to win the Butkus Award, which is bestowed on the nation's top linebacker. He was named an All-American by UPI and Football News in 1991, the same year he earned Big Ten Co-Defensive Player of the Year honors.

goal, but Wheatley again struck on a draw play from 24 yards out to tie the game at 31 going into the fourth quarter. With less than six minutes left, Grbac hit McGee at the Washington 2-yard line, and the big tight end lunged to paydirt to give U-M a 38-31 triumph.

Wheatley was a unanimous pick as the game's MVP with 235 yards rushing — the second-best performance in Rose Bowl history — and three touchdowns. The

MR. SIX

Tailback Tyrone Wheatley possessed a combination of size, speed and power at the tailback position that rarely is seen in college football. He made his mark as a freshman by racing 53 yards for a touchdown against Washington in the 1992 Rose Bowl, and then came back to Pasadena a year later and put on one of the best performances in the game's history. Wheatley rambled for 235 yards and touchdown runs of 56, 88, and 24 yards — the second a Rose Bowl record — in the Wolverines' 38-31 victory over Washington. He set a modern-era U-M record for highest yards-per-rush average (7.34) in 1992 and is one of two Michigan runners to have run for more than 4,000 career rushing yards (4,178). His 47 career rushing touchdowns is also a modern U-M record, 13 more than second-place Rick Leach.

Tyrone Wheatley reached the end zone more times (54) than any other player in Michigan's modern era.

Wolverines finished the season undefeated with a 9-0-3 record and a No. 5 final ranking in the AP poll.

WOLVERINES IN HAPPY VALLEY A 27-23 loss at home to Notre Dame during the second week of the 1993 season made Pasadena feel light years away. Morale suffered more when Michigan performed poorly in a 17-7 loss at Michigan State.

Next up was Michigan's first trip to Penn State, the newest member of the 11-school Big Ten Conference. (Instead of changing the name of the league, conference administrators adopted a new logo with the number 11 tucked between the words Big Ten.)

Michigan welcomed the Big Ten's newest member, Penn State, to the conference in 1993 with a 21-13 win.

The Wolverines wanted nothing to change, while the Nittany Lions entered the league determined to break up the Michigan-Ohio State dominance.

The tide of the 1,000th game in Penn State history turned when U-M's Derrick Alexander raced 48 yards with a punt return for a touchdown just before halftime, narrowing the Penn State lead to 10-7. A 16-yard pass from Collins to Mercury Hayes put the Wolverines up 14-10. But the Nittany Lions drove back down the field to set up a first-and-goal at the Michigan 1-yard line.

Four times Penn State tried the middle of the Michigan defense. Four times, the Wolverines repelled the charge. U-M later scored on a 5-yard swing pass from Collins to fullback Ché Foster for the clinching points in a 21-13 Michigan win.

"What we had in our minds," said Moeller, "was to start out this great rivalry in the right footsteps, so Michigan men could follow and know. That was second in importance to staying up with the Big Ten Conference race."

Moeller's team lost its next two games — to Illinois on a last-second touchdown pass and to Wisconsin — to fall from contention for the 1993 conference title.

EMBARRASSING THE BUCKEYES Michigan regrouped for its home finale with Ohio State, although the Buckeyes had

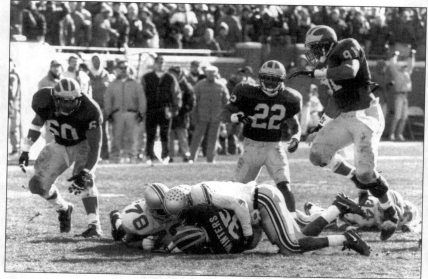

Chuck Winters (on ground) comes up with an interception in the third quarter of U-M's 28-0 blasting of Ohio State in 1993. Defensive captain Buster Stanley (60), defensive back Ty Law (22), and outside linebacker Matt Dyson (91) celebrate the turnover.

more at stake than did the 6-4 Wolverines. Coach John Cooper had not beaten Michigan in five tries at OSU, but the Bucks were undefeated, ranked fifth in the nation, and had the Rose Bowl berth on the line.

Hayes got U-M on the board with an over-the-head 25-yard touchdown catch from Collins in the opening period. Fullbacks Jon Ritchie and Foster each plunged in from a yard out in the second quarter to send U-M on its way to a 28-0 romp.

"This is one of the most embarrassing games I've ever been involved with," Cooper lamented afterward. "They outplayed us on offense, on defense, and in the kicking game. If you'd told me we would come up here and get beat 28-0, I'd have probably stayed home."

Michigan's triumph over Ohio State sent upstart Wisconsin to the Rose Bowl for the first time in 31 years.

MO RETAKES TAMPA Wheatley continued his superb bowl performances, rambling for 124 yards and two touchdowns in a 42-7 rout of North Carolina State in the Hall of Fame Bowl on January 1, 1994, in Tampa. Amani Toomer hauled in a 31-yard pass from Collins for a score on the last play of the first half to put the Wolverines ahead 21-0 at halftime.

"The seniors and the captains gathered everybody up and said, 'Hey, we have to play,' " said Wheatley after U-M won its last four to finish with an 8-4 mark. "Coach Moeller stressed that you just can't lie down and expect everyone else to lie down with us."

BUFFALOED ON A BOMB The 1994 season opened with promise when Remy Hamilton pushed the Wolverines to 2-0 by nailing a 42-yard field goal with two seconds left at Notre Dame in a stunning 26-24 victory, a small payback for the Harry Oliver miracle kick 14 years earlier. The Irish had taken the lead on a touchdown with 52 seconds remaining before Todd Collins engineered a 59-yard drive in five plays to set up Hamilton's dramatic field goal.

"We 'Notre Damed' Notre Dame," Collins said afterward. "There were a couple of games last year that went down to the wire, and we didn't come through. I think this year it will be a little bit different. This team really showed a lot of character."

Two weeks later, Hamilton's heroics were a distant memory. Michigan led seventh-ranked Colorado 26-14 early in the fourth quarter when the Buffaloes staged a staggering comeback. Eventual Heisman Trophy winner Rashaan Salaam scored from a yard out early in the fourth quarter to make the score 26-21, but the Buffaloes

Tyrone Wheatley had a knack for great performances in bowl games. He ranks second on Michigan's all-time rushing list with 4,178 career yards.

Chapter 8: Remaining The Victors **137**

WOLVERINE QUIZ

59. Besides Howard's Heisman Trophy, what other major award was given to a member of the 1991 team?

could manage little more until they regained possession on their own 15-yard line with 15 seconds left.

On the game's final play, Colorado quarterback Kordell Stewart heaved a 64-yard bomb toward the south end zone that bounced off U-M defensive backs Chuck Winters and Ty Law before falling into the hands of Detroit native Michael Westbrook for a 27-26 Colorado victory.

"They made the play when they had to make the play," said a shell-shocked Moeller. "We didn't make the play when we had to make the play."

It was matter-of-fact statement about a season-shattering setback. Players and some coaches later confessed the Wolverines were never the same. Three Big Ten losses, including Michigan's second straight to Wisconsin and its first to a John Cooper-coached Ohio State team, sent the Wolverines to the Holiday Bowl. U-M avoided a fifth loss by handling Colorado State, 24-14, to finish with an 8-4 record.

Tyrone Wheatley, who shocked many by spurning the NFL for a fourth year at Michigan, concluded a stellar career by rushing for 80 yards and a touchdown. Slashing sophomore Tshimanga Biakabutuka led the team with a 6.2 yards-per-carry rushing average and excited Michigan fans as much as his exotic name confounded the media.

MOELLER RESIGNS, CARR PULLS IN
The Colorado miracle and ensuing Big Ten stumbles didn't mark the end of Michigan football tragedy that school year. In an off-season incident at a suburban Detroit restaurant, an intoxicated Moeller was arrested on charges of misdemeanor assault and battery and disorderly conduct.

The incident received massive attention in the local and national media, and athletic director Joe Roberson announced Moeller's resignation on May 4.

Lloyd Carr was named to replace good friend Gary Moeller as Michigan football coach for the 1995 season by athletic director Joe Roberson.

Assistant head coach Lloyd Carr accepted interim command of a program shaken from eight losses over the previous two seasons and the sudden and bizarre departure of its leader. Six months earlier, Moeller had served as the best man in Carr's wedding.

"I would not be honest if I didn't say we are wounded, and we have great pain," Carr said. "We have a program of kids who have great character. They have great courage. They have a great will to win. And Michigan will be back."

BIG COMEBACK MARKS CARR'S START
The first questions about Michigan under Carr were answered in the Pigskin Classic on August 26, 1995, the earliest opening date ever for Michigan football. The Wolverines trailed Virginia 17-0 in the fourth quarter, before redshirt

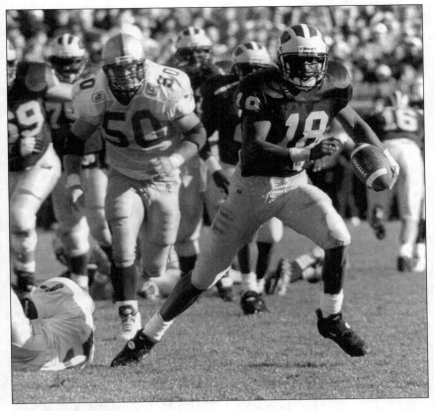

freshman quarterback Scott Dreisbach directed two scoring drives. He then tossed a looping 15-yarder to Hayes in the corner of the end zone on the game's final play to give U-M a miraculous 18-17 win and the biggest come-from-behind win in school history.

"I knew what I had to do," said Dreisbach, who set Michigan records for passing attempts (52) and yards (372) in his debut. "On the touchdown throw, I knew Merc would do his part. I just wanted the ball to stay inbounds."

Michigan won in Dreisbach's first four starts before a thumb injury ended his season. Narrow losses to eventual Big Ten champion Northwestern (19-13), Michigan State (28-25), and Penn State (27-17) dampened Carr's inaugural season.

The U-M players were the loudest celebrants, however, when Roberson officially named Carr head coach after a 5-0 victory over Purdue in a snow and sleet storm at Michigan Stadium.

"I will not rest and I will not be satisfied, until we are in Pasadena and are Rose Bowl champions," Carr said.

Amani Toomer set the single-season standard for Michigan receivers when he garnered 1,096 receiving yards (on 54 receptions) in 1994.

Junior tailback Tshimanga Biakabutuka rushed for 313 yards in Michigan's 31-23 upset of Ohio State to conclude the '95 regular season. He went on to be selected by the Carolina Panthers in the first round (No. 8 overall) of the 1996 NFL Draft.

The appointment of Lloyd Carr as the permanent Michigan football coach was met with over-whelming praise from U-M players.

U-M GIVES BLUES TO OSU, AGAIN Ohio State came to Ann Arbor as a prohibitive favorite with an 11-0 record and a No. 2 national ranking. A win would have sent the Buckeyes to the Rose Bowl for the first time in 11 years.

What happened on that sunny afternoon in November will be remembered for years to come. Running back Tshimanga Biakabutuka rushed for 313 yards, putting on a dazzling display that ranked second in U-M annals only to Ron Johnson's 1968 performance (347 yards) against Wisconsin. Behind Biakabutuka and a tenacious defense, the Wolverines rolled to an exciting 31-23 victory in one of Michigan's finest wins.

"I knew from the first play (a 22-yard run by Biakabutuka) we were going to be able to do some things we wanted to do," said offensive guard and captain Joe Marinaro, whose line cleared the way for 484 total yards of offense. "Fortunately, our coaches realized that, and we beat them up."

Poor kicking and bad field position doomed the Wolverines in the 1995 Builders Square Alamo Bowl,

Mercury Hayes hauled in the game-winning catch in the corner of the end zone at Michigan Stadium as time expired in the Wolverines' 18-17 win against Virginia in the 1996 season opener. After trailing 17-0 in the fourth quarter, Michigan pulled off the greatest comeback in school history.

where Texas A&M handed U-M a 22-20 setback, leaving Carr with a 9-4 record after one season.

THE MICHIGAN TRADITION CONTINUES The Wolverines now look to the future, as they do whether the times be good or bad. The past — a record 37 Big Ten championships, eight national championships, and an ongoing legacy of greatness — allows them to be optimistic. The present steels their effort and enthusiasm.

And the future?

Within the great gray fortress of Schembechler Hall, the players know that those who remember the past are destined to repeat it.

Those who stay will be champions.

WOLVERINE QUIZ

60. Who held the record for the longest touchdown run in a Rose Bowl game before Tyrone Wheatley went 88 yards in 1993?

By the Numbers

The statistics, lists and records that appear in this chapter are taken from the University of Michigan football media guide, which is produced by the U-M Athletic Public Relations Office. The records are updated through the 1995 season.

MICHIGAN FOOTBALL HISTORY

Year	Coach	Overall			Conference				Bowl	Home	Away	Neut.
		W	L	T	W	L	T	Pl				
1879		1	0	1						0-0-0	1-0-0	0-0-1
1880		1	0	0						0-0-0	1-0-0	0-0-0
1881		0	3	0						0-0-0	0-3-0	0-0-0
1882	No outside games											
1883		2	3	0						1-0-0	1-3-0	0-0-0
1884		2	0	0						2-0-0	0-0-0	0-0-0
1885		3	0	0						1-0-0	1-0-0	1-0-0
1886		2	0	0						1-0-0	1-0-0	0-0-0
1887		3	0	0						1-0-0	2-0-0	0-0-0
1888		4	1	0						1-0-0	3-1-0	0-0-0
1889		1	2	0						1-0-0	0-1-0	0-1-0
1890		4	1	0						3-1-0	1-0-0	0-0-0
1891	Mike Murphy/Frank Crawford	4	5	0						4-0-0	0-3-0	0-2-0
1892	Frank E. Barbour	7	5	0						3-0-0	1-3-0	3-2-0
1893	Frank E. Barbour	7	3	0						2-2-0	4-1-0	1-0-0
1894	William L. McCauley	9	1	1						5-0-1	2-1-0	2-0-0
1895	William L. McCauley	8	1	0						6-0-0	1-1-0	1-0-0
1896	W. Douglas Ward	9	1	0	2	1	0	T2		6-0-0	2-1-0	1-0-0
1897	Gustave H. Ferbert	6	1	1	2	1	0	3		5-1-1	0-0-0	1-0-0
1898	Gustave H. Ferbert	10	0	0	3	0	0	T1		7-0-0	2-0-0	1-0-0
1899	Gustave H. Ferbert	8	2	0	1	1	0	T3		6-0-0	1-1-0	1-1-0
1900	Langdon "Biff" Lee	7	2	1	3	2	0	5		6-0-1	0-1-0	1-1-0
1901	Fielding H. Yost	11	0	0	4	0	0	T1	Rose	7-0-0	1-0-0	3-0-0
1902	Fielding H. Yost	11	0	0	5	0	0	1		8-0-0	1-0-0	2-0-0
1903	Fielding H. Yost	11	0	1	3	0	1	T1		10-0-0	1-0-1	0-0-0
1904	Fielding H. Yost	10	0	0	2	0	0	T1		8-0-0	2-0-0	0-0-0
1905	Fielding H. Yost	12	1	0	2	1	0	T2		11-0-0	1-1-0	0-0-0
1906	Fielding H. Yost	4	1	0	1	0	0	T1		3-0-0	1-1-0	0-0-0
1907	Fielding H. Yost	5	1	0						3-1-0	1-0-0	1-0-0
1908	Fielding H. Yost	5	2	1						4-1-0	1-1-1	0-0-0
1909	Fielding H. Yost	6	1	0						3-1-0	3-0-0	0-0-0
1910	Fielding H. Yost	3	0	3						2-0-1	1-0-2	0-0-0
1911	Fielding H. Yost	5	1	2						4-0-1	1-1-1	0-0-0
1912	Fielding H. Yost	5	2	0						4-0-0	1-2-0	0-0-0
1913	Fielding H. Yost	6	1	0						4-1-0	2-0-0	0-0-0
1914	Fielding H. Yost	6	3	0						5-1-0	1-2-0	0-0-0
1915	Fielding H. Yost	4	3	1						4-3-0	0-0-1	0-0-0
1916	Fielding H. Yost	7	2	0						7-1-0	0-1-0	0-0-0
1917	Fielding H. Yost	8	2	0	0	1	0	T8		7-0-0	1-2-0	0-0-0
1918	Fielding H. Yost	5	0	0	2	0	0	T1		4-0-0	1-0-0	0-0-0
1919	Fielding H. Yost	3	4	0	1	4	0	T7		3-2-0	0-2-0	0-0-0
1920	Fielding H. Yost	5	2	0	2	2	0	6		4-1-0	1-1-0	0-0-0
1921	Fielding H. Yost	5	1	1	2	1	1	5		4-1-0	1-0-1	0-0-0
1922	Fielding H. Yost	6	0	1	4	0	0	T1		4-0-0	2-0-1	0-0-0
1923	Fielding H. Yost	8	0	0	4	0	0	T1		6-0-0	2-0-0	0-0-0
1924	George Little	6	2	0	4	2	0	4		3-1-0	3-1-0	0-0-0
1925	Fielding H. Yost	7	1	0	5	1	0	1		5-0-0	2-1-0	0-0-0
1926	Fielding H. Yost	7	1	0	5	0	0	T1		5-0-0	2-1-0	0-0-0
1927	Elton E. "Tad" Wieman	6	2	0	3	2	0	3		5-0-0	1-2-0	0-0-0
1928	Elton E. "Tad" Wieman	3	4	1	2	3	0	T7		3-3-0	0-1-1	0-0-0
1929	Harry G. Kipke	5	3	1	1	3	1	T7		4-1-1	1-2-0	0-0-0
1930	Harry G. Kipke	8	0	1	5	0	0	T1		6-0-1	2-0-0	0-0-0
1931	Harry G. Kipke	8	1	1	5	1	0	T1		6-1-1	2-0-0	0-0-0
1932	Harry G. Kipke	8	0	0	6	0	0	T1		5-0-0	3-0-0	0-0-0
1933	Harry G. Kipke	7	0	1	5	0	1	T1		4-0-1	3-0-0	0-0-0
1934	Harry G. Kipke	1	7	0	0	6	0	10		1-4-0	0-3-0	0-0-0
1935	Harry G. Kipke	4	4	0	2	3	0	T5		2-3-0	2-1-0	0-0-0
1936	Harry G. Kipke	1	7	0	0	5	0	T8		1-4-0	0-3-0	0-0-0

Year	Coach	Overall			Conference			Pl	Bowl	Home	Away	Neut.
		W	L	T	W	L	T					
1937	Harry G. Kipke	4	4	0	3	3	0	T4		1-3-0	3-1-0	0-0-0
1938	H.O. "Fritz" Crisler	5	1	1	3	1	1	T2		4-0-1	1-1-0	0-0-0
1939	H.O. "Fritz" Crisler	6	2	0	6	2	0	T4		4-1-0	2-1-0	0-0-0
1940	H.O. "Fritz" Crisler	7	1	0	3	1	0	2		4-0-0	3-1-0	0-0-0
1941	H.O. "Fritz" Crisler	6	1	1	3	1	1	T2		3-1-1	3-0-0	0-0-0
1942	H.O. "Fritz" Crisler	7	3	0	3	2	0	T3		6-1-0	1-2-0	0-0-0
1943	H.O. "Fritz" Crisler	8	1	0	6	0	0	T1		5-1-0	3-0-0	0-0-0
1944	H.O. "Fritz" Crisler	8	2	0	5	2	0	2		5-1-0	3-1-0	0-0-0
1945	H.O. "Fritz" Crisler	7	3	0	5	1	0	2		5-1-0	2-1-0	0-1-0
1946	H.O. "Fritz" Crisler	6	2	1	5	1	1	2		4-2-1	2-0-0	0-0-0
1947	H.O. "Fritz" Crisler	10	0	0	6	0	0	1	Rose	6-0-0	3-0-0	1-0-0
1948	Bennie G. Oosterbaan	9	0	0	6	0	0	1		5-0-0	4-0-0	0-0-0
1949	Bennie G. Oosterbaan	6	2	1	4	1	1	T1		4-1-1	2-1-0	0-0-0
1950	Bennie G. Oosterbaan	6	3	1	4	1	1	1	Rose	4-2-0	1-1-1	2-0-0
1951	Bennie G. Oosterbaan	4	5	0	4	2	0	4		3-3-0	1-2-0	0-0-0
1952	Bennie G. Oosterbaan	5	4	0	4	2	0	T4		4-2-0	1-2-0	0-0-0
1953	Bennie G. Oosterbaan	6	3	0	3	3	0	T5		6-0-0	0-3-0	0-0-0
1954	Bennie G. Oosterbaan	6	3	0	5	2	0	T2		4-2-0	2-1-0	0-0-0
1955	Bennie G. Oosterbaan	7	2	0	5	2	0	3		6-1-0	1-1-0	0-0-0
1956	Bennie G. Oosterbaan	7	2	0	5	2	0	2		5-2-0	2-0-0	0-0-0
1957	Bennie G. Oosterbaan	5	3	1	3	3	1	6		3-2-1	2-1-0	0-0-0
1958	Bennie G. Oosterbaan	2	6	1	1	5	1	8		2-4-0	0-2-1	0-0-0
1959	Chalmers W. "Bump" Elliott	4	5	0	3	4	0	7		2-4-0	2-1-0	0-0-0
1960	Chalmers W. "Bump" Elliott	5	4	0	2	4	0	T5		5-1-0	0-3-0	0-0-0
1961	Chalmers W. "Bump" Elliott	6	3	0	3	3	0	6		5-2-0	1-1-0	0-0-0
1962	Chalmers W. "Bump" Elliott	2	7	0	1	6	0	10		2-3-0	0-4-0	0-0-0
1963	Chalmers W. "Bump" Elliott	3	4	2	2	3	2	T5		2-3-2	1-1-0	0-0-0
1964	Chalmers W. "Bump" Elliott	9	1	0	6	1	0	1	Rose	5-1-0	3-0-0	1-0-0
1965	Chalmers W. "Bump" Elliott	4	1	0	2	5	0	T7		2-4-0	2-2-0	0-0-0
1966	Chalmers W. "Bump" Elliott	6	1	0	4	3	0	T3		3-3-0	3-1-0	0-0-0
1967	Chalmers W. "Bump" Elliott	4	6	0	3	4	0	T5		2-4-0	2-2-0	0-0-0
1968	Chalmers W. "Bump" Elliott	8	2	0	6	1	0	2		5-1-0	3-1-0	0-0-0
1969	Glenn E. "Bo" Schembechler	8	3	0	6	1	0	T1	Rose	5-1-0	3-1-0	0-1-0
1970	Glenn E. "Bo" Schembechler	9	1	0	6	1	0	T2		6-0-0	3-1-0	0-0-0
1971	Glenn E. "Bo" Schembechler	11	1	0	8	0	0	1	Rose	7-0-0	4-0-0	0-1-0
1972	Glenn E. "Bo" Schembechler	10	1	0	7	1	0	T1		6-0-0	4-1-0	0-0-0
1973	Glenn E. "Bo" Schembechler	10	0	1	7	0	1	T1		6-0-1	4-0-0	0-0-0
1974	Glenn E. "Bo" Schembechler	10	1	0	7	1	0	T1		6-0-0	4-1-0	0-0-0
1975	Glenn E. "Bo" Schembechler	8	2	2	7	1	0	2	Orange	4-1-2	4-0-0	0-1-0
1976	Glenn E. "Bo" Schembechler	10	2	0	7	1	0	T1	Rose	7-0-0	3-1-0	0-1-0
1977	Glenn E. "Bo" Schembechler	10	2	0	7	1	0	T1	Rose	7-0-0	3-1-0	0-1-0
1978	Glenn E. "Bo" Schembechler	10	2	0	7	1	0	T1	Rose	5-1-0	5-0-0	0-1-0
1979	Glenn E. "Bo" Schembechler	8	4	0	6	2	0	3	Gator	5-2-0	3-1-0	0-1-0
1980	Glenn E. "Bo" Schembechler	10	2	0	8	0	0	1	Rose	5-1-0	4-1-0	1-0-0
1981	Glenn E. "Bo" Schembechler	9	3	0	6	3	0	T3	Bluebonnet	4-2-0	4-1-0	1-0-0
1982	Glenn E. "Bo" Schembechler	8	4	0	8	1	0	1	Rose	5-1-0	3-2-0	0-1-0
1983	Glenn E. "Bo" Schembechler	9	3	0	8	1	0	2	Sugar	6-0-0	3-2-0	0-1-0
1984	Glenn E. "Bo" Schembechler	6	6	0	5	4	0	T6	Holiday	5-2-0	1-3-0	0-1-0
1985	Glenn E. "Bo" Schembechler	10	1	1	6	1	1	2	Fiesta	6-0-0	3-1-1	1-0-0
1986	Glenn E. "Bo" Schembechler	11	2	0	7	1	0	T1	Rose	6-0-0	5-1-0	0-1-0
1987	Glenn E. "Bo" Schembechler	8	4	0	5	3	0	4	Hall of Fame	5-2-0	2-2-0	1-0-0
1988	Glenn E. "Bo" Schembechler	9	2	1	7	0	1	1	Rose	5-1-0	3-1-1	1-0-0
1989	Glenn E. "Bo" Schembechler	10	2	0	8	0	0	1	Rose	5-1-0	5-0-0	0-1-0
1990	Gary O. Moeller	9	3	0	6	2	0	T1	Gator	4-2-0	4-1-0	1-0-0
1991	Gary O. Moeller	10	2	0	8	0	0	1	Rose	5-1-0	5-0-0	0-1-0
1992	Gary O. Moeller	9	0	3	6	0	2	1	Rose	5-0-1	4-0-2	1-0-0
1993	Gary O. Moeller	8	4	0	5	3	0	T4	Hall of Fame	5-2-0	2-2-0	1-0-0
1994	Gary O. Moeller	8	4	0	5	3	0	3	Holiday	3-3-0	4-1-0	1-0-0
1995	Lloyd H. Carr	9	4	0	5	3	0	T3	Alamo	6-1-0	3-2-0	0-1-0
Totals		**756**	**250**	**36**	**385**	**146**	**18**					

THE MICHIGAN COACHES

Years	Coach	Won	Lost	Tied	Pct
1879-90	No Coaches	23	10	1	.691
1891	Mike Murphy & Frank Crawford	4	5	0	.444
1892-93	Frank E. Barbour (Yale '92)	14	8	0	.632
1894-95	William L. McCauley (Princeton '94)	17	2	1	.875
1896	William Douglas Ward (Princeton '95)	9	1	0	.900
1897-99	Gustave H. Ferbert (Michigan '97)	24	3	1	.875
1900	Landon "Biff" Lea (Princeton)	7	2	1	.750
1901-23, '25-26	Fielding H. Yost (West Virginia)	165	29	10	.833
1924	George Little (Ohio Wesleyan '12)	6	2	0	.750
1927-28	Elton E. "Tad" Wieman (Michigan '21)	9	6	1	.593
1929-37	Harry G. Kipke (Michigan '24)	46	26	4	.631
1937-47	H.O. "Fritz" Crisler (Chicago '22)	71	16	3	.805
1948-58	Bennie G. Oosterbaan (Michigan '28)	63	33	4	.650
1958-68	Chalmers W. "Bump" Elliott (Michigan '48)	51	42	2	.547
1969-89	Glenn E. "Bo" Schembechler (Miami '51)	194	48	5	.796
1990-94	Gary O. Moeller (Ohio State '63)	36	9	3	.781
1995-	Lloyd H. Carr (Northern Michigan '68)	9	4	0	.692

8 NATIONAL CHAMPIONSHIPS

Year	Coach
1901	Fielding H. Yost
1902	Fielding H. Yost
1903	Fielding H. Yost
1904	Fielding H. Yost
1932	Harry G. Kipke
1933	Harry G. Kipke
1947	H.O. "Fritz" Crisler
1948	Bennie G. Oosterbaan

FINAL NATIONAL RANKINGS

Year	AP	UPI	USA/CNN	Year	AP	UPI	USA/CNN
1936	NR	-	-	1966	NR *	NR	-
1937	NR	-	-	1967	NR *	NR	-
1938	16	-	-	1968	12	15	-
1939	20	-	-	1969	9	8	-
1940	3	-	-	1970	9	7	-
1941	5	-	-	1971	6	4	-
1942	9	-	-	1972	6	6	-
1943	3	-	-	1973	6	6	-
1944	8	-	-	1974	3	5	-
1945	6	-	-	1975	8	8	-
1946	6	-	-	1976	3	3	-
1947	2	-	-	1977	9	8	-
1948	1	-	-	1978	5	5	-
1949	7	-	-	1979	18	19	-
1950	9	6	-	1980	4	4	-
1951	NR	NR	-	1981	12	10	-
1952	NR	NR	-	1982	NR	NR	21
1953	20	19	-	1983	8	9	7
1954	15	15	-	1984	NR	NR	NR
1955	12	13	-	1985	2	2	3
1956	7	7	-	1986	8	7	8
1957	NR	NR	-	1987	19	18	19
1958	NR	NR	-	1988	4	4	5
1959	NR	NR	-	1989 ^	7	8	8
1960	NR	NR	-	1990	7	8	8
1961	NR	NR	-	1991~	6	6	6 ~
1962	NR *	NR	-	1992	5	5	5
1963	NR *	NR	-	1993	21	19	19
1964	4 *	4	-	1994	12	9	12
1965	NR *	NR	-	1995	17	19	19

NR not ranked
* only 10 teams ranked
^ beginning in 1989, AP began selecting the top 25
   teams instead of 20
~ USA Today/CNN took over as coaches poll in 1991

MICHIGAN'S 37 BIG TEN TITLES

Year	Conf. Record	Coach
1898	3-0-0	Gustave Ferbert
1901 *	4-0-0	Fielding H. Yost
1902	5-0-0	Fielding H. Yost
1903 *	3-0-1	Fielding H. Yost
1904 *	2-0-0	Fielding H. Yost
1906 *	1-0-0	Fielding H. Yost
1918 *	2-0-0	Fielding H. Yost
1922 *	4-0-0	Fielding H. Yost
1923 *	4-0-0	Fielding H. Yost
1925	5-1-0	Fielding H. Yost
1926 *	5-0-0	Fielding H. Yost
1930 *	5-0-0	Harry G. Kipke
1932	6-0-0	Harry G. Kipke
1933 *	5-0-1	Harry G. Kipke
1943 *	6-0-0	H.O. "Fritz" Crisler
1947	6-0-0	H.O. "Fritz" Crisler
1948	6-0-0	Bennie G. Oosterbaan
1949 *	4-1-1	Bennie G. Oosterbaan
1950	4-1-1	Bennie G. Oosterbaan
1964	6-1-0	Chalmers W. "Bump" Elliott
1969 *	6-1-0	Glenn E. "Bo" Schembechler
1971	8-0-0	Glenn E. "Bo" Schembechler
1972 *	7-1-0	Glenn E. "Bo" Schembechler
1973 *	7-0-1	Glenn E. "Bo" Schembechler
1974 *	7-1-0	Glenn E. "Bo" Schembechler
1976 *	7-1-0	Glenn E. "Bo" Schembechler
1977 *	7-1-0	Glenn E. "Bo" Schembechler
1978 *	7-1-0	Glenn E. "Bo" Schembechler
1980	8-0-0	Glenn E. "Bo" Schembechler
1982	8-1-0	Glenn E. "Bo" Schembechler
1986 *	7-1-0	Glenn E. "Bo" Schembechler
1988	7-0-1	Glenn E. "Bo" Schembechler
1989	8-0-0	Glenn E. "Bo" Schembechler
1990 *	6-2-0	Gary O. Moeller
1991	8-0-0	Gary O. Moeller
1992	6-0-2	Gary O. Moeller
Totals	**37 Titles**	

* - shared conference title

Year	Bowl	Opponent	Result	Score
1902	Rose	Stanford	W	49-0
1948	Rose	Southern Cal	W	49-0
1951	Rose	California	W	14-6
1965	Rose	Oregon State	W	34-7
1970	Rose	Southern Cal	L	3-10
1972	Rose	Stanford	L	12-13
1976	Orange	Oklahoma	L	6-14
1977	Rose	Southern Cal	L	6-14
1978	Rose	Washington	L	20-27
1979	Rose	Southern Cal	L	10-17
1979	Gator	North Carolina	L	15-17
1981	Rose	Washington	W	23-6
1981	Bluebonnet	UCLA	W	33-14
1983	Rose	UCLA	L	14-24
1984	Sugar	Auburn	L	7-9
1984	Holiday	Brigham Young	L	17-24
1986	Fiesta	Nebraska	W	27-23
1987	Rose	Arizona State	L	15-22
1988	Hall Of Fame	Alabama	W	28-24
1989	Rose	Southern Cal	W	22-14
1990	Rose	Southern Cal	L	10-17
1991	Gator	Mississippi	W	35-3
1992	Rose	Washington	L	14-34
1993	Rose	Washington	W	38-31
1994	Hall Of Fame	N.C. State	W	42-7
1994	Holiday	Colorado State	W	24-14
1995	Alamo	Texas A&M	L	20-22

MICHIGAN STADIUM'S LARGEST CROWDS

Ohio State	1993	106,867*
Notre Dame	1993	106,851
Penn State	1994	106,832
Michigan State	1992	106,788
Minnesota	1992	106,579
Illinois	1992	106,481
Colorado	1994	106,427
Illinois	1993	106,385
Ohio State	1995	106,288
Michigan State	1994	106,272
Ohio State	1979	106,255
Wisconsin	1994	106,209
Michigan State	1988	106,208
Michigan State	1990	106,188
Ohio State	1991	106,156
Florida State	1991	106,145
Michigan State	1986	106,141
Notre Dame	1991	106,138
Ohio State	1989	106,137
Iowa	1992	106,132
Ohio State	1983	106,115
Michigan State	1982	106,113
Indiana	1988	106,104
Ohio State	1985	106,102
Notre Dame	1987	106,098
Indiana	1991	106,097
Ohio State	1981	106,043
Ohio State	1987	106,031
Ohio State	1977	106,024

* - NCAA Regular-Season Record

RETIRED JERSEY NUMBERS

Through 115 illustrious seasons of Michigan football, only five jersey numbers have been retired — 11, 47, 48, 87, and 98. These five numbers honor seven players, because three of these Wolverines, the Wistert brothers (Francis, Albert, and Alvin), each wore No. 11.

Jersey No. 47 recognizes Bennie Oosterbaan, who achieved greatness as a U-M player and coach,

while No. 48 honors Gerald R. Ford, U-M's team MVP in 1934 who went on to become the President of the United States in 1974. Ron Kramer's No. 87 will never be worn by another Wolverine, nor will Tom Harmon's "Old 98."

MICHIGAN'S 102 ALL-AMERICANS

(Position By Position)

Quarterbacks (6) — Benny Friedman, 1925-26; Harry Newman, 1932; Pete Elliott, 1948; Robert Timberlake, 1964; Rick Leach, 1978; Jim Harbaugh, 1986

Halfbacks (12) — William Heston, 1903-04; James Craig, 1913; John Maulbetsch, 1914; Harry Kipke, 1922; Thomas Harmon, 1939-40; Robert Chappuis, 1947; Chalmers Elliott, 1947; James Pace, 1957; Ron Johnson, 1968; Billy Taylor, 1971; Rob Lytle, 1976; Butch Woolfolk, 1981

Fullbacks (4) — Cedric Smith, 1917; Frank Steketee, 1918; Robert Westfall, 1941; William Daley, 1943

Receivers/Ends (16) — Neil Snow, 1901; Stanfield Wells, 1910; Paul Goebel, 1922; Bennie Oosterbaan, 1925-26-27; Ted Petoskey, 1932-33; Edward Frutig, 1940; Elmer Madar, 1946; Richard Rifenburg, 1948; Lowell Perry, 1951; Ronald Kramer, 1955-56; John Clancy, 1966; Jim Mandich, 1969; Jim Smith, 1976; Anthony Carter, 1980-81-82; Desmond Howard, 1991; Derrick Alexander, 1992

Centers (11) — William Cunningham, 1898; Germany Schulz, 1907; Henry Vick, 1921; Jack Blott, 1923; Robert Brown, 1925; Maynard Morrison, 1931; Charles Bernard, 1932-33; Walt Downing, 1977; George Lilja, 1980; Tom Dixon, 1983; John Vitale, 1988

Offensive Guards (14) — Albert Benbrook, 1909-10; Ernest Allmendinger, 1917; Frank Culver, 1917; E.R. Slaughter, 1924; Harry Hawkins, 1925; Ralph Heikkinen, 1938; Julius Franks, 1942; Reggie McKenzie, 1971; Mark Donahue, 1976-77; Kurt Becker, 1981; Stefan Humphries, 1983; Dean Dingman, 1990; Matt Elliott, 1991; Joe Cocozzo, 1992

Offensive Tackles (16) — Miller Pontius, 1913; Tom Edwards, 1925; Otto Pommerening, 1928; Francis Wistert, 1933; Albert Wistert, 1942; Mervin Preguiman, 1943; Alvin Wistert, 1948-49; Allen Wahl, 1949-50; Arthur Walker, 1954; Dan Dierdorf, 1970; Paul Seymour, 1972; Bill Dufek, 1976; Ed Muransky, 1981; William "Bubba" Paris, 1981; John "Bubba" Elliott, 1986-87; Greg Skrepenak, 1990-91

Defensive Tackles (6) — William Yearby, 1964-65; Dave Gallagher, 1973; Curtis Greer, 1979; Mike Hammerstein, 1985; Mark Messner, 1987-88; Chris Hutchinson, 1992

Defensive Guards (1) — Henry Hill, 1970

Linebackers (6) — Marty Huff, 1970; Mike Taylor, 1971; Calvin O'Neal, 1976; John Anderson, 1977; Ron Simpkins, 1979; Erick Anderson, 1991

Defensive Backs (9) — Richard Volk, 1966; Tom Curtis, 1969; Thom Darden, 1971; Randy Logan, 1972; Dave Brown, 1973-74; Don Dufek, 1975; Brad Cochran, 1985; Garland Rivers, 1986; Tripp Welborne, 1989-90; Ty Law, 1994

Placekickers (1) — Remy Hamilton, 1994

MICHIGAN INDIVIDUAL RECORDS

(All records since 1938 unless otherwise noted)   ** *Denotes Big Ten Conference Record*

RUSHING, GAME

Attempts — 42, Ron Johnson vs. Northwestern, 11-4-67
Yards — 347, Ron Johnson vs. Wisconsin, 11-16-68
Average Gain (Min. 5 carries) — 18.3, Leroy Hoard vs. Indiana (7-128), 10-22-88
Average Gain (Min. 10 carries) — 18.0, Rob Lytle vs. Michigan State (10-180), 10- 9-76
Touchdowns — 5, Ron Johnson vs. Wisconsin, 11-16-68

RUSHING, SEASON

Attempts — 303, Tshimanga Biakabutuka, 1995
Yards — 1818, Tshimanga Biakabutuka, 1995
Average Yards Per Play (Min. 500 yards) — 7.34, Tyrone Wheatley (185-1357), 1992
Average Yards Per Game (Min. 500 yards) — 141.9, Jamie Morris (12-1703), 1987
Touchdowns — 19, Ron Johnson, 1968
Most Games, 100+ Yards Rushing — 10, Jamie Morris (12 games), 1987
Most Games, 150+ Yards Rushing — 5, Rob Lytle (12 games), 1976, and Jamie Morris (12 games), 1987
Most Games, 200+ Yards Rushing — 2, five times, most recent: Tshimanga Biakabutuka (13 games), 1995

RUSHING, CAREER

Attempts — 809, Jamie Morris, 1984-5-6-7
Yards — 4393, Jamie Morris, 1984-5-6-7
Average Yards Per Play (Min. 1000 yards) — 6.29, Jon Vaughn (226-1421), 1989-90
Average Yards Per Game (Min. 1000 yards) — 102.4, Bill Taylor (30-3072), 1969-70-1
Touchdowns — 47, Tyrone Wheatley, 1991-2-3-4
Most Games, 100 Or More Yards Rushing — 20, Tyrone Wheatley, 1991-2-3-4
Most Games, 150 Or More Yards Rushing — 8, Jamie Morris, 1984-5-6-7
Most Games, 200 Or More Yards Rushing — 3, Ron Johnson, 1966-7-8

TOP 20 RUSHING LEADERS

Yards	Player	Seasons
4,393	Jamie Morris	1984-5-6-7
4,178	Tyrone Wheatley	1991-2-3-4
3,861	Butch Woolfolk	1978-9-80-1
3,317	Rob Lytle	1973-4-5-6
3,072	Bill Taylor	1969-70-1
2,900	Gordon Bell	1973-4-5
2,810	Tshimanga Biakabutuka	1993-4-5
2,751	Lawrence Ricks	1979-80-1-2
2,624	Harlan Huckleby	1975-6-7-8
2,554	Ricky Powers	1990-1-2-3
2,550	Russell Davis	1975-6-7-8
2,440	Ron Johnson	1966-7-8
2,343	Ed Shuttlesworth	1971-2-3
2,247	Tony Boles	1987-8-9
2,206	Stan Edwards	1977-9-80-1
2,176	Rick Leach	1975-6-7-8
2,134	Tom Harmon	1938-9-40
1,981	Chuck Heater	1972-3-4
1,947	Rick Rogers	1981-2-3-4
1,864	Bob Westfall	1939-40-1

PASSING, GAME

Attempts — 52, Scott Dreisbach vs. Virginia, 8-26-95
Completions — 29, Todd Collins vs. Oklahoma State, 9-19-92
Completion Percentage (Min. 10 attempts) — 92.3, Jim Harbaugh vs. Purdue (12-13), 11-9-85
Completion Percentage (Min. 20 attempts) — 90.9, Elvis Grbac vs. Notre Dame (20-22), 9-14-91
Yards — 372, Scott Dreisbach vs. Virginia, 8-26-95
Average Yards Per Completion (Min. 5 completions) — 36.3, Rick Leach vs. Purdue (6-218), 11-8-75
Average Yards Per Completion (Min. 5 completions) — 30.0, Jim Harbaugh at Indiana (10-300), 10-25-86
Touchdown Passes — 4, done 8 times, most recent: Brian Griese vs. Minnesota, 10-28-95

PASSING, SEASON

Attempts — 296, Todd Collins, 1993
Completions — 189, Todd Collins, 1993
Completion Percentage (Min. 100 attempts) — 65.3, Todd Collins (66-101), 1992
Yards — 2729, Jim Harbaugh, 1986
Average Yards Per Completion (Min. 1000 yards) — 18.8, Bob Chappuis (62-1164), 1947
Average Yards Per Game (Min. 1000 yards) — 209.9, Jim Harbaugh (13-2729), 1986
Touchdown Passes — 25, Elvis Grbac, 1991
Touchdown Percentage (Min. 100 attempts) — 12.38, Rick Leach (13-105), 1976
Lowest Interception Percentage (Min. 100 attempts) — 1.60, Wally Gabler (2-125), 1965
Most Games, 150+ Yards Passing — 11, Jim Harbaugh (13 games), 1986; and Todd Collins (12 games), 1994
Most Games, 200+ Yards Passing — 8, Jim Harbaugh (13 games), 1986
Highest Passing Efficiency Rating (Min. 100 attempts) — 173.3, Bob Chappuis, 1947

PASSING, CAREER

Attempts — 835, Elvis Grbac, 1989-90-1-2
Completions — 522, Elvis Grbac, 1989-90-1-2
Completion Percentage (Min. 200 attempts) — 64.3, Todd Collins (457-711), 1991-2-3-4
Yards — 6460, Elvis Grbac, 1989-90-1-2
Average Yards Per Completion (Min. 2000 yards) — 17.1, Rick Leach (250-4284), 1975-6-7-8
Average Yards Per Game (Min. 2000 yards) — 175.8, Jim Harbaugh (31-5449), 1983-4-5-6
Touchdown Passes — 71, Elvis Grbac, 1989-90-1-2
Touchdown Percentage (Min. 200 attempts) — 8.9, Rick Leach (48-537), 1975-6-7-8
Lowest Interception Percentage (Min. 200 attempts) — 2.5, Michael Taylor (7-275), 1986-7-8-9
Most Games, 150+ Yards Passing — 23, Elvis Grbac, 1989-90-1-2; and Todd Collins, 1991-2-3-4
Most Games, 200+ Yards Passing — 14, Todd Collins, 1991-2-3-4
Highest Passing Efficiency Rating (Min. 200 attempts) — 148.1, Elvis Grbac, 1989-90-1-2

MICHIGAN'S TOP 15 PASSING LEADERS

Yards	Player	Seasons
6,460	Elvis Grbac	1989-90-1-2
5,858	Todd Collins	1991-2-3-4
5,449	Jim Harbaugh	1983-4-5-6
4,860	Steve Smith	1980-1-2-3
4,284	Rick Leach	1975-6-7-8
2,994	John Wangler	1976-7-9-80
2,550	Don Moorhead	1968-9-70
2,533	Dennis Brown	1966-7-8
2,441	Dick Vidmer	1965-6-7
2,285	Dennis Franklin	1972-3-4
2,256	Bob Chappuis	1942-6-7
2,224	Chuck Ortmann	1948-9-50
2,194	Michael Taylor	1986-7-8-9
2,026	Demetrius Brown	1986-7-8
1,656	Bob Timberlake	1962-3-4

TOP 15 COMPLETION LEADERS

Comp.	Player	Seasons
522	Elvis Grbac	1989-90-1-2
457	Todd Collins	1991-2-3-4
387	Jim Harbaugh	1983-4-5-6
324	Steve Smith	1980-1-2-3
250	Rick Leach	1975-6-7-8
200	Don Moorhead	1968-9-70
197	John Wangler	1976-7-9-80
194	Dennis Brown	1966-7-8
186	Dick Vidmer	1965-6-7
163	Michael Taylor	1986-7-8-9
153	Dennis Franklin	1972-3-4
142	Bob Chappuis	1942-6-7
142	Chuck Ortmann	1948-9-50
133	Bob Timberlake	1962-3-4
128	Demetrius Brown	1986-7-8

TOP 15 PASSING ATTEMPTS

Att.	Player	Seasons
835	Elvis Grbac	1989-90-1-2
711	Todd Collins	1991-2-3-4
648	Steve Smith	1980-1-2-3
620	Jim Harbaugh	1983-4-5-6
537	Rick Leach	1975-6-7-8
425	Don Moorhead	1968-9-70
389	Dennis Brown	1966-7-8
380	Dick Vidmer	1965-6-7
346	John Wangler	1976-7-9-80
333	Chuck Ortmann	1948-9-50
294	Dennis Franklin	1972-3-4
275	Michael Taylor	1986-7-8-9
269	Bob Timberlake	1962-3-4
266	Bob Chappuis	1942-6-7
252	Demetrius Brown	1986-7-8

RECEIVING, GAME

Receptions — 12, Brad Myers at Ohio State, 11-22-58
Yards — 197, Jack Clancy vs. Oregon State, 9-17-66
Touchdowns — 4, Derrick Alexander vs. Minnesota, 10-24-92

RECEIVING, SEASON

Receptions — 76, Jack Clancy, 1966
Yards — 1096, Amani Toomer, 1994
Average Yards Per Reception (Min. 20 receptions) — 28.3, Jim Smith (24-680), 1975
Touchdowns — 19 **, Desmond Howard, 1991
Most Games, 75+ Yards Receiving — 7, five times, most recent: 7, Amani Toomer (12 games), 1994
Most Games, 100+ Yards Receiving — 5, Anthony Carter (12 games), 1982

RECEIVING, CAREER

Receptions — 161, Anthony Carter, 1979-80-1-2
Yards — 3076, Anthony Carter, 1979-80-1-2
Average Yards Per Reception (Min. 50 receptions) — 23.4, John Kolesar (61-1425), 1985-6-7-8
Touchdowns — 37 **, Anthony Carter, 1979-80-1-2
Most Games, 75+ Yards Receiving — 20, Anthony Carter, 1979-80-1-2
Most Games, 100+ Yards Receiving — 14, Anthony Carter, 1979-80-1-2

TOP 15 RECEIVING LEADERS (CATCHES)

Catches	Player	Seasons
161	Anthony Carter	1979-80-1-2
143	Amani Toomer	1992-3-4-5
134	Desmond Howard	1989-90-1
132	Jack Clancy	1963-5-6
125	Derrick Alexander	1989-90-1-2-3
124	Mercury Hayes	1992-3-4-5
119	Jim Mandich	1967-8-9
111	Greg McMurtry	1986-7-8-9
99	Jamie Morris	1984-5-6-7
93	Vince Bean	1981-2-3-4
84	Sim Nelson	1982-3-4
74	Jay Riemersma	1992-3-4-5
73	Jim Smith	1973-4-5-6
72	Walter Smith	1991-2-3-4
71	Lowell Perry	1950-1-2

TOP 15 RECEIVING LEADERS (YARDS)

Yards	Player	Seasons
3,076	Anthony Carter	1979-80-1-2
2,657	Amani Toomer	1992-3-4-5
2,163	Greg McMurtry	1986-7-8-9
2,146	Desmond Howard	1989-90-1
2,144	Mercury Hayes	1992-3-4-5
1,977	Derrick Alexander	1989-90-1-2-3
1,919	Jack Clancy	1963-5-6
1,687	Jim Smith	1973-4-5-6
1,514	Vince Bean	1981-2-3-4
1,508	Jim Mandich	1967-8-9
1,425	John Kolesar	1985-6-7-8
1,393	Ralph Clayton	1976-7-8-9
1,261	Lowell Perry	1950-1-2
1,088	Paul Jokisch	1984-5-6
1,011	Dick Rifenburg	1944-6-7-8

TOTAL OFFENSE, GAME

Plays — 61, Dennis Brown vs. Indiana, 10-21-67
Yards — 358, Scott Dreisbach vs. Virginia, 8-26-95

TOTAL OFFENSE, SEASON

Plays — 380, Don Moorhead, 1969
Yards — 2847, Jim Harbaugh, 1986
Average Yards Per Play (Min. 1500 yards) — 7.63, Jim Harbaugh (373-2847), 1986
Average Yards Per Game (Min. 1500 yards) — 219.0, Jim Harbaugh (13-2847), 1986

TOTAL OFFENSE, CAREER

Plays — 1034, Rick Leach, 1975-6-7-8
Yards — 6554, Steve Smith, 1980-1-2-3
Average Yards Per Play (Min. 2500 yards) -7.02, Todd Collins (812-5702), 1991-2-3-4
Average Yards Per Game (Min. 2500 yards) — 186.6, Jim Harbaugh (31-5784), 1983-4-5-6

ALL-PURPOSE, GAME

(Rushing, receiving, returning)
Plays — 44, Ron Johnson vs. Northwestern, 11-4-67
Yards — 387, Ron Johnson vs. Wisconsin, 11-16-68

Plays — 309, Jamie Morris, 1987; and Tshimanga
Biakabutuka, 1995
Yards — 1972, Jamie Morris, 1987

ALL-PURPOSE, CAREER

Plays — 960, Jamie Morris, 1984-5-6-7
Yards — 6201, Jamie Morris, 1984-5-6-7

SCORING, GAME

Points — 30, Ron Johnson vs. Wisconsin, 11-16-68
Touchdowns — 5, Ron Johnson vs. Wisconsin,
11-16-68
Field Goals — 5, Mike Gillette vs. Minnesota,
11-5-88; and J.D. Carlson vs. Illinois, 11-10-90
PATs — 10, Ali Haji-Sheikh vs. Illinois, 11- 7-81

SCORING, SEASON

Points — 138 , Desmond Howard, 1991
Touchdowns — 23, DesmondHoward, 1991
Field Goals — 25 **, Remy Hamilton, 1994
Field Goal Percentage (Min. 10 attempts) — 92.9,
J.D. Carlson (13-14), 1989
PATs — 55 **, Dana Coin, 1971; and Bob Wood, 1976
Pat Conversion Percentage (Min. 25 attempts) —
100.0, Dana Coin (55-55), 1971; J.D. Carlson
(52-52), 1991; J.D. Carlson (47-47), 1990; Ali
Haji-Sheikh (41-41), 1982; Ali Haji-Sheikh
(35-35), 1981; Rick Sygar (32-32), 1966; and
Mike Gillette (26-26), 1986

SCORING, CAREER

Points — 324, Tyrone Wheatley, 1991-2-3-4
Touchdowns — 54, Tyrone Wheatley, 1991-2-3-4
Field Goals — 57, Mike Gillette, 1985-6-7-8
Field Goal Percentage (Min. 15 attempts) — 82.9,
Bob Bergeron (29-35), 1981-2-3-4
PATs -137, J. D. Carlson, 1988-9-90-1
Pat Conversion Percentage (Min. 50 attempts) —
98.6, J.D. Carlson (137-139), 1988-9-90-1
Most Consecutive PATs — 126 **, J.D. Carlson,
1988-9-90-1

TOUCHDOWNS, CAREER

TDs	Player	Years
72	Willie Heston	1901-04
54	Tyrone Wheatley	1991-93
40	Anthony Carter	1979-82
39	Al Herrnstein	1898-02
37	Desmond Howard	1989-91
35	John Curtis	1903-06
34	Tom Hammond	1903-05
34	Rick Leach	1975-78
33	Tom Harmon	1938-40
32	Bill Taylor	1969-71
31	Steve Smith	1980-83
30	John Maulbetsch	1914-16
29	Gordon Bell	1973-75
29	Rob Lytle	1973-76
29	Butch Woolfolk	1978-81
28	Jamie Morris	1984-87

TOUCHDOWNS, SEASON

TDs	Player	Years
26	Al Herrnstein	1902
23	Desmond Howard	1991
21	Willie Heston	1904
20	Willie Heston	1901
19	Neil Snow	1901
19	Ron Johnson	1968
17	Tyrone Wheatley	1992
16	Willie Heston	1903
16	Tom Harmon	1940
16	Rob Lytle	1976
15	Willie Heston	1902
15	Herb Graver	1903
15	Tom Hammond	1903
15	John Curtis	1905
15	Jamie Morris	1987

TOUCHDOWNS, GAME

TDs	Player	Opponent	Year
7	Al Herrnstein	Michigan Ag.	1902
6	Al Herrnstein	Beloit	1901
6	Willie Heston	Kalamazoo	1904
6	Sam Davison	Kentucky	1908
5	Neil Snow	Stanford	1901
5	Al Herrnstein	Buffalo	1901
5	Al Herrnstein	Ohio State	1902
5	Willie Heston	Beloit	1903
5	Tom Hammond	Albion	1903
5	Herb Graver	Ohio State	1903
5	Harry Hammond	Kalamazoo	1904
5	John Curtis	West Virginia	1904
5	Fred Norcross	West Virginia	1904
5	Paul Magoffin	Michigan Ag.	1907
5	Archie Weston	Mt. Union	1917
5	Ron Johnson	Wisconsin	1968

PUNTING, GAME

Punts — 24, Chuck Ortmann at Ohio State,11-25-50
Yards — 723, Chuck Ortmann at Ohio State, 11-25-50
Average (Min. 3 punts) — 56.3, Don Bracken vs.
Northwestern (3-169), 10-24-81

PUNTING, SEASON

Punts — 66, Bill Billings, 1951; and Mark Werner,
1968
Yards — 2705, Monte Robbins, 1984
Average (Min. 30 punts) — 43.63, Monte Robbins
(62-2705), 1984

PUNTING, CAREER

Punts — 203, Don Bracken, 1980-1-2-3
Yards — 8562, Monte Robbins, 1984-5-6-7
Average Yards Per Punt (Min. 75 punts) — 42.8,
Monte Robbins (200-8562), 1984-5-6-7

PUNT RETURNS, GAME

Returns — 8, Brian Carpenter vs. Notre Dame,
9-19-81
Yards — 140, George Hoey vs. Minnesota, 10-28-67
Average Yards Per Return (Min. 2 returns) — 49.5,
George Hoey vs. Navy (2-99), 10-5-68

PUNT RETURNS, SEASON

Returns — 32, Tripp Welborne, 1989
Yards — 455, Tripp Welborne, 1990
Average Yards Per Return (Min. 15 returns) — 15.7,
Desmond Howard (18-282), 1991
Touchdowns — 3, Gene Derricotte, 1947

PUNT RETURNS, CAREER

Returns — 81, Anthony Carter, 1979-80-1-2
Yards — 904, Anthony Carter, 1979-80-1-2
Average Yards Per Return (Min. 30 returns) — 17.3, George Hoey (31-537), 1967-8
Touchdowns — 4, Gene Derricotte, 1944-6-7-8; and Derrick Alexander, 1989-90-1-2-3

KICKOFF RETURNS, GAME

Returns — 5, Glenn Doughty at Michigan State, 10-18-69; Ron Johnson vs. Michigan State, 10-14-67; and Seth Smith at Ohio State, 11-19-94
Yards — 135, Desmond Howard vs. Michigan State, 10-13-90
Average Yardage Per Return (Min. 2 returns) — 62.5, Gil Chapman at Illinois (2-125), 10-21-72

KICKOFF RETURNS, SEASON

Returns — 26, Ron Johnson, 1967
Yards — 504, Desmond Howard, 1990
Average Yardage Per Return (Min. 10 returns) — 30.8, Dave Raimey (10-308), 1961
Touchdowns — 1, 10 times, most recent: Seth Smith, 1994

KICKOFF RETURNS, CAREER

Returns — 63, Anthony Carter, 1979-80-1-2
Yards — 1606, Anthony Carter, 1979-80-1-2
Average Yards Per Return (Min. 20 returns) — 26.9, Desmond Howard (45-1211), 1989-90-1
Touchdowns — 2, Desmond Howard, 1989-90-1

DEFENSE (SINCE 1966)

INTERCEPTIONS, GAME

Most — 3, 10 times, most recent: Andy Moeller at Wisconsin, 10- 4-86
Yards Returned — 95, Tom Harmon vs. Iowa, 10-14-39

INTERCEPTIONS, SEASON

Interceptions — 10, Tom Curtis, 1968
Yards Returned — 182, Tom Curtis, 1968
Touchdowns — 2, Thom Darden, 1971

INTERCEPTIONS, CAREER

Interceptions — 25, Tom Curtis, 1967-8-9
Yards Returned — 431, Tom Curtis, 1967-8-9
Touchdowns — 2, Thom Darden, 1969-70-1; and Lance Dottin, 1988-9-90-1

MOST TACKLES

Game — 24, Calvin O'Neal at Purdue, 11- 6-76
Season — 174, Ron Simpkins, 1977
Career — 516, Ron Simpkins, 1976-7-8-9

MOST TACKLES FOR LOSS (SINCE 1978)

Game — 6, Mark Messner vs. Northwestern (26 yds), 10-31-87; and Will Carr vs. Minnesota (34 yds), 10-28-95
Season — 26, Mark Messner, 1988
Career — 70, Mark Messner, 1985-6-7-8

MOST TACKLES FOR LOSS YARDAGE

Season — 122, Jason Horn, 1995
Career — 376, Mark Messner, 1985-6-7-8

MOST SACKS (SINCE 1978)

Game — 5, Mark Messner vs. Northwestern (25 yds), 10-31-87
Season (Since 1980) — 11, Mark Messner, 1985; Chris Hutchinson, 1992; and Jason Horn, 1995
Career — 36, Mark Messner, 1985-6-7-8

MOST SACK YARDAGE (SINCE 1980)

Season — 99, Chris Hutchinson, 1992
Career — 273, Mark Messner, 1985-6-7-8

MOST PASSES BROKEN UP

Game — 5, Thom Darden vs. Purdue, 31-20, 10-11-69
Season — 14, Marion Body, 1982; and Alfie Burch, 1993
Career — 26, Marion Body, 1979-80-1-2

TOP 10 CAREER TACKLE LEADERS

Tackles	Player	Years
516	Ron Simpkins	1976-7-8-9
428	Erick Anderson	1988-9-90-1
414	Paul Girgash	1979-80-1-2
396	Mike Mallory	1982-3-4-5
385	Andy Cannavino	1977-8-9-80
378	Calvin O'Neal	1974-5-6
369	Mike Boren	1980-1-2-3
360	Steve Morrison	1990-1-2-3-4
336	Greg Morton	1974-5-6
334	Jarrett Irons	1993-4-5

MICHIGAN'S ALL-TIME FOOTBALL LETTERMEN

This listing of all-time football letter winners was compiled by the University of Michigan's Athletic Public Relations Office and is as complete and accurate as historical records allow. It includes the years lettered and position for each of the more than 1,500 letter winners who have played at the University of Michigan since 1879. In each entry, the year is listed for each letter won (For example, in the listing for Cliff Wise, the years are 1940-42, meaning he lettered in 1940 and 1942, but not 1941). This list does not include team managers.

A Abbott, Howard, QB, 1889-90-91; Abrahams, Morris, T, 1969; Abrams, Bobby E., OLB, 1986-87-88-89; Adami, Zachary T., G, 1994-95; Adams, Theo., LG, 1918; Aghakhan, Ninef F., DT, 1991-92-93; Akers, Jeffery, L., ILB, 1983-84-85; Albertson, John W., PK, 1991; Aldrich, William, T, 1893; Alexander, Derrick S., WR, 1989-90-92-93; Aliber, James, QB, 1943-44; Alix, Dennis, QB, 1963; Allen, Frank, Forward, 1878-79-80-81; Allerdice, Dave, HB, 1907-08-09; Allis, Henry, E, 1948-49-50; Allmendinger, Ernest, G, 1911-12-13; Amrine, Robert, HB, 1934; Amstutz, Ralph, G, 1942-43; Anderson, Deollo, SS, 1993-94-95; Anderson, Erick S., ILB, 1988-89-90-91; Anderson, John, OLB, 1974-75-76-77; Anderson, Steve, MG, 1976; Anderson, Timothy, ILB, 1982-83-84; Andrews, Phil, FB, 1976; Anthony, Mel, FB, 1962-63-64; Arbeznik, John, OG, 1977-78-79; Armour, James, OG, 1973-74; Armstrong, Greg, FB, 1982-83-84; Arnold, David P., DB, 1985-86-87-88; Atchinson, Jim, T, 1948-49; Auer, Howard, T, 1929-30-31; Aug, Vincent, HB, 1934-35; Austin, Tom, T, 1932-33-34; Ayers, Norwood, E, 1896-97; Ayres, John, Forward, 1881; Azcona, Eduardo, P, 1990-91-92.

B Babcock, Dick, T, 1923-24-25; Babcock, R.S., Substitute, 1887; Babcock, Samuel, HB, 1925; Baer, Fred, FB, 1952-53-54; Baer, Ray, T, 1925-26-27; Bahlow, Edward, E, 1946; Bailey, Don, OG, 1964-65-66; Baird, James, QB, 1893-94-95; Baker, Fred, G, 1895-96; Baker, Kraig W., P/PK, 1994; Baker, William, T, 1897-98; Baldacci, Lou, QB, 1953-54-55; Ball, William, FB, 1888-89; Ballou, Robert, T, 1946; Balog, Jim, T, 1951-52-53; Balourdos, Art, C/OG, 1981-82-83-84; Balourdos, John S., LB, 1986; Balzhiser, Dick, FB, 1952-53; Banar, Jim, DT, 1968-69; Banks, Theodore, QB , 1920-21; Banks, Charles, Forward, 1885-86; Banks, Harry, DB, 1971-72-74; Banks, Larry, DE, 1974; Barabee, Clifford, HB, 1897-98; Barclay, William, QB, 1935-36-37; Barlow, Alfred, QB, 1905; Barmore, Edmund, HB/QB, 1879-80; Barr, Terry, HB, 1954-55-56; Barry, Paul J., OG, 1995; Bartells, A.D., HB, 1893; Bartholomew, Bruce, T, 1951; Bartlett, William., QB, 1948-49; Bartnick, Greg, OG, 1976-77-78; Barton, Charles, E/T, 1912; Bass, Mike, DB, 1964-65-66; Bastian, Clyde, HB, 1914-15; Bates, Brad, DB, 1980; Bates, Jim, C, 1952-54-55; Batsakes, John, HB, 1958; Bauman, Clem, T, 1943-44; Baumgartner, Bob, OG, 1967-68-69; Beach, Elmer, Forward, 1882-83; Beach, Raymond, QB, 1882-83-84-85; Bean, Vince, SE, 1981-82-83-84; Beard, Chester, G, 1933-34; Beaumont, J.A., Member, 1877; Becker, Kurt, OG, 1978-79-80-81; Beckman, Tom, DT, 1969-70-71; Begle, Ned, HB, 1900; Beison, Richard, G, 1951-52-53; Bell, Gene, S, 1977-78; Bell, Gordon, TB, 1973-74-75; Belsky, Jerome, G, 1936-37; Benbrook, Al, LG, 1908-09-10; Bennett, Don, T, 1951-52-53; Bennett, Edwin, G, 1898; Bennett, John, E, 1896-97-98; Benton, Leland, E, 1913-14-15; Benton, Lou, E, 1914; Bentz, Warren, HB, 1944-45; Berger, Tom, G, 1956-57; Bergeron, Robert, PK, 1983-84; Berline, Jim, OE, 1967; Bernard, Charles, C, 1931-32-33; Berutti, Bill, WB, 1969-70; Bettis, Roger, QB, 1977; Betts, Jim, S, 1968-69-70; Betts, Norm, TE, 1979-80-81; Biakabutuka, Tshimanga, TB, 1993-94-95; Bickle, Doug, E, 1961; Billings, Bill, QB, 1951-52; Bird, James, Substitute, 1892;

Bishop, Allen B., DB, 1984-86-87; Bishop, Harry, QB/HB, 1906; Bissell, Frank, G, 1934-35; Bissell, Geoffrey J., WR, 1987; Bitner, Harry, Forward, 1881-82; Blackwell, Brent, SS, 1994-95; Blakenship, Joel A. Tony, FS, 1991-92-93; Blanchard, Don, T, 1962; Bloomingston, John, FB, 1895; Blott, Jack, C, 1922-23; Bochnowski, Alex, G, 1956-57; Bock, Ernest F., QB, 1956-57; Boden, Marshall, E, 1928; Body, Marion, DB, 1979-80-81-82; Bogle, Thomas, G/C, 1910-1911; Bohn, Christopher R., ILB, 1988-89-90; Bolach, Mark P.., OT, 1993-94-95; Bolas, George, QB/HB, 1934; Bolden, Jim, DB, 1974-75-76; Boles, Tony L., RB, 1988-89; Boor, Don, FB, 1941-42; Borden, Hugh, Rusher, 1882-83; Boren, Mike, ILB, 1980-81-82-83; Borgmann, Bill, G, 1933-34; Borleske, Stanley, E, 1910-1911; Borowski, Andrew E., C, 1985-86-87; Boshoven, Bob, E, 1957; Bostic, Keith, SS, 1979-80-81-82; Bostic, Carlitos R.., OLB, 1985-87; Boutwell, Ben, C, 1889; Bovard, Alan, C, 1927-28-29; Boville, Edwin;1918, , RE; Bowens, Dave, OLB, 1995; Bowers, Dave, E, 1956-57; Bowman, Jim, C, 1955; Boyd, Alan, T, 1916-17; Boyden, Joel M., OLB, 1988; Boyle, Michael, HB, 1912; Bracken, Don, P, 1980-81-82-83; Bradford, Wes, HB, 1950-51; Braman, Mark, DB, 1977-78-79; Brandon, Dave, DE, 1973; Brandstatter, Jim, OT, 1969-70-71; Branoff, Tony, HB, 1952-53-54-55; Brennan, John, G, 1936-37-38; Brielmaier, Jerry, C, 1944; Brieske, Jim, C, 1942-46-47; Brigstock, Tom, HB, 1965; Broadnax, Stan, OG, 1967-68; Brock, Henry, Forward, 1884; Brockington, Fred, WR, 1980-81; Brooks, Charlie, E, 1954-55-56; Brooks, Kevin, DT, 1982-83-84; Brooks, Todd A., WR, 1995; Brown, Corwin, FS, 1989-90-91-92; Brown, David, S, 1972-73-74; Brown, Demetrius J., QB, 1987-88; Brown, Dennis, QB, 1967-68; Brown, Jeffrey F., TE, 1985-86-87-88; Brown, Henry, C, 1898-1900; Brown, Randolph, HB, 1880; Brown, Rick, MG, 1969; Brown, Robert J., C, 1923-24-25; Brown, Robert M., E, 1961-62; Brown, Woody, C, 1977; Brumbaugh, Phil, DB, 1975; Bryan, Fred, T, 1943; Buff, Ron L., FB, 1992-93; Bunch, Jarrod R., FB, 1987-88-89-90; Burch, Alfie L., CB, 1991-92-93; Burg, George, G, 1944-46; Burgei, Jerry, DB, 1980-81-82; Burgess, Fritz, QB, 1982-83; Burkholder, Marc J., TE, 1990-91-92-93; Burks, Roy, DB, 1972-73; Bush, Eric A., FS, 1988-90; Bushnell, Tom, HB, 1912-13-14; Bushong, Jared, T, 1957-58-59; Bushong, Reid, HB, 1958-59-60; Butler, Dave, G, 1964; Butler, Jack, T, 1940; Butterfield, Tyrone A., WR, 1995; Buzynski, John, C, 1966; Byers, Jim, C, 1956-57-58.

C Cable, Ben, Member, 1874; Cachey, Ted, G, 1952-53-54; Cade, Mike, RB, 1979; Caldarazzo, Dick, OG, 1968-69; Caley, William, HB, 1898; Calindrino, Gaspare, DB, 1978; Call, Norm, HB, 1940; Callahan, Alex, G, 1957-58-59; Callahan, Bob, C, 1945-46; Calloway, Christopher R.., WR, 1987-88-89; Campbell, Charles, HB, 1878-79; Campbell, John Erik, DB, 1984-85-86; Campbell, Mark, TE, 1995; Campbell, Robert, HB, 1935-37; Cannavino, Andy, ILB, 1978-79-80; Cantrill, Cecil, G, 1931-32; Cappon, Frank, FB, 1920-21-22; Caputo, David, F., MG, 1989; Carlson, John D., PK, 1989-90-91; Carpenter, Brian, DB, 1979-80-81; Carpenter, Butch, DE, 1969-70-71; Carpenter, Jack, T, 1946; Carpell, Otto, HB, 1911-12; Carr, Bert, C, 1895-96-97; Carr, Jason L., QB, 1993-94-95; Carr, William, DT, 1993-94-95; Carraway, Winfred, DT, 1979-80-81-82; Carter, Anthony, WR, 1979-80-81-82; Carter, Charles, G, 1902-04; Carthens, Milton, TE, 1982-83; Cartwright, Oscar, E, 1917; Cary, John, E, 1919; Casey, Kevin, QB, 1971; Casey, William, T, 1907-08-09; Catlett, James, HB, 1913-14-15; Cechini, Tom, C, 1963-64-65; Ceddia, John, QB, 1976; Cederberg, Jon, TB, 1973; Ceithaml, George, QB, 1940-41-42; Cernak, Robert A.., TE, 1987; Chadbourne, Tom, C, 1890; Chandler, Bob, QB, 1961-62-63; Chapman, Gil, WB,

1972-73-74; Chapman, Harvey Sr., E, 1932-33; Chapman, Harvey Jr., HB, 1961-62-63; Chappuis, Bob, HB, 1942-46-47; Charles, Jean-Agnus, CB, 1992-93-94-95; Chase, John, Rusher/HB, 1878-79-80; Cherry, John, OT, 1973; Chester, David D., OG, 1985-86-87-88; Chiames, George, G, 1945; Christian, Chuck;1979-80, , TE; Chubb, Ralph, HB, 1944-46; Cipa, Larry, QB, 1971-72-73; Clancy, Jack, E, 1963-65-66; Clark, Fay, FB, 1909; Clark, Oswald, E, 1948-49-50; Clark, William, E, 1904-05; Clayton, Ralph, WB, 1977-78-79; Clement, Carl, C, 1906; Cline, Dan;1952-53-54, , HB; Coakley, Gary, SE, 1971-72; Cochran, Bradley M., DB, 1983-84-85; Cochran, William, T, 1913-14-15; Cocozzo, Joseph T., OT, 1989-90-91-92; Cohen, Jeff, DB, 1980-82-83; Cohn, Abe, HB, 1917-18-20; Coin, Dana, K/LB, 1969-70-71; Colby, Branch, Member, 1876; Cole, Harry, T, 1912; Cole, Walter, , 1913 ; Cole, Wheaton, T, 1910; Coleman, Don, DE, 1972-73; Coles, Cedric, DT, 1979-80-81; Collette, William, HB, 1912; Collins, Jerry, SE, 1975; Collins, Shawn, OLB, 1992; Collins, Todd S., QB, 1991-92-93-94; Conklin, Fredric, T, 1909-10-11; Conley, Jim, E, 1962-63-64; Conlin, John, T, 1951-52; Coode, Jim, OT, 1971-72-73; Cooper, Evan, DB, 1980-81-82-83; Cooper, Keith B., OLB, 1987; Cooper, Pierre, TE, 1993-94; Cooper, Robert, HB, 1936; Copeland, Ernie, Member, 1876; Copenhaver, Clint, LB, 1995; Corbin, Scott, FB, 1974-75; Corey, George, HB, 1954-55; Cornwell, Arthur, C, 1910; Cornwell, Francis, E, 1928-29-30; Corona, Clement, G, 1955-56; Cowan, Keith, E, 1959-60; Cowan, Keith, OLB, 1984-85; Cox, Roderick, FB, 1930-32; Coyle, Tom, OG, 1970-71-72; Cragin, Raymond, C, 1928; Craig, Jim, HB, 1911-12-13; Crandell, John, C, 1943; Crane, Fenwick, E, 1943-46; Craw, Garvie, FB, 1967-68-69; Cress, Elmer, C, 1919; Crumpacker, Maurice, T, 1908; Cruse, William, HB/FB, 1917-18-19; Culligan, Bill, HB, 1944-46; Culver, Frank, G/C, 1917-19; Cunningham, Leo, T, 1941; Cunningham, William, C, 1896-97-98-99; Curran, Louis, E, 1921-22-23; Curtis, Guy, T, 1959-60-61; Curtis, John, T, 1903-04-05-06; Curtis, Tom, DB, 1967-68-69; Czak, Edward, E, 1939-40; Czarnota, Mike, ILB, 1981; Czirr, Jim, C, 1973-74-75; Czysz, Frank, G, 1918-19.

Dahlem, Alvin, B, 1928-29; Daley, Bill, FB, 1943; Dames, Michael K., OG, 1985-86-87-88; Damm, Russell, T, 1932; Danhof, Jerome, C, 1966; Daniels, John, SE, 1970-72; Daniels, Norm, E, 1929-30-31; Darden, Thom, DB, 1969-70-71; Daugherty, Douglas R., OG, 1989; Davies, Jim, T, 1955-56-57; Davis, Edward D., TB, 1992-93-94-95; Davis, J. Nathaniel, TB, 1982; Davis, Martin J., OLB, 1989-90-91-92; Davis, Rickey, WR, 1982; Davis, Russell, FB, 1975-76-77-78; Davis, Tim, MG, 1973-74-75; Davison, Samuel, FB, 1908; Day, Floyd, G, 1965; Day, Mike;1973, , LB; Dayton, Joe, C, 1965-66-67; Deacon, Andy, Member , 1876-77-78; Dean, Walter, FB, 1921; DeBaker, Charles, HB, 1930-31-32; Decker, Daniel J., QB, 1983; DeFelice, Vincent, DT, 1982-83-84; DeHaven, George, E, 1887-88-89; Dehlin, Chuck, LB, 1963-64-66; DeLong, Nathan, P-PK, 1995; DeMassa, Tom, G, 1959; DenBoer, Greg, TE, 1972-73-74; Denby, Edwin, C, 1895; Dendrinos, Peter, T, 1947; Denson, Damon M., OG/DT, 1993-94-95; Denzin, John, C, 1968; DePont, Edward, Substitute, 1891-92; DePuy, Richard, Rusher, 1878-79-80-81-82; DePuy, William, Substitute, 1881; D'Eramo, Paul, C, 1965-66; Derricotte, Gene, HB, 1944-46-47-48; Derleth, Robert, T, 1942-43-45-46; DeSantis, Mark, OLB, 1976-77-78; Deskins, Don, T, 1958-59; DeStafano, Guy, FB, 1960; Detwiler, Jim, HB, 1964-65-66; Dever, David S., OG, 1987; Devich, David, LB, 1974-75; Dewey, Syd, G, 1924-25-26; Dickey, B.J., QB, 1977-78-79-81; Dickey, Jim, C, 1956-57-58; Diebolt, David B., TE, 1988-89-90-91; Dierdorf, Dan, OT, 1968-69-70; Diggs, Gerald, DB, 1978-79-80; Dingman, Bob, E, 1951-52; Dingman, Dean R., OG, 1987-88-89-90; Diorio, Jerry, OG, 1980-82-83;

Dixon, Tom, C, 1980-81-82-83; Doane, Tom, LB, 1968; Dobreff, David A., ILB, 1990-92; Dodd, Bill, HB, 1962-63; Doherty, Robert C., OT, 1989-90-91-92; Dohring, Thomas E., OT, 1987-88-89-90; Domhoff, Vic, QB/HB, 1924-26-27; Donahue, Mark, OG, 1975-76-77; Dorn, Edward, Forward, 1884; Dott, Richard, HB, 1880; Dottin, Lance D., DB, 1988-89-90-91; Doty, Alfred, SB, 1967; Dotzauer, Barry, DB, 1971-72-73; Dougall, William, QB, 1961; Douglass, Leslie, G, 1930-31; Douglass, Prentiss, HB, 1908; Doughty, Glenn, WB, 1969-70-71; Downing, Walt, C, 1975-76-77; Drake, Tom, DB, 1971-73-74; Draveling, Leo, T, 1928-29-30; Drehmann, Peter, OT, 1967-68; Dreisbach, Scott, QB, 1995; Dreyer, Walter, HB, 1943; Drumheller, Tom, QB, 1895-96; Dudlar, Gannon, DT/OLB, 1991-92-93; Duerr, John M., OLB, 1987; Dufek, Bill, OT, 1974-75-76-78; Dufek, Don E., FB, 1948-49-50; Dufek, Don P., WB, 1973-74-75; Duff, William, HB, 1884; Duffy, Ignatius, FB, 1896; Duffy, James, Goalkeeper, 1885; Duffy, John, HB, 1885-86-87-88; Duffy, Mark, C, 1971; Dugger, Don, G, 1951-52-53; Dunaway, Craig, TE, 1980-81-82; Dunleavy, George, FB, 1922; Dunn, John, QB, 1920; Dunn, Roland, T, 1916-19; Dunne, Maurice, E, 1914-15-16; Dunne, Robert, E, 1918-19-20-21; Dutcher, Jerry, DB, 1970; Dutter, George, E, 1952-53; Dworsky, Dan, C, 1945-46-47-48; Dyer, Horace, HB, 1893-94; Dygert, George, HB, 1891-92-93-94; Dyson, Matt, OLB, 1991-92-93-94.

Eastman, Harry, HB, 1930; Eaton, Don, DE, 1970-71-73; Edmunds, William, T/E, 1909-10; Edwards, R.T., Rusher, 1877-78-79; Edwards, Stan, TB, 1977-79-80-81; Edwards, Thomas, T, 1924-25; Egan, John, Member, 1895; Eldred, Dale, T, 1955; Elezovic, Peter, PK, 1992-93; Elliott, Bruce, DB, 1969-70-71; Elliott, Chalmers Bump, HB, 1946-47; Elliott, Dave, DB, 1971-73-74; Elliott, Eric M., OG/C, 1988-89-90-91; Elliott, John S. Jumbo, OT, 1984-85-86-87; Elliott, Matt, OL, 1991-92; Elliott, Pete, QB, 1945-46-47-48; Ellis, Greg, MG, 1970-71-72; Ellis, Joseph, QB/HB, 1934; Ellison, John L., WR, 1991; Elston, Michael J., OLB, 1994-95; Elzinga, Mark, QB, 1974-75; Embs, William, E, 1907-08; English, Joseph, FB, 1982; Erben, Robert, C, 1948-49; Erhardt, Mark D., OT, 1987; Evans, Michael J., DT, 1988-89-90-91; Evans, Stephen, DT, 1994; Evashevski, Forest Jr., QB, 1962-63-64; Evashevski, Forest Sr., QB, 1938-39-40; Everhardus, Chris, HB, 1934-35; Everhardus, Herman, HB, 1931-32-33; Everitt, Steven M., C, 1989-90-91-92; Eyke, Walter, G/T, 1906.

Farabee, Ben, E, 1962-63-64; Farabee, Dave, HB, 1968; Farmer, Douglas, FB, 1937; Farnham, Thad, E, 1895-96; Farrand, Royal, QB, 1887; Farrer, Dick, C, 1948-49-50; Faul, Larry, G, 1955-56-57; Fay, Stanley, HB, 1931-32-33; Feaster, Curtis C., LB, 1989; Feaster, Rodney, LB, 1978-79-80; Feazell, Juaquin, DT, 1995; Federico, Eric, FB, 1968-69; Fediuk, Art, TE, 1973; Feely, Thomas J., PK, 1995; Felten, Jeff, C, 1979-80; Felver, Howard, QB, 1896-97; Ferbert, Gustave, HB, 1893-94-95-96; Ferens, John A., DB, 1983; Fichtner, Rustin W., LB, 1988-89; Fillichio, Mike, G, 1957-58-59; Finkbeiner, Donald, T, 1919; Fischer, Brad, QB, 1981; Fischer, Robert, G, 1943; Fisher, Dave, FB, 1964-65-66; Fitch, Alan, G, 1949; Fitzgerald, Dennis, HB, 1959-60; Fitzgerald, J. Patrick, WR, 1987; Flanagan, Dennis, G, 1965; Flora, Bob, T, 1939-40-41; Flora, William E, 1924-25-26; Floyd, Christopher M., RB, 1994-95; Folkertsma, David L., DT, 1985-86-87; Foltz, James, FB, 1945; Fonde, Henry, HB, 1945-46-47; Ford, Gerald, C, 1932-33-34; Ford, Len, E, 1945-46-47; Fortune, William, G, 1917-18-19; Foster, Brian W., FS, 1992; Foster, Ché A., FB, 1992-93-94; Fox, Jim, G, 1953-54-55; France, Richard, G, 1898-99; Francis, Al, MG, 1968-69; Franklin, Dennis, QB, 1972-73-74; Franks, Dennis, C, 1972-73-74; Franks, Julius, G, 1941-42; Fraumann, Harlin E, 1940-41; Frazer, Richard, OL, 1984; Freedman, Zack D., SS, 1993;

Freehan, Bill, E, 1960; Freeman, J. Paul, RG, 1918; Freeney, Charles, FB, 1909; Freihofer, Cecil, G, 1944-45; Freihofer, Walt, G, 1942; Freund, Raynor, Reserve, 1892-93-94-95; Friedman, Benny, QB, 1924-25-26; Fritz, Ralph, G, 1938-39-40; Froemke, Gerald, HB, 1917-19; Frutig, Edward, E, 1938-39-40; Frysinger, Terry, DT, 1968; Fuller, Frederic, HB, 1925-27; Fuog, Russell, C, 1932-33-34.

Gabel, Norman, T, 1925-26-27; Gabler, John, WB, 1967-68-69; Gabler, Wally, QB, 1965; Gagalis, Peri, FB, 1952-53-54; Gallagher, Dave, DT, 1971-72-73; Gallagher, John, G, 1943; Galt, Martin, HB, 1913; Gant, Anthony K., DB, 1982-83-84-85-86; Garbar, Jesse, G, 1935-36; Garfield, Stephen, T, 1922; Garrels, Allen, G/E, 1911; Garrels, John, E, 1905-06; Garrett, Edward, FB, 1982-83-84; Garrity, Tom, OT, 1979-81-82; Gasperoni, Sergio, TE, 1993; Gear, Kenney, WR, 1980; Gedeon, Elmer, E, 1936-37-38; Geistert, Walter, HB, 1928; Gembis, Joseph, B, 1927-28-29; Gemmell, Robert, HB, 1882-83; Genebach, Lowell, QB, 1917; Genyk, George, G, 1957-58-59; Geyer, Ron, T, 1952-53-54; Ghindia, John, QB, 1948-49; Ghindia, John, OG, 1984; Giesler, Jon, OT, 1976-77-78; Gilbert, Louis, HB, 1925-26-27; Gill, David, E, 1899; Gillette, V. Michael, PK, 1985-86-87-88; Gilmore, Tom, Goalkeeper, 1881-82-83; Girgash, Paul, ILB, 1979-80-81-82; Glidden, Steve, E, 1889; Glinka, Dave, QB, 1960-61-62; Godfrey, Chris, DT, 1977-78-79; Goebel, Jerry, C, 1954-55-57; Goebel, Paul, E, 1920-21-22; Goetz, Angus, E, 1917-18-19-20; Goldsmith, DuVal, T, 1931; Gooding, Cecil, G, 1903; Goodwell, John;1916-17, , T; Goodwin, Harold R., OG, 1995; Gorte, Mike, HB, 1964; Goss, Tom, DT, 1966-67-68; Gottschalk, Luther, Substitute, 1885; Gracey, Clifford, G, 1916; Graham, Walter, T, 1904-05-06-07; Grambau, Fred, DT, 1969-71-72; Grant, James J., ILB, 1986-87-88-89; Grant, Todd, C, 1959-60-61; Graver, Herb, E, 1901-02-03; Graves, Steve, MG, 1976-77; Graves, W. Eric, MG, 1992; Gray, Jim, T, 1958; Gray, Joseph, MG, 1982-83-84; Grbac, Elvis, QB, 1989-90-91-92; Green, Donald, FB, 1909-10; Green, Jim, C, 1962-63; Green, Merritt, E, 1950-51-52; Greene, John, T, 1943; Greenleaf, George, , 1893-94-95-96; Greenwald, Harold, HB, 1926; Greenwood, John, HB, 1955-56; Greer, Curtis, DT, 1976-77-78-79; Greer, Edward, E, 1944; Gregory, Bruce, HB, 1924-25; Gregory, George, C, 1901-02-03; Griese, Brian D., QB, 1994-95; Griffin, Charles, C, 1891-92-93; Grinnell, Henry, T, 1926-27; Groce, Alvin, HB, 1957-58; Grosh, Lawrence, HB, 1890-91-92-93; Grube, Charles, E, 1923-24-25; Gusich, Frank, WB, 1969-70-71; Gustafson, Larry, WB, 1971-72-73; Gutzwiller, Mark G., DB, 1988; Guynes, Thomas V., OG/OT, 1993-94-95.

Hackett, Jim, C, 1976; Hadden, Harry, T, 1894; Hagle, Anson, T, 1888-89; Hahn, Richard, G, 1962-63-64; Hainrihar, Gary, OG, 1972-73; Haji-Sheikh, Ali, PK, 1979-80-81-82; Hall, Ben, G, 1959-60-61; Hall, David, QB, 1982-83; Hall, Forrest, G, 1895; Hall, James, OT, 1974-75; Hall, Werner, OG, 1968-69-70; Halstead, John, E, 1958-59-60; Hamilton, Remy M., PK, 1994-95; Hammels, James, T, 1919; Hammerstein, Mark S., OT, 1983-84-85-86; Hammerstein, Mike, OT, 1981-82-83-84-85; Hammond, Harry, E, 1904-05-06-07; Hammond, Thomas, HB, 1903-04-05; Hanish, Joseph, HB, 1916-17; Hankins, Woodrow, TB, 1993-94-95; Hankwitz, Mike, TE, 1967-68-69; Hanlon, Mickey, WR, 1982; Hanna, Henry, OG, 1965; Hannah, Don, QB, 1959-60; Hannan, Frederic, FB, 1897; Hanshue, Cloyce, G, 1934-35; Hanzlik, Robert, T, 1943; Harbaugh, James J., QB, 1983-84-85-86; Harden, Linwood, DB, 1972; Harden, Mike, DB, 1977-78-79; Harding, Dave, ILB, 1977; Harding, Frank, C, 1892-93; Hardy, William, OT, 1965-66; Harless, William, G, 1886-87-90; Harmon, Tom, HB, 1938-39-40; Harper, Darrell, HB, 1957-58-59; Harpring, Jack, OT, 1968-69-70; Harrigan, Frank, HB, 1927;

Harris, Stu, DB, 1978-79-81; Harris, Bill, SE, 1968-69-70; Harris, William F., MG, 1984-85-86-87; Harrison, Greg, DB, 1970; Hart, Bill, C, 1970-71-72; Hartman, Jerry, DB, 1966-67-68; Haslerig, Clint, WB, 1971-72-73; Hassel, Richard A., DB, 1986-87-88; Hassel, Tom, OLB, 1980-81-82-83; Hatheway, E., FB, 1880; Hawkins, Harry, G, 1923-24-25; Hayden, Edward, T, 1929; Hayes, Mercury, WR, 1992-93-94-95; Hayes, Ralph, E, 1891; Hayman, Wayne, Member, 1873; Haynes, Gary Duke, FB, 1982; Healy, Brian, DB, 1967-68-69; Heater, Chuck, FB, 1972-73-74; Heath, William, T/FB, 1926; Hedding, Kevin A., TE, 1991; Heffelfinger, Jon, DE, 1967; Heikkinen, Ralph, G, 1937-38; Hendershot, Fred, RE, 1916-17-18; Henderson, Anthony J., MG, 1991-92-93-94; Henderson, John, E, 1963-64; Henderson, William, E, 1919; Hendricks, Tom, HB, 1954-55; Heneveld, Lloyd, G, 1947-48-49; Hennessy, John, DT, 1974-75-76; Henning, Charles, Member, 1877; Henninger, Fred, T, 1893-94-95-96; Henry, Preston, WB, 1969-70; Heren, Dieter E., DB, 1983-84-85-86; Herrala, Scott W., DB, 1987; Herrick, David, OT/DT, 1984-85; Herrmann, Jim, ILB, 1980-81-82; Herrmann, John H., DT, 1986-87-88; Herrnstein, A.E., HB, 1901-02; Herrnstein, John, FB, 1956-57-58; Herrnstein, William, HB/E, 1923-24-25; Hershberger, Don, E, 1945-46-47-48; Hess, John, T, 1949-50; Heston, John, HB, 1931-32-33; Heston, LeRoy, E, 1926-27; Heston, William Jr., HB, 1929-30; Heston, Willie, HB, 1901-02-03-04; Hetzler, Howard, Substitute, 1885; Hewitt, William, E, 1929-30-31; Hewlett, Rich, DB, 1979-80-82-83; Heynen, Dick, T, 1955-56-57; Hickey, Ed, HB, 1953-54-55; Hicks, Dwight, S, 1974-75-76-77; Hicks, Ivan L., DB, 1984-85-86; Higgins, Francis, Forward, 1885-86; Higgins, Kenneth E., SE, 1985-86; Hidlebrand, Willard H., G/T, 1932-33-34; Hidlebrand, Willard R., T, 1958-59-60; Hilkene, Bruce, T, 1944-46-47; Hill, Dave, FB, 1954-55; Hill, Henry, MG, 1968-69-70; Hill, Richard, G, 1954-55-56; Hinton, Gene, T, 1945-49; Hirsch, Elroy, HB, 1943; Hoard, Leroy, FB/TB, 1987-88-89; Hoban, Bill, DT, 1972-73-75; Hoban, Mike, OG, 1971-72-73; Hoey, George, DB, 1967-68; Hoffman, Leo, QB, 1926-27; Hogg, James, FB, 1896-97; Holden, George, QB, 1890; Holdren, Nathan T., ILB, 1991-92; Holgate, Jim, HB, 1943; Holland, Joseph H., OLB, 1986-87-88; Hollis, Pete, QB, 1965; Hollister, John, HB, 1893-95; Hollway, Bob, E, 1947-48-49; Hollway, Bob K., OLB, 1978; Holmes, Daniel, G, 1928; Holmes, Mike, DE, 1974-75; Holtry, Jeff, OLB, 1994; Hood, Ed, HB, 1961-62; Hood, Edward J., DB, 1985; Hook, Wally, FB, 1936-38; Hooper, James, G, 1895; Horn, Jason R., DT, 1992-93-94-95; Horn, T. Chris, RB, 1988; Horton, Walter, QB, 1880-81; Houtman, John, T, 1960-61-63; Howard, Christopher L., RB, 1994-95; Howard, Derek, DB, 1974-75-76-77; Howard, Desmond K., WR, 1989-90-91; Howell, Frank, HB, 1950-51-52; Howell, George W., ILB/FB, 1994-95; Hoyne, Jeff, E, 1963-64-65; Hozer, Stan, HB/E, 1928-30-31; Hribal, Jim, OT, 1966; Huckleby, Harlan, TB, 1975-76-77-78; Hudson, Roy, FB, 1929-30-31; Huebel, Herbert, QB, 1911-12; Huff, Benjamin J., DT/OLB, 1994-95; Huff, Marty, LB, 1968-69-70; Hughitt, Ernest, QB, 1913-14-15; Huiskens, Tom, TE, 1970; Hulbert, Bruce, T, 1928; Hulke, Scott, OT, 1971; Hull, G.M., G, 1888; Humphries, Derrick, OE, 1966; Humphries, Jim, MG, 1978; Humphries, Stefan, OG, 1980-81-82-83; Hurley, Bob, FB, 1952-53; Husar, Michael A., OT, 1985-86-87-88; Hutchinson, Christopher H., DT, 1989-90-91-92; Hutchinson, Loomis, E, 1897; Hynes, Michael L., DB, 1994.

Imsland, Jerry, SE, 1968-69; Ingalls, Don, C, 1939-40-41; Ingram, Jerald, FB, 1979-80-81; Irons, Jarrett D., ILB, 1993-94-95.

Jackson, Allen, G, 1948-49-50; Jackson, Norm, FB, 1950; Jackson, Tony, DB, 1978-79-80-81; Jackson, William, DT, 1976; Jacobson, Tage, T, 1933-34; Jacoby, Mark, WB, 1974; Jaeckin, John P., TE, 1992-93; James,

Doug, OG, 1981-82-83-84; James, Efton, E, 1913; James, Hugh, QB, 1903; James, John, , 1903; Janke, Fred, T, 1936-37-38; Jansen, Jon, OT, 1995; Jaycox, John, HB, 1884-85-86; Jefferis, A.W., Substitute, 1891-92; Jefferson, Allen L., TB, 1987-88-89-90; Jenkins, Trezelle, OT, 1992-93-94; Jennings, Ferris, QB, 1934; Jensen, Tom, OG, 1973-74-75; Jewett, George, HB, 1890-92; Jilek, Dan, DE, 1973-74-75; Jobson, Tom, T, 1958-59-60; Johns, James, T, 1920-21-22; Johnson, Deon, CB, 1991-92-93-94; Johnson, Earl, FB, 1955; Johnson, Ernest, E, 1935; Johnson, Farnham, E, 1943; Johnson, Gene, TE, 1975-76-77-78; Johnson, George, T, 1945-47; Johnson, Gilvanni, WR, 1984-85; Johnson, Irvin, ILB, 1979; Johnson, Jesse W., TB, 1991-92; Johnson, Keith, DE, 1973-74-75; Johnson, Larry, DE, 1973-74; Johnson, Livetius H., WR, 1991; Johnson, Oliver, OLB, 1980; Johnson, Paul, OT, 1965-67; Johnson, Raymond, DB, 1977; Johnson, Robert, E, 1958-59-60; Johnson, Ron, RB, 1966-67-68; Johnson, Roy, T, 1919; Johnson, Stacy, QB, 1976; Johnson, Steven, DB/WB, 1982; Johnson, Tom, T, 1949-50-51; Johnson, Walt, E, 1956-57-58; Johnston, Collins, HB, 1878-81; Johnston, Jim, WB, 1972; Jokisch, Daniel E., TE/WB, 1988-89-90; Jokisch, Paul H., SE, 1984-85-86; Jolly, Mike, DB, 1976-77-78-79; Jones, Dennis, HB, 1962; Jones, Joe, LB, 1969; Jones, Paul, FB, 1902; Jordan, Forrest, G, 1939; Jordan, John, C, 1936; Julian, Fred, HB, 1957-58-59; Juttner, Charles, Reserve, 1897-99.

K Kadela, Dave, OT, 1977; Kamhout, Carl, T, 1955; Kampe, Kurt Jr., G, 1947; Kampe, Kurt III, DB, 1974-75; Kane, Gary, E, 1958-59; Karpus, Arthur, HB, 1918; Karwales, Jack, E, 1941-42; Kasparek, Ed, WR, 1978; Kattus, Eric, TE, 1981-83-84-85; Kayner, Howard, T/G, 1911; Keating, Tom, T, 1961-62-63; Keating, Bill, G, 1964-65; Kee, Tom, LB, 1970-71-72; Keefer, Jackson, HB, 1922; Keena, Leo, FB, 1897-99; Keitz, Dale, DT, 1977-78-79; Keller, Mike, DE, 1969-70-71; Keller, Tom, OLB, 1979; Kelsey, Ray, G, 1949-50-51; Kelto, Reuben, T, 1939-40-41; Kemp, Stan, E, 1964-65-66; Kempthorn, Dick, FB, 1947-48-49; Kenaga, Ray, QB, 1953; Kenn, Mike, OT, 1975-76-77; Kennedy, Charles, HB, 1942; Kennedy, Ted, C, 1940-41; Kennedy, Robert, T, 1943; Keough, Kelly, DT, 1980; Kern, Frank, T, 1943; Kerr, Tom, C, 1960; Ketterman, Dick, E, 1957; Key, David R., DB, 1987-88-89-90; Khan, Gulam A., PK, 1989; Kiesel, George, QB, 1947; Kieta, Bob, RB, 1968; Killian, Tim, K/OG, 1968-69-70; Killiea, Henry, C, 1884; Kines, Chuck, T, 1964-65; King, Kevin, FB, 1976-77; King, Steven R., OT, 1973-74-75; King, Stephen L., FS, 1993-94-95; Kinyon, Pete, G, 1950-51; Kipke, Harry, HB, 1921-22-23; Kirby, Craig, E, 1963-64-65; Kirk, Bernard, E, 1921-22; Kiskadden, Alex, Forward, 1886; Knickerbocker, Stan, HB, 1952-54-55; Knight, David M., WR, 1989; Knode, Ken, QB, 1918-19; Knode, Robert, QB/HB, 1921; Knuth, Eric C., MG, 1990; Knutson, Gene, E, 1951-52-53; Kocan, Ron, E, 1962; Koceski, Leo, HB, 1948-49-50; Kodros, Archie, C, 1937-38-39; Kohl, Harry, HB, 1940; Kohl, Ralph, T, 1947-48; Kolesar, Bob, G, 1940-41-42; Kolesar, John C., WR, 1985-86-87-88; Kolesar, William, T, 1953-54-55; Korowin, Jim, E, 1959-61; Koschalk, Rick, MG, 1974-75; Koss, Greg, S, 1972-73; Kovacevich, Dave, G, 1962-63; Kovacs, Louis, DB, 1962; Kowalik, John Jr., HB, 1962; Kowalik, John, G, 1931-32-33; Kraeger, George, G, 1943-46; Kramer, Jon, DE, 1966-67; Kramer, Melvin, T, 1935; Kramer, Ron, E, 1954-55-56; Krauss, Michael G., OG, 1985; Kreager, Carl, C, 1949-50; Krejsa, Bob, HB, 1940; Kress, Ted, HB, 1952-53; Kromer, Paul, HB, 1938-39-40; Krueger, Fred, E, 1957; Kuick, Don, HB, 1947; Kunow, Walter, T, 1923-24; Kunsa, Joe, OG, 1968; Kupec, C.J., TE, 1972; Kurtz, Dave, G, 1961-62-63; Kuzma, Tom, HB, 1941-42.

L Labun, Nick, PK, 1977; LaFountaine, Sean, DB, 1987-88; Laine, John, G, 1941; LaJeunesse, Omer, G, 1930-31; Lambert, Oscar, C, 1917; Landsittel, Tom, OG, 1966; Lang, Bob, OT, 1974-75-76; Lantry, Mike, PK, 1972-73-74; Laskey, Bill, E, 1962-63-64; Lavine, Louis, QB, 1936-37-38; Law, Tajuan E. Ty, CB, 1992-93-94; Lawrence, James, FB, 1902; Lawton, George, FB, 1910; Lazetich, Milan, C, 1944; Leach, Rick, QB, 1975-76-77-78; LeClaire, Larry, FB, 1950-51-52; Lee, Louis, DB, 1964-65-66; Legette, Burnie A., FB, 1989-90-91-92; Lehr, John, T, 1961; Leith, Jerry, HB, 1959; Lemirande, Mike, OLB, 1979-80-81-82; Lentz, Charlie, HB, 1948-49; Leonard, H.B., HB, 1892-93-94; Leoni, Mike, OT, 1978-79; Leoni, Tony, TB, 1978-79; LeRoux, Art, T, 1944; Lessner, Donald G., DB, 1987; Lewandowski, Phillip, ILB, 1984; Lewis, Kirk, OG, 1973-74-76; Lewis, Michael J., OT, 1992; Lightner, Henry, E, 1913; Lilja, George, C, 1977-78-79-80; Lincoln, James, T, 1935-36; Lindsay, Rock, OG, 1978; Linthicum, Frank, E, 1908-09-10; Linton, John, G, 1944-45-46; Lockard, Harold, HB, 1940-41; Loell, John, FB, 1906-07; Logan, Randy, DB, 1971-72; Logas, Phillip L., SE, 1986; Logue, Ben, RB, 1983-84; Longman, Frank, FB, 1903-04-05; Lott, John, DB, 1980-81-82-83; Loucks, Alvin, G, 1919; Lousma, Jack, QB, 1956; Lovell, Erik, PK, 1992-94; Lovette, John, G, 1925-26; Luby, Earle, T, 1935-36-37; Lukz, Joe, OG, 1969; Lund, Don, FB, 1942-43-44; Lyall, Jim, DT, 1973; Lyles, Rodney, OLB, 1982-83-84; Lynch, John, DB, 1968; Lyons, John, E, 1913-14; Lytle, Rob, TB, 1974-75-76.

M Mace, William, Member, 1882; Mack, Hugh, QB, 1943; Mack, Tom, T, 1964-65; Mackall, Rex, ILB, 1975-76; MacPhee, Bill, C, 1958; MacPherran, Ed, HB, 1887-88-89; Madar, Elmer, E, 1941-42-46; Maddock, Jim, QB, 1954-55-56; Maddock, Joseph, T, 1902-03; Mader, Jerry, T, 1962-63-64; Madsen, Edgar, E, 1924; Maentz, Scott, E, 1959-60-61; Maentz, Tom, E, 1954-55-56; Magidsohn, Joe, HB, 1909-10; Magoffin, Paul, HB, 1905-06-07; Mair, Peter, OT, 1966-67; Malinak, Tim, ILB, 1978; Mallory, Curtis S., ILB, 1989; Mallory, Douglas S., DB, 1984-85-86-87; Mallory, Mike, ILB, 1982-83-84-85; Maloney, Frank, C, 1961; Maloney, Patrick M., SS, 1990-91-92; Malveaux, Felman, WR, 1991-92; Mandel, David M., TE, 1987; Mandel, Scott H., TE, 1987; Mandich, Jim, TE, 1967-68-69; Mann, Bob, E, 1946-47; Manning, Paul J., OG/C, 1991-92; Mans, George, E, 1959-60-61; Manuel, Warde J., DT, 1987-88; Marciniak, Jerry, T, 1956-57-58; Marcovsky, Abraham, G, 1932; Marcum, John, G, 1962-63-64; Marinaro, Joseph C., OG, 1992-93-94-95; Marion, Bob, G, 1954-55; Marion, Phillip, FB, 1923-24; Markray, Triando, WR, 1983-84; Marks, Tom, G, 1900; Marsh, Doug, TE, 1977-78-79; Marshall, Alex C., DT, 1988-89-90-91; Martens, Albert, E, 1916; Marzonie, George A., 1936-37; Matheson, Bob, G, 1951-52; Maulbetsch, John, HB, 1914-15-16; Maves, Earl, FB, 1943; Mayes, Eric, DB, 1995; McBride, Jack, QB, 1970; McClelland, Don, G, 1947-48-49; McCoy, Dick, DT, 1968-69-70; McCoy, Ernie, HB, 1957; McCoy, Matthew S., DT, 1989; McDonald, Charles, T, 1898-99; McDonald, Duncan, QB, 1951-52-53-54; McGee, Tony L., TE, 1989-90-91-92; McGugin, Dan, G, 1901-02; McHale, Frank, G, 1913-14; McIntyre, A. Andree, ILB, 1984-85-86-87; McIntyre, Kent, G, 1926; McKean, Tom, E, 1890; McKenzie, Reggie, OG, 1969-70-71; McLean, John, HB, 1898-99; McLenna, Bruce, HB, 1961; McMillan, Neil, QB , 1910-11; McMurtry, Gregory W., SE, 1986-87-88-89; McNeal, Tom, QB, 1883-84-85; McNeill, Ed, E, 1945-46-47-48; McNitt, Gary, FB, 1958-59-60; McPhearson, Jim, QB, 1959; McRae, Bennie, HB, 1959-60-61; McThomas, Gregory, OLB, 1991-92; McWilliams, Dick, G, 1949-50; Meads, Ed, T, 1953-54-55; Meek, Richard, FB, 1911; Mehaffey, Howard, G, 1938-44; Melchiori, Wayne, C, 1952; Melita, Tom, MG, 1977; Melnyk, Michel, PK, 1984; Melzow, William, G, 1939-40-41; Mercer, Brian, TB, 1982-83; Meredith, David, DT, 1982-83-84; Messner, Mark W., DT, 1985-86-87-88; Meter, Jerry, ILB, 1976-77-78; Metz, Dave,

OG, 1972-73-74; Meyer, Jack, QB, 1938; Meyers, Earl, HB, 1935; Middlebrook, John, LB, 1971; Mielke, Bob, DT, 1964-65-66; Mihic, John H., OL, 1985; Miklos, Jerry, DG, 1966-67-68; Miles, Les, OG, 1974-75; Milia, Marc J., C, 1991-92-93; Miller, Clay, OT, 1981-82-83-84-85; Miller, James R., QB, 1925-26-27; Miller, James J., RE/QB, 1907-09; Miller, James K., QB, 1923-24; Miller, Shawn C., OG, 1991-92-93; Miller, Wallace, T, 1930; Milligan, John D., ILB, 1987-88-89-90; Minko, John, G, 1960-61-62; Mitchell, Alan, WR, 1978-79-80; Mitchell, Anthony L., DB, 1987-88; Mitchell, Charles, Goalkeeper, 1878-79; Mitchell, Keith A., TE, 1987-88; Moeller, Andrew G., ILB, 1982-84-85-86; Molenda, John, FB, 1925-26; Momsen, Anton, C, 1945-46-49-50; Monthei, Dennis, MG, 1967; Moons, Patrick J., PK, 1985-86; Moore, Albert, HB, 1883; Moore, Ed, LB, 1968-69-70; Moorhead, Don, QB, 1968-69-70; Morgan, Dennis, LB, 1965-66-67; Morgan, Robert, T/E, 1930; Morris, James W., TB, 1984-85-86-87; Morrison, Chester, RT, 1917-18; Morrison, Maynard, C, 1929-30-31; Morrison, Steven C., ILB, 1990-91-92-93-94; Morrow, Gordon, C, 1957; Morrow, John, T, 1953-54-55; Morrow, William, QB, 1885-86; Morton, Greg, DT, 1974-75-76; Morton, Leon D., DB, 1990; Mouton, Kenneth L., DB, 1986; Mowrey, Harry, T, 1891; Mroz, Vincent, E, 1943; Muelder, Wesley, HB, 1945; Muir, William, C, 1962-64; Muirhead, Stan, T, 1921-22-23; Muransky, Ed, OT, 1979-80-81; Murdock, Guy, C, 1969-70-71; Murray, Vada, FS, 1988-89-90; Musser, James, C, 1912-13; Mutch, Craig, LB, 1972-73; Myers, Brad, HB, 1957-58-59; Myll, Clifton, E, 1943.

N Naab, Fred, T, 1943; Nadlicki, Michael A., FB/OLB, 1992; Nauta, Steve, C, 1975-76-78; Neal, Tom, OT, 1981; Needham, Ben, ILB, 1978-79-81; Negus, Fred, C/T, 1943; Neisch, LeRoy, E, 1921-22-23; Nelson, David, HB, 1940-41; Nelson, Doug, SB, 1967; Nelson, Sim, TE, 1982-83-84; Nelson, Viggo, FB, 1920; Newell, Pete, DT, 1968-69-70; Newman, Harry Jr., HB, 1958-59; Newman, Harry Sr., QB, 1930-31-32; Newton, Fred, E/T, 1906; Nicholson, John, E, 1937-38-39; Nicolau, Dave, DT, 1979-80; Nielsen, Paul, E, 1939; Nieman, Tom, TE, 1970; Niemann, Walter, C, 1915-16; Ninde, Daniel, G, 1894; Noble, Tyrone L., CB, 1994; Nolan, Del, G, 1961; Norcross, Fred, QB, 1903-04-05; Norton, John, , 1951; Noskin, Stan, QB, 1957-58-59; Nunley, Frank, LB, 1964-65-66; Nussbaumer, Bob, HB, 1943-44-45; Nyland, Herman, E, 1926-27; Nyren, Mary, G, 1955-56-57.

O Oade, James, T, 1925; O'Donnell, Joe, G, 1960-62-63; Ohlenroth, Bill, T, 1948-49-50; Olcott, William, FB, 1881; Oldham, Don, HB, 1950-51-52; Oldham, Mike, SE, 1969-70-71; Olds, Fred, G, 1937-38-39; Oliver, Russ, FB, 1932-33-34; Olshanski, Henry, E, 1943; Olszewski, Patrick J., OT, 1988; O'Neal, Calvin, LB, 1974-75-76; Oosterbaan, Bennie, E, 1925-26-27; Oppman, Doug, G, 1958; Ortmann, Chuck, HB, 1948-49-50; Orwig, Jim, T, 1955-56-57; Osbun, Tony, DT, 1980-81; O'Shaughnessy, Dick, C, 1951-52-53; Osman, Todd J., DT, 1987-88-89-90; Osterman, Russ, E, 1950-51; Owen, Kevin D., WR, 1990; Owens, Mel, OLB, 1977-79-80.

P Pace, Jim, HB, 1955-56-57; Padjen, John, C, 1950; Page, Craig, TB, 1978; Palmaroli, John, G, 1926-27; Palmer, Paul, QB, 1959; Palmer, Pete, QB, 1950; Palomaki, Dave, T, 1960; Parini, Sean A., OLB, 1994-95; Paris, William Bubba, OT, 1978-79-80-81; Parker, Fred, HB, 1924-25; Parker, Noah, OG, 1995; Parker, Ray, G, 1929; Parkhill, Tom, E, 1965; Parks, Dan, DT, 1968-69; Partchenko, John M., OT, 1994-95; Patanelli, Matt, E, 1934-35-36; Patchen, Brian, C, 1963-64; Paterson, George, C, 1911-12-13; Patrick, Harry, T, 1905-06; Pattengill, Vic, RE, 1909-10; Paul, Louis, HB, 1893-93; Pavloff, Lou, G, 1959-62; Payne, David, ILB, 1979; Payne, Reginald G., C, 1993-94-95; Peach, Willard, E,

1916-19; Pearson, William, Substitute, 1891-92-93; Peckham, John, C, 1953-54-55; Pederson, Bernhardt, T, 1951-52; Pederson, Chip, TE, 1978; Pederson, Ernest, G, 1935-37; Penksa, Bob, OT, 1967-68; Peoples, Shonte, SS, 1991-92-93; Peristeris, Paul A., P, 1995; Perlinger, Jeff, DT, 1973-74-75; Perrin, John, HB, 1920; Perry, Lowell, E, 1950-51-52; Perryman, Robert L., FB, 1983-84-85-86; Peterson, Donald, HB, 1949-50-51; Peterson, Tom, FB, 1944-47-48-49; Petoskey, Fred, E, 1931-32-33; Petoskey, Jack, E, 1943; Petro, Charles, G, 1921; Petroff, Frank L., DL, 1988; Petterson, Chad M., WR, 1993-94; Phelps, Eric, DE, 1975; Phillips, Ed, FB, 1936-38; Phillips, Ray, OG, 1965-66-67; Picard, Frank, QB, 1910-11; Pickard, Frederick P., E, 1949-50-51; Pickens, Jim, DB, 1975-76-77; Pierson, Barry, DB, 1967-68-69; Pighee, John, S, 1972; Plate, S. Troy, OT, 1992; Plate, William T., DB, 1988-89-90; Poe, Howard, G, 1927-28-29; Pommerening, Otto, T, 1927-28; Pond, Irving, Rusher, 1879; Ponsetto, Joseph, QB, 1943-44-45; Pontius, Miller, E, 1911-12-13; Poorman, Edwin, T, 1928-29; Poplawski, Tom, OT, 1971-72; Popowski, Robert, OG, 1984; Popp, Herb, E, 1949-50; Porter, Dave, DT, 1966-67; Poulos, Paul, G, 1958-59-60; Powers, Bobby, ILB, 1991-92-93-94; Powers, Hiram, E, 1891-92-93; Powers, John, G, 1949-50; Powers, John J., OG, 1977-78-80; Powers, Richard A., TB, 1990-91-92-93; Prahst, Gary, E, 1956-57-58; Prashaw, Milton, C, 1945; Pregulman, Mervin, C/T, 1941-42-43; Prettyman, Horace, Member, 1882-83-85-86-88-89-90; Prichard, Tom, QB, 1961-62-63; Pritula, Bill, T, 1942-46-47; Pryce, Trevor N., OLB, 1993-94; Pryor, Cecil, DE, 1968-69; Przygodski, George, TE, 1973-74-75; Ptacek, Bob, HB, 1956-57-58; Puckelwartz, Bill, HB, 1925-27; Pullen, Tom, E, 1965; Purdum, Claire, G, 1930; Purucker, Norm, HB, 1937-38; Putich, Bill, QB, 1949-50-51.

Q Quaerna, Jerold O., OT, 1985-86; Quinn, Clement, G, 1910-11-12; Quinn, Cyril, FB, 1912-13; Quinn, Gary, OG, 1979; Quinn, Terrence G., WR, 1995.

R Radigan, Tim, FB, 1965; Raeder, Jim, FB, 1959-60-61; Raimey, Dave, HB, 1960-61-62; Ramirez, Marcelino, C/G, 1988-89; Randall, Gregory, DB, 1984-85; Randolph, Chuck, DT, 1975; Ranney, Leroy, LE, 1908-09; Rather, Dave, SE, 1970-71-72; Ray, Marcus K., SS, 1995; Raymond, Philip, HB, 1916; Raynsford, Jim, T, 1912-13-14; Redden, Curtis, E, 1901-02-03; Redner, Arthur, HB, 1900-01; Reed, Frank, HB, 1878-79; Reeves, Jeff, DB, 1979-80-81; Regeczi, John, FB, 1932-33-34; Rehor, Fred, G, 1915-16; Reid, Lawrence, FB, 1978-79; Reimann, Lewis, T, 1914-15; Rein, Russell, QB, 1984; Reinhold, Michael W., ILB, 1983-85; Rekowski, Stephen M., DT, 1990-91-92-93; Remias, Steve, F, 1934-35; Renda, Hercules, HB, 1937-38-39; Rennebohm, Bob, E, 1943; Renner, Art, E, 1943-44-45-46; Renner, William, QB, 1933-35; Rentschler, Dave, E, 1955-56; Rescarla, Russ, FB, 1951-52; Reynick, Charles, Member, 1877-78; Reynolds, John, FB, 1966; Rheinschild, Walter, T/E, 1905-07; Rice, Daniel, RB, 1982; Rich, George, FB, 1926-27-28; Richards, J.D., QB, 1894-95-96-97; Richards, Todd W., WR, 1993-94-95; Richardson, A.E., HB, 1899; Richardson, Max, FL, 1974-75-76-77; Ricks, Lawrence, TB, 1979-80-81-82; Riemersma, A. Jay, QB/TE, 1992-93-94-95; Ries, Dick, G, 1963; Ries, Joseph R., C, 1995; Rifenburg, Dick, E, 1946-47-48; Riley, Tom, RG, 1908; Rinaldi, Joe, C, 1935-36-37; Rindfuss, Dick, HB, 1962-63-64; Rio, Tony, FB, 1957-59; Ritchie, Jon D., FB, 1993; Ritchie, Stark, HB, 1935-36-37; Ritley, Bob, OT, 1969; Ritter, Chuck, G, 1954; Ritter, David R., SS, 1988-89-90-91; Rivers, Garland A., DB, 1983-84-85-86; Roach, Tom, T, 1929; Robbins, Dammond R. Monte, P, 1984-85-86-87; Roberts, Scott, TE, 1982; Roberts, Willis, Member, 1876; Robinson, Don, HB, 1941-42-46; Roby, Doug, HB , 1921-22; Rockwell, F.A., QB, 1923-24; Rodgers, Nathaniel, MG, 1982-83-84; Roehm, Laurence, QB, 1915; Rogers, Joe, E, 1939-40-41; Rogers, Rick, RB,

1981-82-83-84; Root, Edgar, Member, 1874; Rosatti, Rudy, T, 1922; Rose, Carlton, OLB, 1980-81-82-83; Rosema, Bob, DE, 1971; Rosema, Rocky, DE, 1965-66-67; Rotunno, Mike, E, 1954-55-56; Rowser, John, DB, 1963-65-66; Rumney, Mason, LE, 1906-07; Rundell, Warren, G, 1893-94; Runyan, Jon D., OT/OG, 1993-94-95; Russ, Carl, LB, 1972-73-74; Ruzicka, Chuck, T, 1963-65; Rye, Harold, E, 1917-19.

S Safley, Ben, Member, 1872-76; Sample, Fred, C, 1968; Samuels, Tom, T, 1930-31; Sanders, Ernest, FS, 1994-95; Sanderson, Ed, QB, 1892-93; Sarantos, Pete, C, 1969; Sansom, Elijah, DE, 1968; Savage, Carl, G, 1932-33; Savage, Mike, E, 1933-34-35; Savilla, Roland, T, 1937-38-39; Scarcelli, James J., OLB, 1983-84-85; Scheffler, Lance, TB, 1968-69-70; Schick, Gary, E, 1965; Schlicht, Leo, E, 1951; Schlopy, R. Todd;1983-84 , , PK; Schmerge, Mark, TE, 1975-76-77-78; Schmerge, Paul, TE, 1984-85; Schmidt, Paul, T, 1961; Schoenfeld, John, C, 1926-27; Schopf, Jon, T, 1959-60-61; Schram, Dick, T, 1962; Schulte, Henry, G, 1903-04-05; Schulte, Timothy M., OLB, 1984-85-86; Schulte, Todd M., ILB, 1985-86; Schulz, Germany, C, 1904-05-07-08; Schumacher, Jerry, OG, 1970-71-72; Schuman, Stanton, C/G, 1935; Scott, Spencer, T, 1913; Seabron, Tom, OLB, 1975-76-77-78; Seal, Paul, TE, 1971-72-73; Searle, John, HB, 1921; Sears, Harold, G, 1934; Senter, Henry, E, 1893; Sessa, Michael, WR, 1984; Sexton, Walt, MG, 1971-72; Seyferth, Fritz, FB, 1969-70-71; Seymour, Paul, OT, 1970-71-72; Seymour, Phil, DE, 1967-68-70; Shannon, Ed, HB, 1954-55-56; Sharpe, Ernie, RB, 1965-66-67; Sharpe, Phil, E, 1941-42; Shatusky, Mike, HB, 1956-57; Shaw, Jeff, MG, 1980; Shaw, Walt, HB, 1900; Sherman, Roger, E, 1891-93; Sherman, Sam, E, 1889-90; Shields, Edmund, Reserve, 1895; Shimko, Martin J., DT, 1985; Shorts, Bruce, T, 1900-02; Shuttlesworth, Ed, FB, 1971-72-73; Sickels, Quentin, G, 1944-46-47-48; Siegel, Don, T, 1936-37-38; Siegmund, Rudolph, G, 1899; Sigler, William, G, 1943; Sigman, Lionel, T, 1955-56; Sikkenga, Jay, G, 1931; Simkus, Arnold, T, 1962-64; Simmons, Rasheed C., OLB, 1995; Simon, David, C, 1984; Simpkins, Ron, ILB, 1976-77-78-79; Simpson, Cornelius, OLB, 1987-89-90-91; Simrall, James, QB, 1928-29-30; Sincich, Al, MG, 1981-82-83-84; Singer, Oscar, G, 1932-33; Sipp, Warren, FB, 1966-67-68; Sirosky, Dennis, LB, 1968; Sisinyak, Gene, FB, 1956-57-58; Skene, Douglas C., OG/OT, 1989-90-91-92; Skinner, James, Forward, 1885; Skorput, Ante, OG, 1993-94; Skrepenak, Gregory A., OT, 1988-89-90-91; Slade, Tom, QB, 1971-72-73; Slaughter, E.R., C, 1922-23-24; Slezak, Dave, C, 1961; Smeja, Rudy, E, 1941-42-43; Smick, Dan, E, 1936-37-38; Smith, Andrew, C, 1909; Smith, Cedric, FB, 1915-16-17; Smith, Frederic, C, 1888-89; Smith, Jim, WB, 1973-74-75-76; Smith, Jeff, E, 1961; Smith, Jerry, C, 1958-59-60; Smith, John, G, 1945; Smith, Kerry, RB, 1980-82-83; Smith, Kevin, DB, 1981; Smith, Mike, FL, 1977; Smith, Roosevelt, TB, 1977-78-79; Smith, Seth A., WR, 1994; Smith, Steve B., QB, 1980-81-82-83; Smith Steve C., E, 1963-64-65; Smith, Tony, DT, 1970-71-72; Smith, Walter R., WR, 1991-92-93-94; Smith, William, T, 1937-38-39; Smith, Willie, T, 1956-57-58; Smithers, John, HB, 1935-36; Smykowski, Scott A., ILB, 1989; Snider, Gene, C, 1954-56-57; Snover, Edward, Member, 1876; Snow, Muir, G, 1896-97; Snow, Neil, FB, 1898-99-00-01; Soboleski, Joe, T, 1945-46-47-48; Sobsey, Solomon, E, 1935; Sollom, Kenneth H., QB, 1988-89-90-91; Soodik, Eli, G, 1932; Sorenson, T.C., T, 1929; Spacht, Ron, HB, 1961; Spahn, Jeff, QB, 1974; Sparkman, Wayne, FB, 1962-63; Sparks, Cliff, QB, 1916-17-19; Spearman, Clint, DE, 1970-71-72; Spencer, Marc A., LB, 1988-89; Spencer, Royce, E, 1967; Spidel, John, QB, 1956-57-58; Splawn, Laurence, FB, 1914; Sprague, Ernest, Forward, 1887-88; Springer, Jeffrey M., ILB, 1994-95; Squier, George, G, 1926-28; Staatz, Karl, E, 1914-15; Stabb, Chester, E, 1936; Stamman, Carl, E, 1924-25; Stamos, John, QB, 1959-60-61; Stanford, Thad,

E, 1951-52-53; Stanley, Sylvester, DT, 1989-91-92-93; Stanton, Ed, FB, 1936-37; Stapleton, Christopher J., P, 1989-91-92-93; Stark, Randolph W., OLB, 1990-91; Staroba, Paul, SE, 1968-69-70; Stawski, Willard, T, 1961; Steckle, Allen, T, 1897-98-99; Steele, Harold, G, 1922-23-24; Steele, James L., DT, 1994-95; Steger, Geoff, WB, 1971-73-74; Steger, Herb, HB, 1922-23-24; Steinke, Alfred, G, 1928-29; Steketee, Frank, FB, 1918-20-21; Stenberg, Bob, FB, 1942-43; Stephenson, Curt, WR, 1975-76-77; Stetten, Maynard, T, 1958; Steuk, William, OLB, 1992; Stieler, Steve, C, 1959; Stincic, Tom, DE, 1966-67-68; Stine, William, T, 1958-59-60; Stites, Richard L., ILB, 1987; Stites, Robert W., ILB, 1987; Strabley, Mike, LB, 1975; Straffon, Ralph, FB, 1949-50; Straub, Harvey, QB, 1928; Street, Charles, QB, 1888-89; Streets, Tai, WR, 1995; Strenger, Rich, OT, 1980-81-82; Stribe, Ralph, T, 1950-51-52; Strinko, Greg, DE, 1975; Strinko, Steve, LB, 1972-73-74; Strobel, Jack, HB, 1960-61-62; Strong, Dave, HB, 1938-39; Strozewski, Dick, T, 1950-52-53; Stuart, Ted, E/HB, 1904-05; Sukup, Milo, G, 1938-39-40; Sullivan, John, Reserve, 1907-08; Sullivan, Michael D., OT, 1993-94-95; Sutherland, C.J., G, 1889-90; Sutkiewicz, Rick A., PK, 1985-86-87; Sutton, John, Substitute, 1889; Swan, Don, G , 1921-24; Swearengin, Julian, WR, 1992; Sweeley, Everett, E, 1899-00-01-02; Sweeney, Larry, C, 1980-81-82-83; Sweet, Cedric, FB, 1934-35-36; Swett, Robert S., ILB, 1994-95; Swift, Tom, G, 1944; Sword, Sam, ILB, 1995; Sygar, Dick, DB, 1964-65-66; Syring, Dick, G, 1958-60; Sytek, Jim, QB, 1958; Szafranski, Roger, MG, 1976; Szara, Gerry, OG, 1975-76-77; Szydlowski, Ron, WB, 1973; Szymanski, Dick, C, 1961-62-63.

T Tabachino, Robert, OG, 1984-85; Takach, Tom, DE, 1969; Talcott, William, QB, 1898; Taylor, Billy, TB, 1969-70-71; Taylor, Daydrion, DB, 1995; Taylor, Kip, E, 1927; Taylor, Michael A., QB, 1987-88-89; Taylor, Mike, LB, 1969-70-71; Tech, Karl, PK/P, 1981; Tedesco, Dominic, OLB, 1976-77; Teeter, Michael L., LB/TE, 1986-87-88-89; Teetzel, Clayton, E, 1897; Teninga, Walt, HB, 1945-47-48-49; Tessmer, Estel, QB, 1930-31-33; Teuscher, Charlie, E, 1957; Thibert, Steven J., OLB, 1984-85-86-87; Thisted, Carl, C, 1925; Thomas, John E., C, 1973; Thomas, John R., QB, 1968; Thomas, Joseph, Reserve, 1896; Thompson, Clarence, FS, 1993-94-95; Thompson, Robert C., OLB, 1979-80-81-82; Thomson, George, FB, 1910-11-12; Thornbladh, Bob, FB, 1971-72-73; Timberlake, Bob, QB, 1962-63-64; Timm, Bob, G, 1950-51-52; Tinker, Horace, C, 1938-39; Tinkham, Dave, FB, 1950-51-52; Titas, Frank, OG/PK, 1967-68-69; Tomasi, Dom, G, 1945-46-47-48; Toomer, Amani, WR, 1992-93-94-95; Topor, Ted, QB, 1950-51-52; Topp, Gene, E, 1952-53; Torbet, Roy, E, 1911-1912-13; Torzy, Mark, OT, 1978; Totzke, John, HB, 1928; Townsend, Brian L., OLB, 1988-89-90-91; Townsend, Frederic, Forward, 1881; Trainer, David, T, 1889-90; Traphagan, Roice, G, 1913; Traupe, Eric H., ILB, 1989-90; Trgovac, Mike, MG, 1977-78-79-80; Triplehorn, Howard, HB, 1934; Triplett, Todd, OLB, 1982; Trosko, Fred, HB, 1937-38-39; Troszak, Doug, DT, 1971-72-73; Trowbridge, W.R., Substitute, 1886; Trump, Jack, G, 1943; Truske, Joe, E, 1926-28-29; Tucker, Curtis, OT, 1971-72-73; Tuman, Jerame D., TE, 1995; Tumpane, Pat, OT, 1973-74; Tunnicliff, Bill, FB, 1959-60-61; Tupper, Virgil, G, 1892; Tureaud, Ken, FB, 1959-60-61; Tyng, Alexander, Member, 1870.

U Ulevitch, Herman, G, 1937; Usher, Edward, HB/FB, 1918-20-21; Utz, Irwin, QB, 1921-22-23.

V Valek, Vincent, E, 1938; Valpey, Art, E, 1935-36-37; Vanderbeek, Michael J., ILB, 1993-94; Vander Leest, Robert A., TE, 1993-94-95; VanDervoort, Ed, T, 1922-23; VandeWater, Clarence, G, 1936-37; VanDyne, Rudd, FB, 1959-60; VanDyne, Yale F., WR, 1989-90-91; VanOrden, Bill, G, 1920-21-22; VanPelt, Jim, QB, 1955-

56-57; VanSummern, Bob, HB, 1948-49; Vaughn, Johnathon S., TB, 1989-90; Vercel, Jovan, LB, 1973; Vernier, Bob, QB, 1942-46; Veselenak, John, E, 1953-54; Vick, Ernie, FB/C, 1918-19-20-21; Vick, Richard, HB, 1923; Vidmer, Dick, QB, 1965-66-67; Viergerer, John, T, 1933-34-35; Villa, Giovanni, T, 1893-94-95-96; Virgil, Bryan, PK, 1978-79; Vitale, John S., C, 1985-86-87-88; Vogele, Jerry, LB, 1974-75-76; Volk, Rick, DB, 1964-65-66.

W Wade, Mulford, Substitute, 1887; Wadhams, Tim, DB, 1969; Wahl, Charlie, C, 1944; Wahl, Robert, T, 1948-49-50; Walker, Alan, TB, 1971; Walker, Art, T, 1952-53-54; Walker, Derrick N., TE, 1986-87-88-89; Walker, Harlan, QB, 1918; Walker, Jack C., DT, 1986; Walker, John, C, 1958-60-61; Walker, Marcus B., ILB, 1991-92-93; Wallace, Brian E., OT, 1990-91; Wallace, Coleman, CB, 1989-90-91-92; Wallace, Zeke, WR, 1980; Walls, Grant, T, 1960; Wandersleben, Tom, OG, 1980; Wambacker, J.W., C , 1896; Wangler, John, QB, 1979-80; Ware, Dwayne K., CB, 1989-90-91-92; Ward, Carl, RB, 1964-65-66; Ward, Jim, HB, 1960-61-62; Ward, Willis, E, 1932-33-34; Wardley, Frank, HB, 1942; Warner, Don, MG, 1973; Washington, Dennis B., RB, 1990; Washington, Martin, OG, 1968; Washington, Sanford, ILB, 1981; Wasmund, William, QB, 1907-08-09; Watkins, James, FB, 1907-09; Watson, William, G, 1914-15; Watson, Shawn, RB, 1990; Watts, Harold, C, 1943-44-45-46; Weathers, Andre L., CB, 1995; Webb, Phil A., RB, 1985-86-87; Weber, Gary, DT, 1978-79; Weber, Wally, FB, 1925-26; Wedge, Bob, LB, 1966-67-68; Weeks, Alanson, FB, 1898; Weeks, Harold, Reserve, 1907; Weeks, Harrison, 1899-00-01-02, , QB; Weil, David C., OG, 1987-88; Weinmann, Tom, E, 1967; Weisenburger, Jack, FB, 1944-45-46-47; Welborne, Sullivan A. Tripp, SS, 1987-88-89-90; Wells, Rex, G, 1943; Wells, Richard, HB, 1963-64-65; Wells, Stanfield, E, 1909-10-11; Welton, Arthur, Reserve, 1886; Wendt, Eric W., C, 1994; Wentworth, Peter A., QB, 1986; Werner, Mark, DB/P, 1968-69; Weske, Dick, G , 1915-16-17; Westfall, Bob, FB, 1939-40-41; Weston, Archie, HB, 1917-19; Westover, Louis, QB, 1931-32-33; Weyers, John, G, 1944; Whalen, Jim, E, 1915; Wheatley, Tyrone, TB, 1991-92-93-94; Wheeler, Clare, QB, 1928-29-30; White, Brent D., DT, 1986-87-88-89; White, Gerald E., RB, 1984-85-86; White, Howell, T, 1922-23; White, Hugh, T, 1898-00-01; White, John, C, 1946-47; White,

Paul, HB, 1941-42-43-46; White, Richard, SE, 1976-77; White, Robert, DB, 1969; Whiteford, Dave, S, 1975; Whitledge, John R., QB, 1986; Whittle, John, HB, 1927; Widman, Charles, HB, 1893; Wieman, Elton, G, 1916-17-20; Wiese, Bob, FB, 1942-43-44-46; Wikel, Howard, HB, 1943-47; Wilcher, Thomas, TB, 1985-86; Wilhite, Clayton, E, 1964-65-66; Wilhite, Jim, DL, 1967-68; Wilkins, Stu, G, 1945-46-47-48; Williams, Anthony C., WR, 1994-95; Williams, Bryan A., CB, 1995; Williams, Clarence, RB, 1995; Williams, James O., SS, 1988-89-90-91; Williams, Jerry, E, 1953-54; Williams, Richard, G, 1928; Williams, Ron, G, 1952-53; Williams, Timothy L., OLB, 1987-88-89; Williams, Tracy, RB, 1988; Williamson, Ivan, E, 1930-31-32; Williamson, Dick, DT, 1966-67; Williamson, Walt, DE, 1972-73; Willingham, John R., OLB, 1986-87; Willner, Gregg, P/PK, 1977-78; Wilson, Don, B, 1929; Wilson, Ebin, G, 1901; Wilson, Hugh, G , 1919-20-21; Wilson, Michael, DT, 1983; Wine, Ray, C, 1956-57; Wink, Jack, QB, 1943; Winters, Charles, FS, 1993-94-95; Wise, Cliff, HB, 1940-42; Wisniewski, Irv, E, 1947-48-49; Wistert, Albert, T, 1940-41-42; Wistert, Alvin, T, 1947-48-49; Wistert, Francis, T, 1931-32-33; Witherspoon, Tom, HB, 1950-51-52; Wolter, Jim, G, 1949-50-51; Wombacher, John, C, 1895-96; Wood, George, Forward, 1887; Wood, Bob, PK, 1975-76; Woodlock, John S., OG, 1991; Woodruff, P.G., Forward, 1881; Woodson, Charles, CB, 1995; Woodward, Paul, G, 1962-63; Woodworth, Paul, E, 1891-92; Woolfolk, Butch, TB, 1978-79-80-81; Woolley, Ed, DE, 1968; Workman, Harry, QB, 1906; Wormwood, Frank, HB, 1881-82; Wright, Charles, Substitute, 1885-86-87; Wright, Harry, C, 1935; Wright, Ken, DT, 1965-66; Wuerfel, Joshua C., PK/P, 1992.

Y Yanz, John, T, 1962-64; Yanz, Richard, OG, 1967; Yarano, Daniel A., OG, 1983; Yearby, Bill, T, 1963-64-65; Yerges, Howard, QB, 1944-45-46-47; Yont, J.G., T, 1894-95; Yost, Fielding Jr., E, 1931.

Z Zacharis, Steven T., TE, 1989; Zachary, John, HB, 1958; Zan Fagna, Don, HB, 1951; Zatkoff, Roger, T, 1950-51-52; Zeiger, Harold, QB, 1916; Zenkewicz, Trent A., DT, 1992-93-94-95; Ziem, Fred, G, 1936; Zielinski, Ronald W., OT, 1990; Zimmerman, Bob, FB, 1939; Zingales, John S., DB/K, 1985; Zubkus, Jim, E, 1959-61; Zuganelis, George, LB, 1969; Zurbrugg, Christopher M., QB, 1984-85-86

MICHIGAN'S ALL-TIME BEST PLAYERS

Choosing Michigan's all-time best players, in any era, is a difficult proposition. For this daunting task, we turned to Bob Rosiek, a 1970 University of Michigan graduate and preeminent U-M football historian. Through his extensive research and own firsthand viewing of more than 400 U-M football games since the mid-1950s, he has compiled his own listing of Michigan's all-time best players from both the early era (1879-1945) and the modern era (1946-1995) of college football.

While not every reader will agree with all the selections, this certainly is a superb starting point for discussion and debate about the best players ever to don the Maize and Blue for gridiron glory.

ALL-TIME PLAYERS — EARLY ERA (1879-1945)

End — Neil Snow 1901; Stanfield Wells 1911; Paul Goebel 1922; Bennie Oosterbaan 1927

Tackle — John Curtis 1906; Tom Edwards 1925; Francis Wistert 1933; Albert Wistert 1942

Guard — Dan McGugin 1902; Albert Benbrook 1910; Butch Slaughter 1924; Merv Pregulman 1942

Center — Germany Schulz 1908; Chuck Bernard 1933

Quarterback — Boss Weeks 1902; Benny Friedman 1926; Harry Newman 1932; Forest Evashevski 1940

Halfback — Albert Herrnstein 1902; Willie Heston 1904; Jim Craig 1913; Johnny Maulbetsch 1916; Harry Kipke 1923; Tom Harmon 1940

Fullback — Bob Westfall 1941; Bill Daley 1943

Placekicker — Dave Allerdice 1909; Harry Newman 1932

Punter — John Garrels 1906; Harry Kipke 1923

Note: Listings are chronological by position with final varsity season indicated.

ALL-TIME PLAYERS — MODERN ERA (1946-1995)

OFFENSE

End — Dick Rifenburg 1948; Jim Mandich 1969

Tackle — Tom Mack 1965; Dan Dierdorf 1970; Ed Muransky 1981; Greg Skrepanek 1991

Guard — Reggie McKenzie 1971; Mark Donahue 1977; Kurt Becker 1981; Dean Dingman 1990

Center — Tom Dixon 1983; John Vitale 1988

Flanker — Jack Clancy 1966; Jim Smith 1976; Anthony Carter 1986; Desmond Howard 1991

Quarterback — Bob Timberlake 1964; Rick Leach 1978; Jim Harbaugh 1986; Elvis Grbac 1992

Tailback — Bob Chappuis 1947; Chuck Ortmann 1950; Ron Johnson 1968; Rob Lytle 1976; Butch Woolfolk 1981; Tyrone Wheatley 1994

Fullback — Ed Shuttlesworth 1973; Russell Davis 1978

Placekicker — Jim Brieske 1947; J.D. Carlson 1990

DEFENSE

End — Len Ford 1947; Ron Kramer 1956; Mike Keller 1971; Robert Thompson 1982

Line — Alvin Wistert 1949; Bill Yearby 1965; Curtis Greer 1979; Mark Hammerstein 1985; Mark Messner 1988; Chris Hutchinson 1992

Linebacker — Dick Kempthorn 1949; Ron Simpkins 1979; Mike Mallory 1985; Erick Anderson 1991

Back — Bump Elliott 1947; Gene Derricotte 1948; Terry Barr 1956; Rick Volk 1966; Tom Curtis 1969; Thom Darden 1971; Dave Brown 1974; Tripp Welborne 1989

Punter — Don Bracken 1983; Monte Robbins 1987

Note: Listings are chronological by position with final varsity season indicated.

ALL-TIME HEAD COACHES

Fielding Yost 1901-23, 25-26
Fritz Crisler 1938-47
Bo Schembechler 1969-89

TRIVIA ANSWERS

Grading System — 60 Questions

60-54 Correct — Point-A-Minute Man
53-46 Correct — Rose Bowl Bound
45-39 Correct — Part-time Victor
38-32 Correct — Not True Blue
31-25 Correct — Doomed To The Snakepit
24-0 Correct — Must Be A Sparty

1. Racine (Wis.) College. Michigan won on a touchdown and a goal, officially recorded as a 1-0 victory.
2. Irving Pond.
3. Mike Murphy, a trainer at the Detroit Athletic Club, and Frank Crawford, a graduate student from Yale, were Michigan's first coaches in 1891.
4. Oct. 30, 1897. The Michigan varsity was defeated, 15-0, by an alumni team. Three years later, Michigan defeated Purdue at Regents Field in the first Alumni Game played against a college opponent.
5. Charles Baird became Michigan's first athletic director in 1898.
6. 1898.
7. Charles Widman.
8. Louis Elbel, a music student at the University, was so inspired by Michigan's last-minute victory over Chicago in 1898 he wrote the words and music to "The Victors" on his way back to Ann Arbor.
9. Al Herrnstein.
10. The 130-0 humbling of West Virginia in 1904.
11. Willie Heston.
12. Old Ferry Field, or Regents Field, as it was more widely known.
13. 55-1-1.
14. 50.
15. Adolph "Germany" Schulz.
16. In 1924, when Michigan defeated Wisconsin, 21-0, on October 25 before a crowd of 45,000 at Ferry Field.
17. Benny Friedman and Bennie Oosterbaan.
18. 165-29-10.
19. 85,000.
20. Former great U-M running back Harry Kipke.
21. 31-1-3.
22. The Michigan Marching Band.
23. Big Ten regulations on postseason games forced U-M to decline the invitation extended by the Tournament of Roses Association.
24. 25.
25. Fritz Crisler introduced the famed winged helmet when he came to Michigan in 1938.
26. Tom Harmon.
27. Yost stepped down in 1941, following a 40-year

association with Michigan.
28. Michigan played its first night game, a 14-0 victory over Marquette at Marquette Stadium in Milwaukee, in 1944.
29. Bob Ufer.
30. 1947, when the Wolverines defeated Michigan State, 55-0.
31. "The Mad Magicians."
32. Alvin Wistert, 32 years old.
33. Oosterbaan was named College Football Coach of the Year, making Michigan the first school ever to have two different coaches win that honor in successive seasons.
34. Army.
35. Northwestern.
36. Chuck Lentz.
37. Yankee Stadium.
38. Ron Kramer.
39. Fritz Crisler.
40. Dennis Fitzgerald.
41. Navy's Roger Staubach.
42. The assassination of President John F. Kennedy.
43. Bob Timberlake.
44. Mel Anthony.
45. Wisconsin.
46. Miami (Ohio) University.
47. Barry Pierson.
48. Jim Young, who was the head coach at Purdue from 1977-81.
49. Coin converted all 55 of his point-after conversion kicks in the 1971 season.
50. The Rose Bowl. Mark Harmon, the son of U-M Heisman Trophy winner Tom Harmon, was the UCLA quarterback.
51. U-M starting quarterback Dennis Franklin suffered a broken collarbone late in the 10-10 tie with Ohio State.
52. Schembechler owned a 5-4-1 record against Hayes.
53. Fielding H. Yost.
54. Bob Bergeron.
55. Ohio State.
56. Jon Vaughn.
57. The five members of Michigan's offensive line — Greg Skrepenak, Dean Dingman, Tom Dohring, Steve Everitt, and Matt Elliott — shared the award.
58. Boston College.
59. Linebacker Erick Anderson won the Butkus Award as the nation's top linebacker.
60. Michigan's Mel Anthony, 84 yards.

ABOUT THE AUTHORS

JOHN BORTON

John Borton is a 1981 graduate of Siena Heights College in Adrian, Mich. An English and media major, Borton has done sports commentary and production work for radio stations WABJ and WLEN in Adrian and WUOM in Ann Arbor. He was a news reporter and sportswriter for *The Daily Telegram* in Adrian for nine years. Borton has been the editor of *The Wolverine* magazine since 1991 and has been a regular guest on WTKA in Ann Arbor.

PAUL DODD

Paul Dodd is a 1987 graduate of the University of Michigan, where he was a member of the U-M Marching Band for five years and the U-M Basketball Band for four years. A communications major, Dodd was a sportswriter for the *Daily Local News* in West Chester, Pa., from 1988 to 1990. A frequent contributor to WTKA in Ann Arbor, Dodd has served as assistant editor of *The Wolverine* since 1991.

COLLEGE SPORTS HANDBOOKS
Stories, Stats & Stuff About America's Favorite Teams

U. of Arizona	Basketball	Arizona Wildcats Handbook
U. of Arkansas	Basketball	Razorbacks Handbook
Baylor	Football	Bears Handbook
Clemson	Football	Clemson Handbook
U. of Colorado	Football	Buffaloes Handbook
U. of Florida	Football	Gator Tales
Georgia Tech	Basketball	Yellow Jackets Handbook
Indiana U.	Basketball	Hoosier Handbook
Iowa State	Sports	Cyclones Handbook
U. of Kansas	Basketball	Crimson & Blue Handbook
Kansas State	Sports	Kansas St Wildcat Handbook
LSU	Football	Fighting Tigers Handbook
U. of Louisville	Basketball	Cardinals Handbook
U. of Miami	Football	Hurricane Handbook
U. of Missouri	Basketball	Tiger Handbook
U. of Nebraska	Football	Husker Handbook
U. of N. Carolina	Basketball	Tar Heels Handbook
N.C. State	Basketball	Wolfpack Handbook
U. of Oklahoma	Football	Sooners Handbook
Penn State	Football	Nittany Lions Handbook
U. of S. Carolina	Football	Gamecocks Handbook
Stanford	Football	Stanford Handbook
Syracuse	Sports	Orange Handbook
U. of Tennessee	Football	Volunteers Handbook
U. of Texas	Football	Longhorns Handbook
Texas A&M	Football	Aggies Handbook
Texas Tech	Sports	Red Raiders Handbook
Virginia Tech	Football	Hokies Handbook
Wichita State	Sports	Shockers Handbook
U. of Wisconsin	Football	Badgers Handbook

Also:

Big 12 Handbook: Stories, Stats and Stuff About The Nation's Best
Football Conference

The Top Fuel Handbook: Stories, Stats and Stuff About Drag Racing's
Most Powerful Class

For ordering information call Midwest Sports Publications at:

1-800-492-4043